CONTENTS

275 BEST-SELLING CONTEMPORARY DESIGNS

Simple Exterior, Luxurious Interior   P-6595, p. 16

IN THIS ISSUE:

SPECIAL SECTION:
Best-Selling Homes in Full Color! 2

Best-Selling Contemporary Designs..................33

NEW RELEASES!
A debut of more than 30 New Plans 129

More Exciting Contemporary Designs 161

HOW TO ORDER BLUEPRINTS

The "Source 1" Plans Package 12

What You Need to Know Before You Order 14

Blueprint Order Form.......................................15

Distinguished Living   EOF-62, p. 52

Circular Dining Room!   K-663-N, p. 162

President — Jeffrey B. Heegaard
Publisher — Roger W. Heegaard
Associate Publishers — Mark Englund, Wendy Schroeder
Editor — Dianne Talmage
Associate Editors — Pamela Robertson, Eric Englund, Matthew Arthurs, Sharon Teska
Sales Operations Supervisor — Wayne Ramaker
Marketing Associates — Gene Tubbs, Mary Gehlhar, Carrie Morrison, John Lickteig
Controller — Nancy Ness
Financial Analysts — Barbara Marquardt, Jeanne Marquardt, Tom Klauer
Information Systems Analyst — John Herber
Information Systems Associates — Kevin Gellerman, Jeffrey Tindillier
Blueprint Manager — Chuck Lantis
Staff: Amy Berdahl, Brian Boese, Daniel Brown, Tera Girardin, Joan Jerry, Brad Johnson, April Liljedahl, Monita Mohammadian, Michelle Olofson, Kellie Pierce, Michael Romain, Shelley Safratowich, Karen Zambory, Peggy Zambory

Affordable Style and Excitement   B-89054, p. 242

Private Decks Abound   CAR-81007, p. 272

Published by HomeStyles Publishing and Marketing, Inc., Company Leaders Jeffrey B. Heegaard and Roger W. Heegaard. For information on advertising, call Mary Gehlhar at 612-338-8155, P.O. Box 50670, Minneapolis, MN 55405.

A Real Original

- This home's round window, elegant entry and transom windows create an eye-catching, original look.
- Inside, high ceilings and tremendous views let the eyes wander. The foyer provides an exciting look at the expansive deck and the inviting spa through the living room's tall windows. The windows frame a handsome fireplace, while a 10-ft. ceiling adds volume and interest.
- To the right of the foyer is a cozy den or home office with its own fireplace, 10-ft. ceiling and dramatic windows.
- The spacious kitchen/breakfast area features an oversized snack bar island and opens to a large screen porch. Within easy reach are the laundry room and the entrance to the garage.
- The bright formal dining room overlooks the deck and boasts a ceiling that vaults up to 10 feet.
- The secluded master suite looks out to the deck as well, with access through a patio door. The private bath features a dynamite corner spa tub, a separate shower and a large walk-in closet.
- A second bedroom and bath complete the main floor.

Plan B-90065

Bedrooms: 2+	Baths: 2
Living Area:	
Main floor	1,889 sq. ft.
Total Living Area:	**1,889 sq. ft.**
Standard basement	1,889 sq. ft.
Garage	406 sq. ft.
Exterior Wall Framing:	2x6

Foundation Options:

Standard basement
(All plans can be built with your choice of foundation and framing. A generic conversion diagram is available. See order form.)

BLUEPRINT PRICE CODE:	B

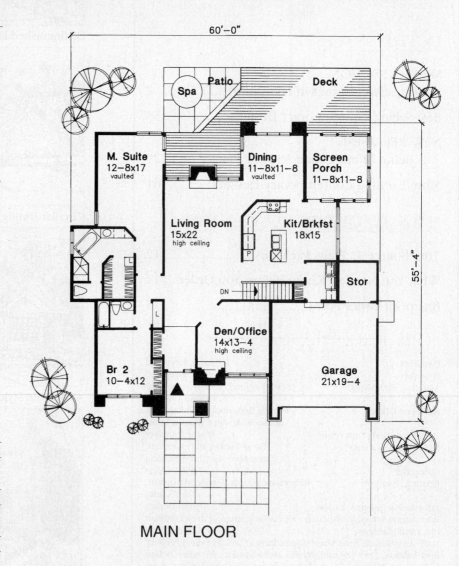

MAIN FLOOR

TO ORDER THIS BLUEPRINT, CALL TOLL-FREE 1-800-547-5570

Plan B-90065

PRICES AND DETAILS ON PAGES 12-15

Take the Plunge!

- From the elegant porte cochere to the striking rooflines, this home's facade is magnificent. But the rear area is equally fine, with its spa, waterfall and pool.
- Double doors lead from the entry into a columned foyer. Beyond the living room is a sunken wet bar that extends into the pool area, allowing guests to swim up to the bar for refreshments.
- The stunning master suite offers views of the pool through a curved window wall, access to the patio and an opulent bath.
- A secluded den, study or guest room is conveniently close to the hall bath.
- The dining room boasts window walls and a tiered pedestal ceiling. The island kitchen easily services both the formal and the informal areas of the home.
- A large breakfast room flows into a warm family room with a fireplace and sliders to the patio and pool.
- A railed staircase leads to the upper floor, where there are two bedrooms, a continental bath and a shared balcony deck overlooking the pool area.
- The observatory features high windows to accommodate an amateur stargazer's telescope. This room could also be used as an activity area for hobbies or games.

Plan HDS-99-154

Bedrooms: 3-4	Baths: 3
Living Area:	
Upper floor	675 sq. ft.
Main floor	2,212 sq. ft.
Total Living Area:	**2,887 sq. ft.**
Garage	479 sq. ft.
Exterior Wall Framing:	2x4
Foundation Options:	

Slab
(Typical foundation & framing conversion diagram available—see order form.)

BLUEPRINT PRICE CODE: D

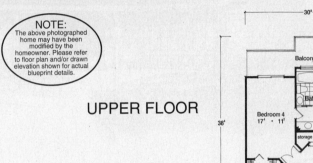

NOTE:
The above photographed home may have been modified by the homeowner. Please refer to floor plan and/or drawn elevation shown for actual blueprint details.

UPPER FLOOR

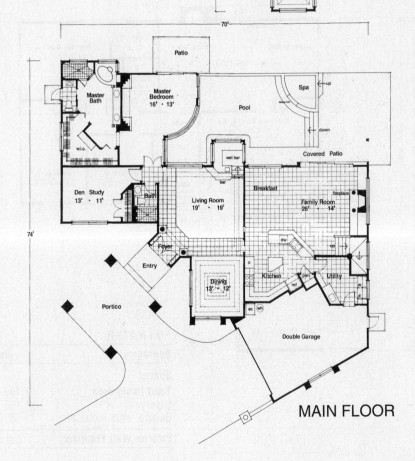

MAIN FLOOR

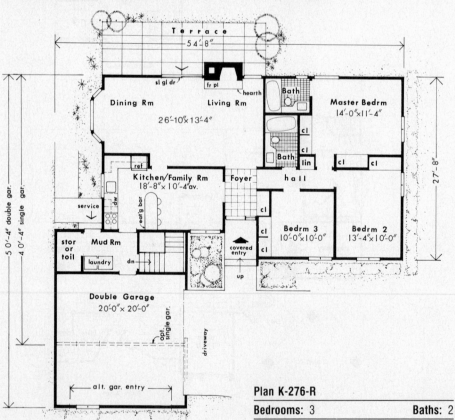

Compact, Economical to Build

- This economically-structured L-shaped ranch puts a great many desirable features into a mere 1,193 sq. ft. of living space. A wood-burning fireplace highlights the living area. Sliding glass doors open to the backyard terrace.
- The kitchen/family room features an eating bar.
- Covered entry welcomes you to the central foyer for easy channeling to any part of the house.
- Located in a wing of their own are three bedrooms and two baths.
- For a narrow lot, the garage door could face the front.

Plan K-276-R

Bedrooms: 3	Baths: 2

Space:	
Total living area:	1,193 sq. ft.
Basement:	1,193 sq. ft.
Garage, mud room, etc.:	551 sq. ft.

Exterior Wall Framing:	2x4 or 2x6

Foundation options:
Standard basement.
Crawlspace.
Slab.
(Foundation & framing conversion diagram available — see order form)

Blueprint Price Code: A

TO ORDER THIS BLUEPRINT, CALL TOLL-FREE 1-800-547-5570

Plan K-276-R

PRICES AND DETAILS ON PAGES 12-15

Designed for Livability

- As you enter this excitingly spacious traditional home, you see through the extensive windows to the backyard.
- This four-bedroom home was designed for the livability of the maturing family with the separation of the master suite.
- The formal dining room expands spatially to the living room while being set off by a decorative column and plant shelves.
- The bay that creates the morning room and the sitting area for the master suite also adds excitement to this plan, both inside and out.
- The master bath offers an exciting oval tub under glass and a separate shower, as well as a spacious walk-in closet and a dressing area.

Plan DD-1696

Bedrooms: 4	Baths: 2
Living Area:	
Main floor	1,748 sq. ft.
Total Living Area:	**1,748 sq. ft.**
Standard basement	1,748 sq. ft.
Garage	393 sq. ft.
Exterior Wall Framing:	2x4

Foundation Options:

Standard basement

Crawlspace

Slab

(All plans can be built with your choice of foundation and framing. A generic conversion diagram is available. See order form.)

BLUEPRINT PRICE CODE: B

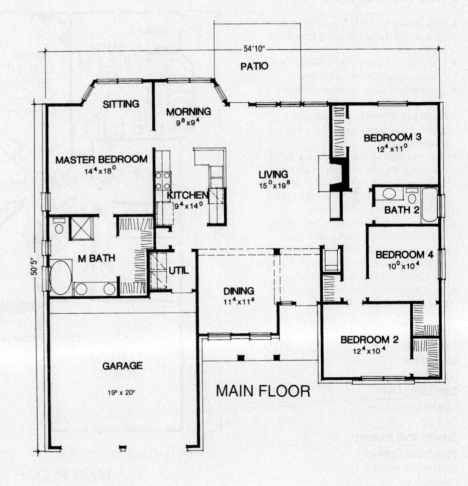

54'10"

PATIO

SITTING

MORNING
9⁸ x 9⁴

MASTER BEDROOM
14⁴ x 18⁰

KITCHEN
9⁴ x 14⁰

LIVING
15⁰ x 19⁸

BEDROOM 3
12⁴ x 11⁰

BATH 2

50'5"

M BATH

UTIL

DINING
11⁴ x 11⁴

BEDROOM 4
10⁰ x 10⁴

GARAGE
19⁸ x 20⁰

MAIN FLOOR

BEDROOM 2
12⁴ x 10⁴

Planned to Perfection

- This attractive and stylish home offers an interior design that is planned to perfection.
- The covered entry and vaulted foyer create an impressive welcome.
- The vaulted Great Room features a corner fireplace, a wet bar and lots of windows. The adjoining dining room offers a bay window and access to a covered patio.
- The gourmet kitchen includes an island cooktop, a garden window above the sink and a built-in desk. The attached nook is surrounded by windows that overlook a delightful planter.
- The master suite boasts a tray ceiling that rises to 9½ ft. and a peaceful reading area that accesses a private patio. The superb master bath features a garden tub and a separate shower.
- Two secondary bedrooms share a compartmentalized bath.

Plan S-4789

Bedrooms: 3	Baths: 2
Living Area:	
Main floor	1,665 sq. ft.
Total Living Area:	**1,665 sq. ft.**
Standard basement	1,665 sq. ft.
Garage	400 sq. ft.
Exterior Wall Framing:	2x6

Foundation Options:

Standard basement
Crawlspace
Slab

(All plans can be built with your choice of foundation and framing. A generic conversion diagram is available. See order form.)

BLUEPRINT PRICE CODE: B

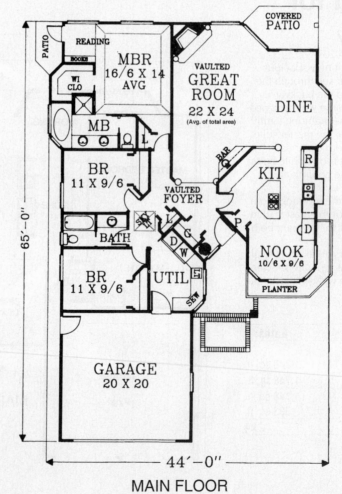

MAIN FLOOR

BASEMENT STAIRWAY LOCATION

TO ORDER THIS BLUEPRINT, CALL TOLL-FREE 1-800-547-5570

Plan S-4789

PRICES AND DETAILS ON PAGES 12-15

Alluring Arches

- Massive columns, high, dramatic arches and expansive glass attract passersby to this alluring one-story home.
- Inside, 12-ft. coffered ceilings are found in the foyer, dining room and living room. A bank of windows in the living room provides a sweeping view of the covered backyard patio, creating a bright, open effect that is carried throughout the home.
- The informal, family activity areas are oriented to the back of the home as well. Spectacular window walls in the breakfast room and family room offer tremendous views. The family room's inviting corner fireplace is positioned to be enjoyed from the breakfast area and the spacious island kitchen.
- Separated from the secondary bedrooms, the superb master suite is entered through double doors and features a sitting room and a garden bath. Another full bath is across the hall from the den, which would also make a great guest room or nursery.

Plan HDS-99-179

Bedrooms: 3+	Baths: 3
Living Area:	
Main floor	2,660 sq. ft.
Total Living Area:	**2,660 sq. ft.**
Garage	527 sq. ft.
Exterior Wall Framing:	2x4

Foundation Options:

Slab

(All plans can be built with your choice of foundation and framing. A generic conversion diagram is available. See order form.)

BLUEPRINT PRICE CODE: D

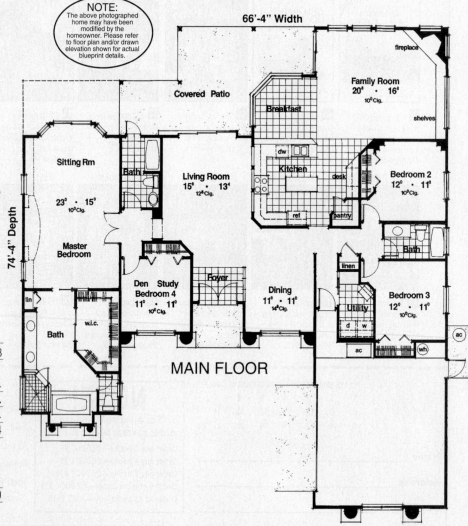

NOTE:
The above photographed home may have been modified by the homeowner. Please refer to floor plan and/or drawn elevation shown for actual blueprint details.

66'-4" Width

74'-4" Depth

Covered Patio

Family Room
20⁸ • 16⁸
10⁰ Clg.

fireplace

shelves

Breakfast

Sitting Rm
23⁰ • 15⁰
10⁰ Clg.

Bath

Living Room
15⁰ • 13⁴
12⁸ Clg.

Kitchen

dw

desk

Bedroom 2
12⁰ • 11⁰
10⁰ Clg.

ref

pantry

Bath

Master Bedroom

lin

Bath

w.i.c.

Den Study
Bedroom 4
11⁰ • 11⁰
10⁰ Clg.

Foyer

Dining
11⁸ • 11⁰
14⁴ Clg.

linen

Utility

d w

Bedroom 3
12⁰ • 11⁰
10⁰ Clg.

ac

ac

wh

ac

MAIN FLOOR

TO ORDER THIS BLUEPRINT,
CALL TOLL-FREE 1-800-547-5570

Plan HDS-99-179

PRICES AND DETAILS
ON PAGES 12-15

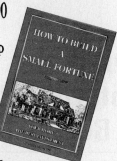

Dramatic Interior Makes a Best-Seller

- An incredible master suite takes up the entire 705 sq. ft. second floor, and includes deluxe bath, huge closet and skylighted balcony.
- Main floor design utilizes angles and shapes to create dramatic interior.
- Extra-spacious kitchen features large island, sunny windows and plenty of counter space.
- Sunken living room focuses on massive fireplace and stone hearth.
- Impressive two-level foyer is lit by skylights high above.
- Third bedroom or den with an adjacent bathroom makes an ideal home office or hobby room.

Photo by Karlis Grants

NOTE:
The above photographed home may have been modified by the homeowner. Please refer to floor plan and/or drawn elevation shown for actual blueprint details.

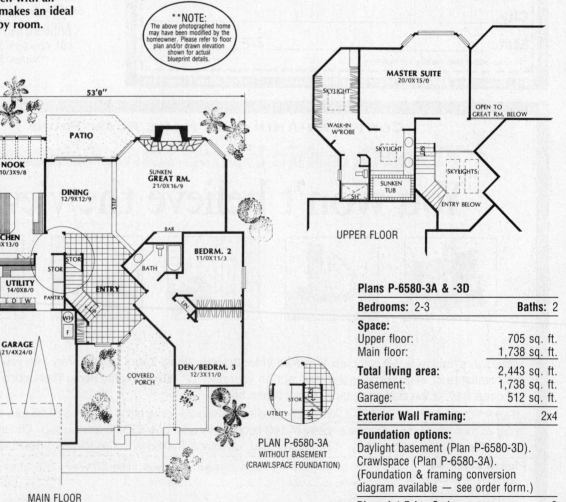

MAIN FLOOR

PLAN P-6580-3A
WITHOUT BASEMENT
(CRAWLSPACE FOUNDATION)

UPPER FLOOR

Plans P-6580-3A & -3D

Bedrooms: 2-3	Baths: 2
Space:	
Upper floor:	705 sq. ft.
Main floor:	1,738 sq. ft.
Total living area:	2,443 sq. ft.
Basement:	1,738 sq. ft.
Garage:	512 sq. ft.
Exterior Wall Framing:	2x4

Foundation options:
Daylight basement (Plan P-6580-3D).
Crawlspace (Plan P-6580-3A).
(Foundation & framing conversion diagram available — see order form.)

Blueprint Price Code:	C

TO ORDER THIS BLUEPRINT,
CALL TOLL-FREE 1-800-547-5570

Plans P-6580-3A & -3D

PRICES AND DETAILS
ON PAGES 12-15

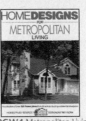

THE "SOURCE 1"

WHAT OUR PLANS INCLUDE

"SOURCE 1" construction blueprints are detailed, clear and concise. All blueprints are designed by licensed architects or members of the A.I.B.D. (American Institute of Building Design), and each plan is designed to meet nationally recognized building codes (either the Uniform Building Code, Standard Building Code or Basic Building Code) at the time and place they were drawn.

The blueprints for most home designs include the following elements, but the presentation of these elements may vary depending on the size and complexity of the home and the style of the individual designer:

1. *Exterior Elevations* show the front, rear and sides of the house, including exterior materials, details and measurements.

2. *Foundation Plans* include drawings for a full, daylight or partial basement, crawlspace, slab, or pole foundation. All necessary notations and dimensions are included. (Foundation options will vary for each plan. If the home you want does not have the type of foundation you desire, a foundation conversion diagram is available from "SOURCE 1".)

3. *Detailed Floor Plans* show the placement of interior walls and the dimensions for rooms, doors, windows, stairways, etc., of each level of the house.

4. *Cross Sections* show details of the house as though it were cut in slices from the roof to the foundation. The cross sections specify the home's construction, insulation, flooring and roofing details.

5. *Interior Elevations* show the specific details of cabinets (kitchen, bathroom, and utility room), fireplaces, built-in units, and other special interior features, depending on the nature and complexity of the item. ***Note:*** *For cost savings and to accommodate your own style and taste, we suggest contacting local cabinet and fireplace distributors for sizes and styles.*

6. *Roof Details* show slope, pitch and location of dormers, gables and other roof elements, including clerestory windows and skylights. These details may be shown on the elevation sheet or on a separate diagram. ***Note:*** *If trusses are used, we suggest using a local truss manufacturer to design your trusses to comply with your local codes and regulations.*

7. *Schematic Electrical Layouts* show the suggested locations for switches, fixtures and outlets. These details may be shown on the floor plan or on a separate diagram.

8. *General Specifications* provide general instructions and information regarding structure, excavating and grading, masonry and concrete work, carpentry and wood, thermal and moisture protection, and specifications about drywall, tile, flooring, glazing, caulking and sealants.

PLANS PACKAGE

OTHER HELPFUL BUILDING AIDS

Every set of plans that you order will contain the details your builder needs. However, "Source 1" provides additional guides and information that you may order, as follows:

1. *Reproducible Blueprint Set* is useful if you will be making changes to the stock home plan you've chosen. This set consists of original line drawings produced on erasable, reproducible paper for the purpose of modification. When alterations are complete, working copies can be made.

2. *Mirror Reversed Plans* are used when building the home in reverse of the illustrated floor plan. Reversed plans are available for an additional one-time surcharge. Since the lettering and dimensions will read backwards, we recommend that you order only one or two reversed sets in addition to the regular-reading sets.

3. *Itemized List of Materials* details the quantity, type and size of materials needed to build your home. (This list is helpful in acquiring an accurate construction estimate.)

4. *Description of Materials* describes the type and quality of materials suggested for the home. This form may be required for obtaining FHA or VA financing.

5. *Typical "How-To" Diagrams — Plumbing, Wiring, Solar Heating, and Framing and Foundation Conversion Diagrams.* Each of these diagrams details the basic tools and techniques needed to plumb, wire and install a solar heating system, convert plans with 2 x 4 exterior walls to 2 x 6 (or vice versa), or adapt a plan for a basement, crawlspace or slab foundation. ***Note: These diagrams are general and not specific to any one plan.**

NOTE: Due to regional variations, local availability of materials, local codes, methods of installation, and individual preferences, it is impossible to include much detail on heating, plumbing, and electrical work on your plans. The duct work, venting, and other details will vary depending on the type of heating and cooling system (forced air, hot water, electric, solar) and the type of energy (gas, oil, electricity, solar) that you use. These details and specifications are easily obtained from your builder, contractor, and/or local suppliers.

PLEASE READ BEFORE YOU ORDER

WHO WE ARE

"Source 1" is a consortium of 45 of America's leading residential designers. All the plans presented in this book are designed by licensed architects or members of the A.I.B.D. (American Institute of Building Designers), and each plan is designed to meet nationally recognized building codes (either the Uniform Building Code, Standard Building Code or Basic Building Code) in effect at the time and place that they were drawn.

BLUEPRINT PRICES

Our sales volume allows us to offer quality blueprints at a fraction of the cost it takes to develop them. Custom designs cost thousands of dollars, usually 5 to 15% of the cost of construction. Design costs for a $100,000 home, for example, can range from $5,000 to $15,000.

Our pricing schedule is based on "Total heated living space." Garages, porches, decks and unfinished basements are not included.

Number of Sets	Price Code Based on Square Feet						
	A under 1,500	B 1,500-1,999	C 2,000-2,499	D 2,500-2,999	E 3,000-3,499	F 3,500-3,999	G 4,000 & up
1	$265	$300	$335	$370	$405	$440	$475
4	$310	$345	$380	$415	$450	$485	$520
7	$340	$375	$410	$445	$480	$515	$550
Reproducible Set	$440	$475	$510	$545	$580	$615	$650

ARCHITECTURAL AND ENGINEERING SEALS

The increased concern over energy costs and safety has prompted many cities and states to require an architect or engineer to review and "seal" a blueprint prior to construction. There may be a fee for this service. Please contact your local lumber yard, municipal building department, Builders Association, or local chapter of the AIBD or AIA (American Institute of Architecture).

Note: (Plans for homes to be built in Nevada may have to be re-drawn and sealed by a Nevada-licensed design professional.)

EXCHANGE INFORMATION

We want you to be happy with your blueprint purchase. If, for some reason, the blueprints that you ordered cannot be used, we will be pleased to exchange them within 30 days of the purchase date. Please note that a handling fee will be assessed for all exchanges. For more information, call us toll-free. **Note: Reproducible Sets cannot be exchanged for any reason.**

ESTIMATING BUILDING COSTS

Building costs vary widely depending on style, size, type of finishing materials you select, and the local rates for labor and building materials. A local average cost per square foot of construction can give you a rough estimate. To get the average cost per square foot in your area, you can call a local contractor, your state or local Builders Association, the National Association of Home Builders (NAHB), or the AIBD. A more accurate estimate will require a professional review of the working blueprints and the types of materials you will be using.

FOUNDATION OPTIONS AND EXTERIOR CONSTRUCTION

Depending on your location and climate, your home will be built with either a slab, crawlspace or basement foundation; the exterior walls will either be 2x4 or 2x6. Most professional contractors and builders can easily adapt a home to meet the foundation and exterior wall requirements that you desire.

If the home that you select does not offer the foundation or exterior wall requirements that you prefer, HomeStyles offers a typical foundation and framing conversion diagram. (See order form.)

HOW MANY BLUEPRINTS SHOULD I ORDER?

A single set of blueprints is sufficient to study and review a home in greater detail. However, if you are planning to get cost estimates or are planning to build, you will need a minimum of 4 sets. If you will be modifying your home plan, we recommend ordering a Reproducible Blueprint Set.

To help determine the exact number of sets you will need, please refer to the Blueprint Checklist below:

BLUEPRINT CHECKLIST

____ **Owner (1 Set)**

____ **Lending Institution (usually 1 set for conventional mortgage; 3 sets for FHA or VA loans)**

____ **Builder (usually requires at least 3 sets)**

____ **Building Permit Department (at least 1 set)**

REVISIONS, MODIFICATIONS AND CUSTOMIZING

The tremendous variety of designs available from "SOURCE 1" allows you to choose the home that best suits your lifestyle, budget and building site. Through your choice of siding, roof, trim, decorating, color, etc., your home can be customized easily.

Minor changes and material substitutions can be made by any professional builder without the need for expensive blueprint revisions. However, if you will be making major changes, we strongly recommend that you order a Reproducible Blueprint Set and seek the services of an architect or professional designer.

**Every state, county and municipality has its own codes, zoning requirements, ordinances, and building regulations. Modifications may be necessary to comply with your specific requirements -- snow loads, energy codes, seismic zones, etc.

COMPLIANCE WITH CODES

Depending on where you live, you may need to modify your plans to comply with local building requirements -- snow loads, energy codes, seismic zones, etc. All "SOURCE 1" plans are designed to meet the specifications of seismic zones I or II. "SOURCE 1" authorizes the use of our blueprints expressly conditioned upon your obligation and agreement to strictly comply with all local building codes, ordinances, regulations, and requirements -- including permits and inspections at the time of construction.

LICENSE AGREEMENT, COPY RESTRICTIONS, COPYRIGHT

When you purchase a "SOURCE 1" blueprint, we, as Licensor, grant you, as Licensee, the right to use these documents to construct a single unit. All of the plans in this publication are protected under the Federal Copyright Act, Title XVII of the United States Code and Chapter 37 of the Code of Federal Regulations. Each "Source 1" designer retains title and ownership of the original documents. The blueprints licensed to you cannot be resold or used by any other person, copied or reproduced by any means. **This does not apply to Reproducible Blueprints.** When you purchase a Reproducible Blueprint Set, you reserve the right to modify and reproduce the plan.

BLUEPRINT ORDER FORM

Ordering your dream home plans is as easy as 1-2-3!

Complete this order form in just 3 easy steps. Then mail in your order, or call 1-800-547-5570 for faster service!

Thank you for your order and good luck with your new home!

1. BLUEPRINTS & ACCESSORIES

BLUEPRINT CHART

SAVE $60! **SAVE $135!**

Price Code	1 Set	4 Sets	7 Sets	Reproducible Set*
A	$265	$310	$340	$440
B	$300	$345	$375	$475
C	$335	$380	$410	$510
D	$370	$415	$445	$545
E	$405	$450	$480	$580
F	$440	$485	$515	$615
G	$475	$520	$550	$650

Prices subject to change.

*A Reproducible Set is produced on erasable paper for the purpose of modification. Available for plans with prefix: A, AG, AGH, AH, AHP, APS, AX, B, BOD, C, CPS, DD, DW, E, EOF, FB, GL, GML, GSA, H, HDS, HFL, J, K, KLF, LMB, LRD, M, NW, OH, PH, PI, PM, S, SDG, THD, U, UDG, V.

ADDITIONAL SETS: Additional sets of the plan ordered are $35 each. Save $60 to $135 when you order the 4-set or 7-set package shown above!

MIRROR REVERSED SETS: $40 Surcharge. From the total number of sets you ordered above, choose the number of these that you want to be reversed. Pay only $40. *Note: All writing on mirror reversed plans is backwards. We recommend ordering only one or two reversed sets in addition to the regular-reading sets.*

ITEMIZED LIST OF MATERIALS: Available for $40; each additional set is $10. Details the quantity, type and size of materials needed to build your home.

DESCRIPTION OF MATERIALS: Sold only in a set of two for $40. (For use in obtaining FHA or VA financing.)

TYPICAL HOW-TO DIAGRAMS: One set $12.50. Two sets $23. Three sets $30. All four sets only $35. General guides on plumbing, wiring, and solar heating, plus information on how to convert from one foundation or exterior framing to another. *Note: These diagrams are not specific to any one plan.*

2. SHIPPING AND HANDLING

Add shipping and handling costs according to chart below:

	1-3 Sets	4-6 Sets	7 Sets or more	Reproducible Set
U.S. Regular (5-6 working days)	$12.50	$15.00	$17.50	$15.00
U.S. Express (2-3 working days)	$25.00	$27.50	$30.00	$27.50
Canada Regular (2-3 weeks)	$12.50	$15.00	$17.50	$15.00
Canada Express (5-6 working days)	$25.00	$30.00	$35.00	$30.00
Overseas/Airmail (7-10 working days)	$50.00	$60.00	$70.00	$60.00

3. PAYMENT INFORMATION

Choose the method of payment you prefer. Send check, money order or credit card information, along with name and address to:

1. COMPLETE THIS FORM

Plan Number_____ Price Code_____

Foundation_____
(Carefully review the foundation option(s) available for your plan -- basement, crawlspace, pole, pier, or slab. If several options are offered, choose only one.)

No. of Sets:
- ☐ One Set
- ☐ Four Sets
- ☐ Seven Sets
- ☐ One Reproducible Set

$_____ (See Blueprint Chart at left)

ADDITIONAL SETS_____ (Quantity) $_____ ($35 each)

MIRROR REVERSED SETS_____ (Quantity) $_____ ($40 Surcharge)

ITEMIZED LIST OF MATERIALS_____ (Quantity) $_____ ($40; $10 for each additional)
(Available on plans with prefix: AH, AHP, APS*, AX*, B*, C, CAR, CDG*, CPS, DD*, DW, E, FB, GSA, H, HFL, I, J, K, LMB*, LRD, N, NW*, P, PH, R, S, THD, U, UDG, VL.)
*Not available on all plans. *Please call before ordering.*

DESCRIPTION OF MATERIALS $_____ ($40 for two sets)
(Available on plans with prefix: AHP, C, DW, H, HFL, J, K, LMB, N, P, PH, VL.)

TYPICAL HOW-TO DIAGRAMS $_____ (All four only $35)
(One set $12.50. Two sets $23. Three sets $30.)
☐ Plumbing ☐ Wiring ☐ Solar Heating ☐ Framing & Foundation Conversion

SUBTOTAL $_____

SALES TAX* $_____ (*MN residents add 6.5% sales tax)

2.
SHIPPING & HANDLING $_____ (See chart at left)

3.
GRAND TOTAL $_____

☐ Check/Money Order enclosed (in U.S. funds)
☐ VISA ☐ MASTERCARD ☐ DISCOVER ☐ AMEX

Credit Card#_____ Exp. Date_____

Name_____

Address_____

City_____ State_____ Country_____

Zip_____ Daytime Phone(___)_____

Check if you are a builder: ☐ Home Phone(___)_____

Mail coupon to: **HomeStyles Plan Service** P.O. Box 50670 Minneapolis, MN 55405

Or Fax to: **(612)338-1626**

FOR FASTER SERVICE CALL 1-800-547-5570

FOR FASTER SERVICE CALL 1-800-547-5570

PGW #27

Simple Exterior, Luxurious Interior

- Modest and unassuming on the exterior, this design provides an elegant and spacious interior.
- Highlight of the home is undoubtedly the vast Great Room/Dining area, with its vaulted ceiling, massive hearth and big bay windows.
- An exceptionally fine master suite is also included, with a large sleeping area, luxurious bath and big walk-in closet.
- A beautiful kitchen is joined by a bright bay-windowed breakfast nook; also note the large pantry.
- The lower level encompasses two more bedrooms and a generously sized game room and bar.

MAIN FLOOR

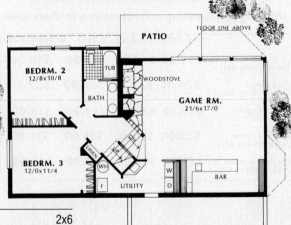

BASEMENT

Plan P-6595-3D

Bedrooms: 3	Baths: 2½

Space:	
Main floor:	1,530 sq. ft.
Lower level:	1,145 sq. ft.
Total living area:	**2,675 sq. ft.**
Garage:	462 sq. ft.

Exterior Wall Framing:	2x6

Foundation options:
Daylight basement only.
(Foundation & framing conversion diagram available — see order form.)

Blueprint Price Code:	D

Plan P-6595-3D

PRICES AND DETAILS ON PAGES 12-15

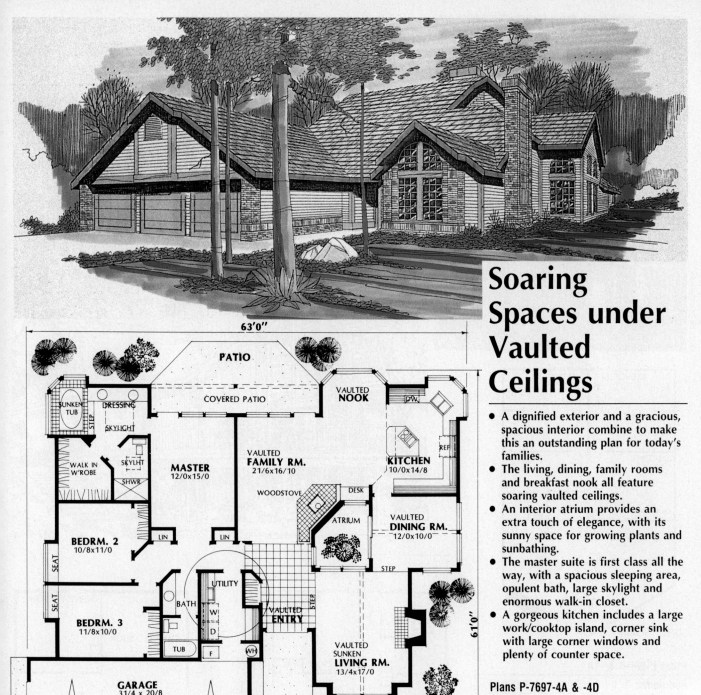

Soaring Spaces under Vaulted Ceilings

- A dignified exterior and a gracious, spacious interior combine to make this an outstanding plan for today's families.
- The living, dining, family rooms and breakfast nook all feature soaring vaulted ceilings.
- An interior atrium provides an extra touch of elegance, with its sunny space for growing plants and sunbathing.
- The master suite is first class all the way, with a spacious sleeping area, opulent bath, large skylight and enormous walk-in closet.
- A gorgeous kitchen includes a large work/cooktop island, corner sink with large corner windows and plenty of counter space.

Plans P-7697-4A & -4D

Bedrooms: 3	Baths: 2

Space:	
Main floor (crawlspace version):	2,003 sq. ft.
Main floor (basement version):	2,030 sq. ft.
Basement:	2,015 sq. ft.
Garage:	647 sq. ft.

Exterior Wall Framing:	2x6

Foundation options:
Daylight basement (Plan P-7697-4D).
Crawlspace (Plan P-7697-4A).
(Foundation & framing conversion diagram available — see order form.)

Blueprint Price Code:	C

Floor Plan Labels

63'0"

PATIO

COVERED PATIO

VAULTED NOOK

DW

SUNKEN TUB

DRESSING

SKYLIGHT

SKYLHT

WALK IN W'ROBE

SHWR

MASTER 12/0x15/0

VAULTED FAMILY RM. 21/6x16/10

KITCHEN 10/0x14/8

REF

WOODSTOVE

DESK

BEDRM. 2 10/8x11/0

LIN

LIN

ATRIUM

VAULTED DINING RM. 12/0x10/0

SEAT

STEP

SEAT

BEDRM. 3 11/8x10/0

UTILITY

W D

BATH

VAULTED ENTRY

STEP

TUB

F

WH

VAULTED SUNKEN LIVING RM. 13/4x17/0

GARAGE 31/4 x 20/8

61'0"

RAILING

DN

BATH

VAULTED ENTRY

W D

PLAN P-7697-4D
WITH DAYLIGHT BASEMENT

Soaring Design
Lifts the Human Spirit

- Suitable for level or sloping lots, this versatile design can be expanded or finished as time and budget allow.
- Surrounding deck accessible from all main living areas.
- Great living room enhanced by vaulted ceilings, second-floor

balcony, skylights and dramatic window wall.
- Rear entrance has convenient access to full bath and laundry room.
- Two additional bedrooms on upper level share second bath and balcony room.

**NOTE: The above photographed home may have been modified by the homeowner. Please refer to floor plan and/or drawn elevation shown for actual blueprint details.

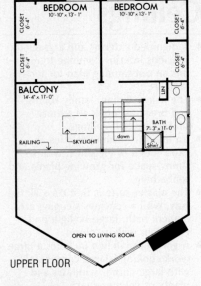

UPPER FLOOR

BEDROOM 10'-10" x 13'-1"
BEDROOM 10'-10" x 13'-1"
CLOSET 6'-4"
CLOSET 6'-4"
CLOSET 6'-4"
CLOSET 6'-4"
BALCONY 14'-4" x 11'-0"
LIN.
BATH 7'-3" x 11'-0"
Shwr.
RAILING
SKYLIGHT
down
OPEN TO LIVING ROOM

Plans H-930-1 & -1A

Bedrooms: 3	Baths: 2

Space:	
Upper floor:	710 sq. ft.
Main floor:	1,210 sq. ft.
Total living area:	**1,920 sq. ft.**
Basement:	605 sq. ft.
Garage/shop:	605 sq. ft.

Exterior Wall Framing:	2x6

Foundation options:
Daylight basement (Plan H-930-1).
Crawlspace (Plan H-930-1A).
(Foundation & framing conversion diagram available — see order form.)

Blueprint Price Code:	
Without basement:	B
With basement:	D

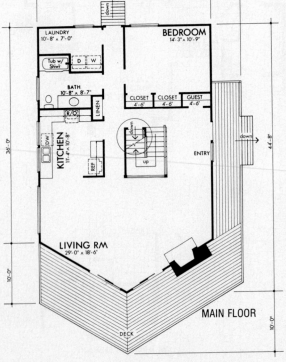

LAUNDRY 10'-8" x 7'-0"
Tub w/ Shwr
D W
BATH 10'-8" x 8'-7"
R/O
LINEN
KITCHEN 11'-4" x 10'-8"
DW
REF
BEDROOM 14'-3" x 10'-9"
CLOSET 4'-6"
CLOSET 4'-6"
GUEST 4'-6"
down
up
ENTRY
down
LIVING RM 29'-0" x 18'-6"
DECK
30'-0"
5'-0"
36'-0"
10'-0"
44'-8"
10'-0"

MAIN FLOOR

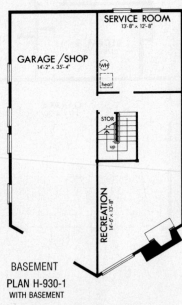

SERVICE ROOM 13'-8" x 12'-8"
GARAGE/SHOP 14'-2" x 35'-4"
WH
heat
STOR
up
RECREATION 14'-6" x 13'-8"

BASEMENT
PLAN H-930-1
WITH BASEMENT

STOR

PLAN H-930-1A
WITHOUT BASEMENT
(CRAWLSPACE FOUNDATION)

TO ORDER THIS BLUEPRINT, CALL TOLL-FREE 1-800-547-5570 **Plans H-930-1 & -1A** *PRICES AND DETAILS ON PAGES 12-15*

Instant Impact

- Bold rooflines, interesting angles and unusual window treatments give this stylish home lots of impact.
- Inside, high ceilings and an open floor plan maximize the home's square footage. At only 28 ft. wide, the home also is ideal for a narrow lot.
- A covered deck leads to the main entry, which features a sidelighted door, angled glass walls and a view of the striking open staircase.
- The Great Room is stunning, with its vaulted ceiling, energy-efficient woodstove and access to a large deck.
- A flat ceiling distinguishes the dining area, which shares an angled snack bar/cooktop with the step-saving kitchen. A laundry/mudroom is nearby.
- Upstairs, the master suite offers a sloped ceiling and a clerestory window. A walk-through closet leads to the private bath, which is enhanced by a skylighted, sloped ceiling.
- Linen and storage closets line the hallway leading to the smaller bedrooms, one of which has a sloped ceiling and double closets.

Plans H-1427-3A & -3B

Bedrooms: 3	Baths: 2½
Living Area:	
Upper floor	880 sq. ft.
Main floor	810 sq. ft.
Total Living Area:	**1,690 sq. ft.**
Daylight basement	810 sq. ft.
Garage	409 sq. ft.
Exterior Wall Framing:	2x4
Foundation Options:	**Plan #**
Daylight basement	H-1427-3B
Crawlspace	H-1427-3A

(All plans can be built with your choice of foundation and framing. A generic conversion diagram is available. See order form.)

BLUEPRINT PRICE CODE:	**B**

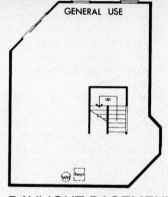

GENERAL USE

DAYLIGHT BASEMENT

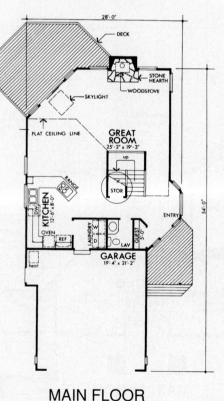

28'-0"

DECK

STONE HEARTH

WOODSTOVE

SKYLIGHT

FLAT CEILING LINE

GREAT ROOM
25'-2" x 19'-3"

RANGE

KITCHEN
12'-6" x 9'-0"

DW

OVEN

REF

LAUNDRY

STOR

CLOSET
5'-0"

ENTRY

LAV

GARAGE
19'-4" x 21'-2"

heat

54'-0"

MAIN FLOOR

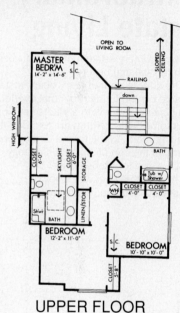

OPEN TO LIVING ROOM

MASTER BEDR'M
14'-2" x 14'-6"

RAILING

down

SLOPED CEILING

HIGH WINDOW

CLOSET 6'-0"

SKYLIGHT

CLOSET 6'-0"

STORAGE

LINEN/STOR

BATH

Tub w/ Shower

CLOSET 4'-0"

CLOSET 4'-0"

WH

BATH

Sh'wr

BEDROOM
12'-2" x 11'-0"

S.C.

BEDROOM
10'-10" x 10'-0"

CLOSET 5'-8"

UPPER FLOOR

STAIRWAY AREA IN CRAWLSPACE VERSION

Photo by Mark Englund/HomeStyles

Extraordinary Estate Living

- Extraordinary estate living is at its best in this palatial beauty.
- The double-doored entry opens to a large central living room that overlooks a covered patio with a vaulted ceiling. Volume 14-ft. ceilings are found in the living room, in the formal dining room and in the den or study, which may serve as a fourth bedroom.
- The gourmet chef will enjoy the spacious kitchen, which flaunts a cooktop island, a walk-in pantry and a peninsula snack counter shared with the breakfast room and family room.
- This trio of informal living spaces also shares a panorama of glass and a corner fireplace centered between TV and media niches.
- Isolated at the opposite end of the home is the spacious master suite, which offers private patio access. Dual walk-in closets define the entrance to the adjoining master bath, complete with a garden Jacuzzi and separate dressing areas.
- The hall bath also opens to the outdoors for use as a pool bath.

Plan HDS-99-177	
Bedrooms: 3+	**Baths:** 3
Living Area:	
Main floor	2,597 sq. ft.
Total Living Area:	**2,597 sq. ft.**
Garage	761 sq. ft.
Exterior Wall Framing:	2x4

Foundation Options:

Slab
(All plans can be built with your choice of foundation and framing. A generic conversion diagram is available. See order form.)

BLUEPRINT PRICE CODE: D

NOTE:
The above photographed home may have been modified by the homeowner. Please refer to floor plan and/or drawn elevation shown for actual blueprint details.

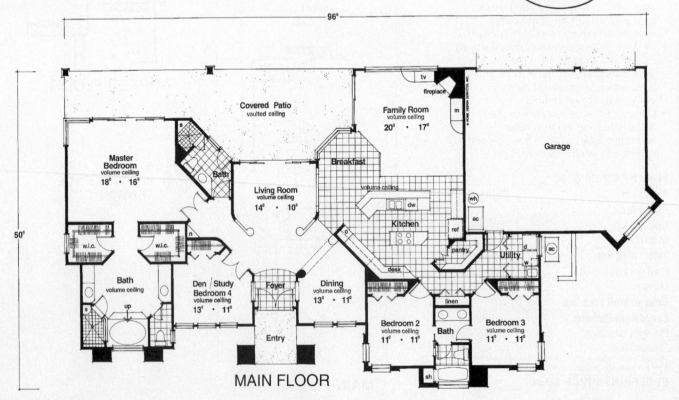

MAIN FLOOR

Plan HDS-99-177

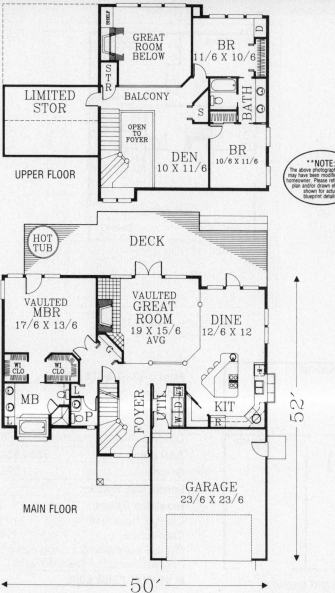

GREAT ROOM BELOW

BR 11/6 X 10/6

LIMITED STOR

STR

BALCONY

BATH

S

OPEN TO FOYER

DEN 10 X 11/6

BR 10/6 X 11/6

UPPER FLOOR

**NOTE:
The above photographed home may have been modified by the homeowner. Please refer to floor plan and/or drawn elevation shown for actual blueprint details.

HOT TUB

DECK

VAULTED MBR 17/6 X 13/6

VAULTED GREAT ROOM 19 X 15/6 AVG

DINE 12/6 X 12

WI CLO

WI CLO

MB

L

P

FOYER

UTIL

W D

KIT

52'

GARAGE 23/6 X 23/6

MAIN FLOOR

50'

Vaulted Great Room

- While the exterior has traditional overtones, this plan is thoroughly modern both inside and out.
- The vaulted Great Room with adjacent kitchen and dining room gives the home an open and spacious feeling.
- The vaulted master suite on the first floor includes walk-in closets and a sumptuous master bath.
- The upper floor includes two more bedrooms, which share a continental bath.
- Also note the den and balcony overlooking the foyer and Great Room below.
- A huge deck with a hot tub can be reached easily from the master suite, the Great Room or the dining room.

Plan S-2100	
Bedrooms: 3	**Baths:** 2½
Living Area:	
Upper floor:	660 sq. ft.
Main floor	1,440 sq. ft.
Total Living Area:	**2,100 sq. ft.**
Standard basement	1,440 sq. ft.
Garage	552 sq. ft.
Exterior Wall Framing:	2x6
Foundation Options:	
Standard basement	
Crawlspace	
Slab	
(Typical foundation & framing conversion diagram available—see order form.)	
BLUEPRINT PRICE CODE:	C

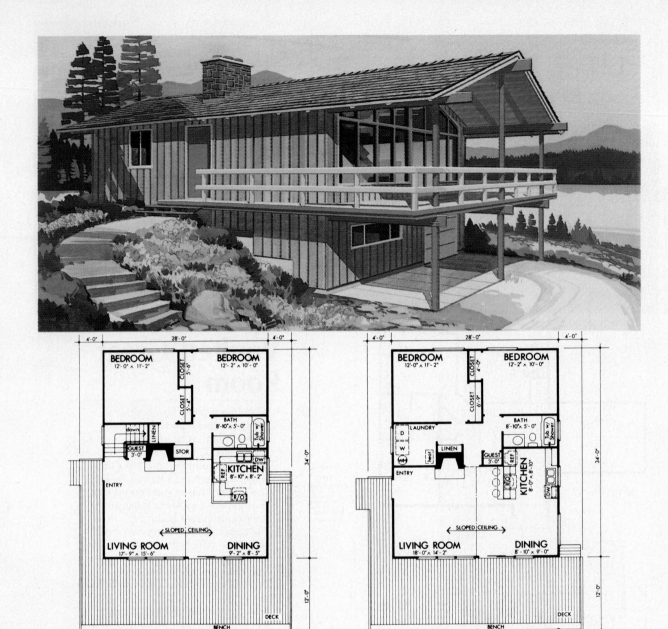

MAIN FLOOR PLAN H-833-7
WITH DAYLIGHT BASEMENT

MAIN FLOOR PLAN H-833-7A
WITHOUT BASEMENT

An Owner-Builder Special

- Everything you need for a leisure or retirement retreat is neatly packaged in just 952 square feet.
- The basic rectangular design features a unique wraparound deck, which is entirely covered by the projecting roof-line.
- Vaulted ceilings and a central fireplace visually enhance the cozy living/dining room.
- The daylight-basement option is suitable for building on a sloping lot.

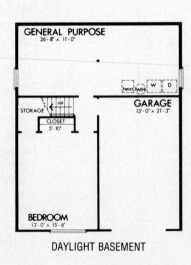

DAYLIGHT BASEMENT

Plans H-833-7 & -7A	
Bedrooms: 2-3	**Baths: 1**
Living Area:	
Main floor	952 sq. ft.
Optional daylight basement	676 sq. ft.
Total Living Area:	**952/1,628 sq. ft.**
Garage	276 sq. ft.
Exterior Wall Framing:	2x6
Foundation Options:	**Plan #**
Daylight basement	H-833-7
Crawlspace	H-833-7A
(Typical foundation & framing conversion diagram available—see order form.)	
BLUEPRINT PRICE CODE:	**A/B**

TO ORDER THIS BLUEPRINT,
CALL TOLL-FREE 1-800-547-5570

Plan H-833-7 & -7A

PRICES AND DETAILS
ON PAGES 12-15

REAR VIEW

Solar Flair

- Full window walls and a sun room with glass roof act as passive energy collectors in this popular floor plan.
- Expansive living room features wood stove and vaulted ceilings.
- Dining room shares a breakfast counter with the merging kitchen.
- Convenient laundry room is positioned near kitchen and garage entrance.
- Second level is devoted entirely to the private master suite, featuring vaulted ceiling and a balcony view to the living room below.

Plans H-877-5A & -5B

Bedrooms: 3-4	Baths: 2-3

Space:

Upper floor:	382 sq. ft.
Main floor:	1,200 sq. ft.
Sun room:	162 sq. ft.
Total living area:	**1,744 sq. ft.**
Basement:	approx. 1,200 sq. ft.
Garage:	457 sq. ft.

Exterior Wall Framing:	2x6

Foundation options:
Daylight basement (Plan H-877-5B).
Crawlspace (Plan H-877-5A).
(Foundation & framing conversion diagram available — see order form.)

Blueprint Price Code:

Without basement:	B
With basement:	D

UPPER FLOOR

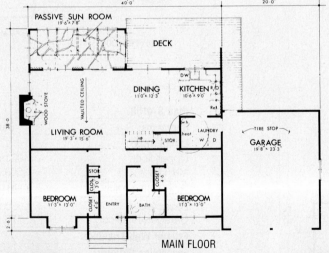

MAIN FLOOR

PLAN H-877-5B
WITH BASEMENT

BASEMENT

FRONT VIEW

Gracious Open-Concept Floor Plan

- A striking and luxurious contemporary, this home offers great space and modern styling.
- A covered entry leads to a spacious foyer, which flows into the sunken dining and Great Room area.
- The vaulted Great Room boasts a spectacular two-story-high fireplace, dramatic window walls and access to a rear deck or patio.
- A bright nook adjoins the open kitchen, which includes a corner window above the sink.
- The den, which could be a guest bedroom, features a bay window overlooking the deck.
- The majestic master bedroom on the second floor offers a 10-ft.-high coved ceiling, a splendid bath, a large closet and a private deck.
- Two other upstairs bedrooms share a second bath and a balcony hallway overlooking the Great Room and entry below.

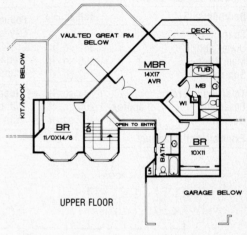

UPPER FLOOR

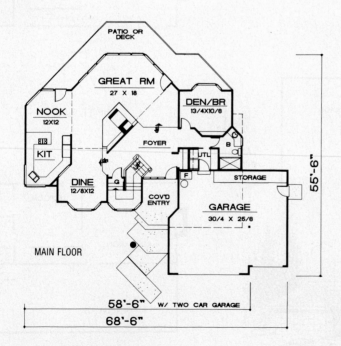

MAIN FLOOR

58'-6" W/ TWO CAR GARAGE

68'-6"

Plan S-41587

Bedrooms: 3-4	**Baths: 3**
Living Area:	
Upper floor:	1,001 sq. ft.
Main floor	1,550 sq. ft.
Total Living Area:	**2,551 sq. ft.**
Basement	1,550 sq. ft.
Garage (three-car)	773 sq. ft.
Exterior Wall Framing:	2x6

Foundation Options:
Daylight basement
Standard basement
Crawlspace
Slab
(Typical foundation & framing conversion diagram available—see order form.)

BLUEPRINT PRICE CODE:	D

Raised Cottage Design Offers Large Covered Porches

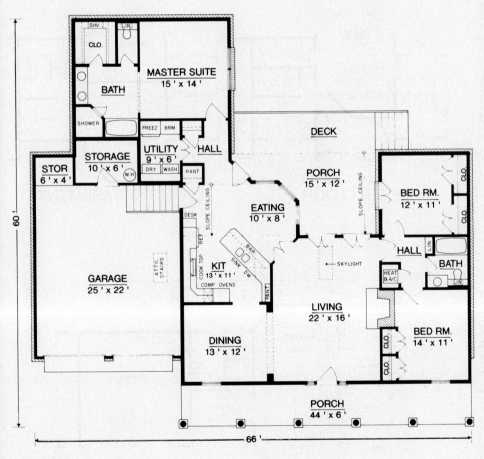

- Twin dormers and covered porch add drama to this raised one-story.
- Large centered living room features 12' ceilings and built-in skylights.
- Kitchen has unusual but functional angular design, sloped ceilings, bar, and eating area that overlooks the adjoining deck.
- Elegant master suite is conveniently located near kitchen.

Plan E-1826

Bedrooms: 3	Baths: 2

Space:	
Total living area:	1,800 sq. ft.
Garage:	550 sq. ft.
Storage:	84 sq. ft.
Porches:	466 sq. ft.

Exterior Wall Framing:	2x6

Foundation options:
Crawlspace.
Slab.
(Foundation & framing conversion diagram available — see order form.)

Blueprint Price Code:	B

Unique and Dramatic

- This home's unique interior and dramatic exterior make it perfect for a sloping, scenic lot.
- An expansive and impressive Great Room, warmed by a woodstove, flows into an island kitchen that's completely open in design.
- The passive-solar sun room is designed to collect and store heat from the sun, while providing a good view of the surroundings.
- Upstairs, you'll see a glamorous, skylighted master suite with a private bath and a huge walk-in closet.
- A skylighted hall bath serves the bright second bedroom.
- The daylight basement adds a sunny sitting room, a third bedroom and a large recreation room.

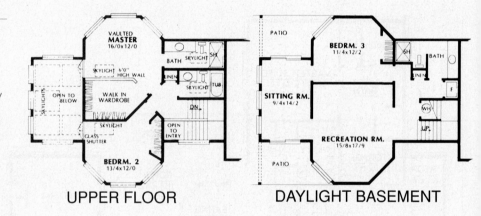

UPPER FLOOR

DAYLIGHT BASEMENT

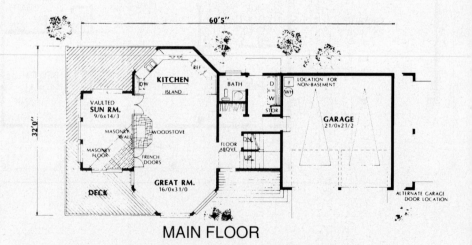

MAIN FLOOR

Plans P-536-2A & -2D

Bedrooms: 2+		**Baths:** 2½-3½
Living Area:		
Upper floor		642 sq. ft.
Main floor		863 sq. ft.
Daylight basement		863 sq. ft.
Total Living Area:		**1,505/2,368 sq. ft.**
Garage		445 sq. ft.
Exterior Wall Framing:		2x6
Foundation Options:		**Plan #**
Daylight basement		P-536-2D
Crawlspace		P-536-2A

(All plans can be built with your choice of foundation and framing. A generic conversion diagram is available. See order form.)

BLUEPRINT PRICE CODE:	**B/C**

Plans P-536-2A & -2D

PRICES AND DETAILS ON PAGES 12-15

Free-Flowing Floor Plan

- A fluid floor plan with open indoor/outdoor living spaces characterizes this exciting luxury home.
- The stylish columned porch opens to a spacious living room and dining room expanse that overlooks the outdoor spaces. The breathtaking view also includes a dramatic corner fireplace.
- The dining area opens to a bright kitchen with an angled eating bar. The overall spaciousness of the living areas is increased with high 12-ft. ceilings.
- A sunny, informal eating area adjoins the kitchen, and an angled set of doors opens to a convenient main-floor laundry room near the garage entrance.
- The vaulted master bedroom has a walk-in closet and a sumptuous bath with an oval tub.
- A separate wing houses two additional bedrooms and another full bath.
- Attic space is accessible from stairs in the garage and in the bedroom wing.

Plan E-1710

Bedrooms: 3	Baths: 2

Living Area:

Main floor	1,792 sq. ft.
Total Living Area:	**1,792 sq. ft.**
Standard basement	1,792 sq. ft.
Garage	484 sq. ft.
Storage	96 sq. ft.

Exterior Wall Framing:	2x6

Foundation Options:

Standard basement
Crawlspace
Slab

(All plans can be built with your choice of foundation and framing. A generic conversion diagram is available. See order form.)

BLUEPRINT PRICE CODE:	B

REAR VIEW

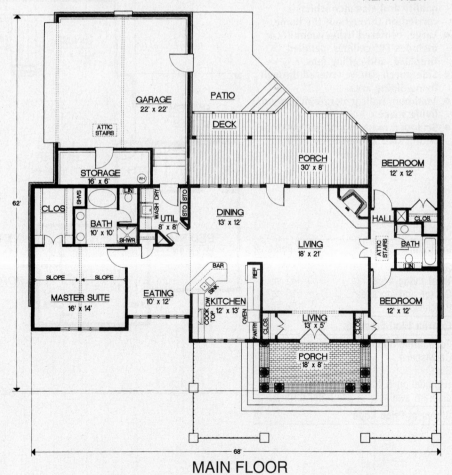

MAIN FLOOR

The Solid Look of Permanence

- Exterior design lends an air of quality and elegance which is carried on throughout the home.
- Large, centered living room decor includes 10' ceilings, detailed fireplace, and ceiling fans.
- Side porch can be entered through living/dining area.
- Minimum halls generate maximum living space.
- Secluded master suite has romantic sitting area and designer bath.

Plan E-1435

Bedrooms: 3	Baths: 2

Space:	
Total living area:	1,442 sq. ft.
Garage and storage:	516 sq. ft.
Porches:	128 sq. ft.

Exterior Wall Framing:	2x4

Foundation options:
Crawlspace.
Slab.
(Foundation & framing conversion diagram available — see order form.)

Blueprint Price Code:	A

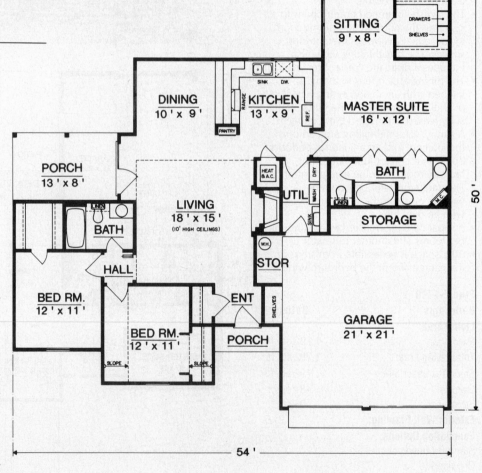

Plan E-1435

Outstanding Floor Plan

- This sharp, stately one-story design is attractively accented with brick.
- The focal point of the interior is a grand, spacious family room with a beamed cathedral ceiling, a slate-hearth fireplace and sliding glass doors to a backyard terrace.
- The adjoining kitchen has a curved snack bar and opens to a sunny dinette

area that is framed by a curved wall of windows overlooking the terrace.
- The formal living spaces grace the front of the home. The large living room features a sloped ceiling and dramatic, high windows. The spacious dining room has easy access to the kitchen.
- Included in the sleeping wing is a luxurious master suite with a private bath. A big walk-in closet and a skylighted dressing room are featured.
- The two secondary bedrooms share a hall bath that has a dual-sink vanity. A half-bath is near the mudroom.

Plan K-278-M	
Bedrooms: 3	**Baths:** 2½
Living Area:	
Main floor	1,803 sq. ft.
Total Living Area:	**1,803 sq. ft.**
Standard basement	1,778 sq. ft.
Garage and storage	586 sq. ft.
Exterior Wall Framing:	2x4 or 2x6
Foundation Options:	

Standard basement
Slab
(All plans can be built with your choice of foundation and framing. A generic conversion diagram is available. See order form.)

BLUEPRINT PRICE CODE:	B

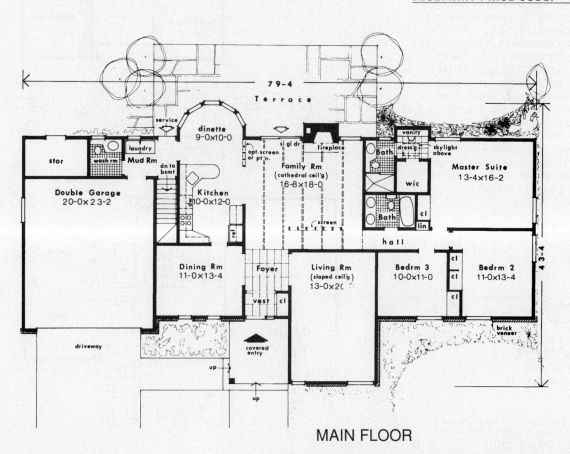

MAIN FLOOR

Photo by Mark Englund/HomeStyles

Stately Elegance

- The elegant interior of this home is introduced by the barrel vault and stately columns at the front entry.
- Double doors open from the entry to the two-story-high foyer, where a half-round transom window brightens the central open-railed stairway.
- Off the foyer, the living room is separated from the sunny dining room by impressive columns.
- The island kitchen offers a bright corner sink, a walk-in pantry and a bayed breakfast area that merges with the spacious family room.
- A door opens from the family room to the backyard patio, plus a wet bar and a fireplace enhance the whole area.
- Upstairs, the master suite boasts a wall of windows and a private bath with two walk-in closets, a corner garden tub and a separate shower. Three additional bedrooms have private access to one of two more full baths.

Plan DD-2968-A

Bedrooms: 4+	Baths: 3½
Living Area:	
Upper floor	1,382 sq. ft.
Main floor	1,586 sq. ft.
Total Living Area:	**2,968 sq. ft.**
Standard basement	1,586 sq. ft.
Garage	521 sq. ft.
Exterior Wall Framing:	2x4

Foundation Options:

Standard basement

Crawlspace

Slab

(All plans can be built with your choice of foundation and framing. A generic conversion diagram is available. See order form.)

BLUEPRINT PRICE CODE: D

NOTE:
The above photographed home may have been modified by the homeowner. Please refer to floor plan and/or drawn elevation shown for actual blueprint details.

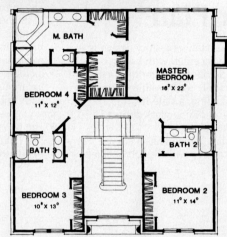

UPPER FLOOR

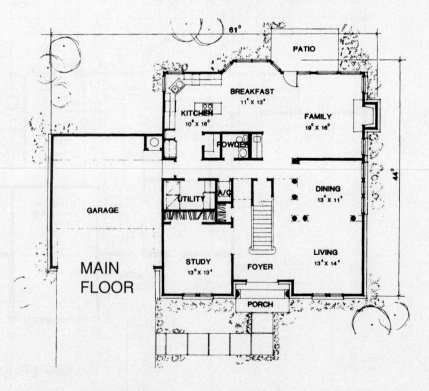

MAIN FLOOR

TO ORDER THIS BLUEPRINT, CALL TOLL-FREE 1-800-547-5570

Plan DD-2968-A

PRICES AND DETAILS ON PAGES 12-15

Build It on Weekends

- The basic design and use of truss roof framing promote easy and speedy erection.
- See-through kitchen allows a look into the living or dining rooms.
- Living room reveals the outdoors and surrounding deck through sliding glass doors.
- Separate bedroom/bathroom area eliminates cross-room traffic and wasted hall space.
- Plan H-921-2A utilizes the sealed crawlspace as an air distribution chamber for a Plen-Wood heating system.
- Plan H-921-1A has a standard crawlspace foundation and optional solar heating system.

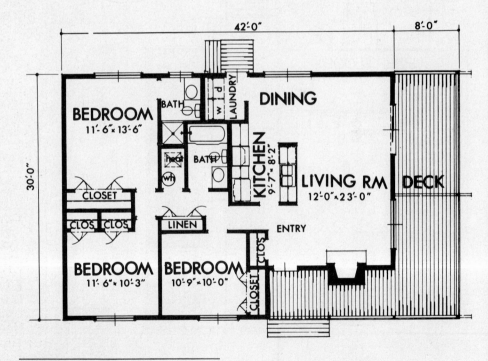

Plans H-921-1A & -2A

Bedrooms: 3	Baths: 2

Space:

Main floor:	1,164 sq. ft.
Total living area:	**1,164 sq. ft.**

Exterior Wall Framing:	2x6

Foundation options:
Plen-Wood crawlspace system (Plan H-921-2A).
Standard crawlspace (Plan H-921-1A).
(Foundation & framing conversion diagram available — see order form.)

Blueprint Price Code: A

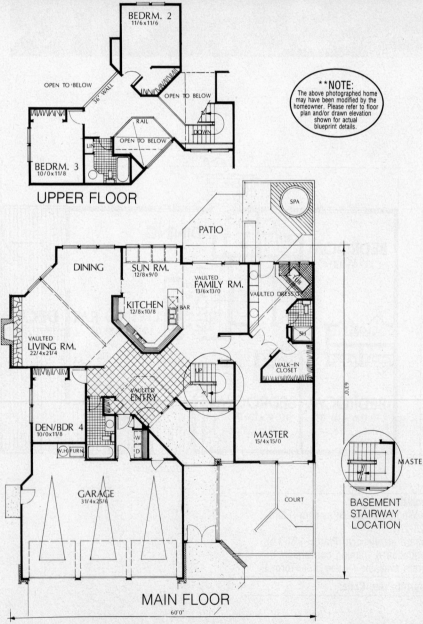

BEDRM. 2
11/6 x 11/6

OPEN TO BELOW

36 WALL

OPEN TO BELOW

RAIL

LIN

OPEN TO BELOW

DOWN

BEDRM. 3
10/0 x 11/8

UPPER FLOOR

**NOTE:
The above photographed home
may have been modified by the
homeowner. Please refer to floor
plan and/or drawn elevation
shown for actual
blueprint details.

SPA

PATIO

DINING

SUN RM.
12/8 x 9/0

VAULTED
FAMILY RM.
13/6 x 13/0

VAULTED DRESS.

KITCHEN
12/8 x 10/8

BAR

VAULTED
LIVING RM.
22/4 x 21/4

SH

UP

WALK-IN
CLOSET

VAULTED
ENTRY

DEN/BDR 4
10/0 x 11/8

W D

MASTER
15/4 x 15/0

W.H FURN

63'0"

GARAGE
31/4 x 25/6

COURT

MASTER

BASEMENT
STAIRWAY
LOCATION

MAIN FLOOR

60'0"

Privacy and Luxury

- This home's large roof planes and privacy fences enclose a thoroughly modern, open floor plan.
- A beautiful courtyard greets guests on their way to the secluded entrance. Inside, a vaulted entry area leads directly into the living and dining rooms, which also boast a vaulted ceiling, plus floor-to-ceiling windows, a fireplace and a wall-length stone hearth.
- A sun room next to the spacious, angular kitchen offers passive solar heating and natural brightness.
- The vaulted family room features access to a rear patio through sliding glass doors.
- The main-floor master bedroom boasts sliders to a secluded portion of the front courtyard. The vaulted master bath includes a walk-in closet, a raised tub, a separate shower and access to a private sun deck with a hot tub.
- Upstairs, two bedrooms are separated by a bridge hallway that overlooks the rooms below.

Plans P-7663-3A & -3D

Bedrooms: 3+	Baths: 3
Living Area:	
Upper floor	569 sq. ft.
Main floor	2,039 sq. ft.
Total Living Area:	**2,608 sq. ft.**
Daylight basement	2,039 sq. ft.
Garage	799 sq. ft.
Exterior Wall Framing:	2x4
Foundation Options:	**Plan #**
Daylight basement	P-7663-3D
Crawlspace	P-7663-3A
(Typical foundation & framing conversion diagram available—see order form.)	
BLUEPRINT PRICE CODE:	D

Dramatic Dining Room

- The highlight of this lovely one-story design is its dramatic dining room, which boasts a high ceiling and a tall wall of windows.
- The soaring foyer ushers guests through an arched opening and into the vaulted Great Room, which is warmed by a showy fireplace.
- The kitchen features a large pantry, a serving bar and a handy pass-through to the family room. The bright breakfast area offers outdoor access and a convenient laundry closet.
- The two secondary bedrooms share a compartmentalized bath.
- The master suite is unsurpassed, with its sitting room, plant shelves and volume ceilings. A gorgeous corner tub is found in the luxurious master bath.

Plan FB-5008-ALLE

Bedrooms: 3	Baths: 2
Living Area:	
Main floor	1,715 sq. ft.
Total Living Area:	**1,715 sq. ft.**
Daylight basement	1,715 sq. ft.
Garage	400 sq. ft.
Exterior Wall Framing:	2x4

Foundation Options:

Daylight basement

Crawlspace

Slab

(All plans can be built with your choice of foundation and framing. A generic conversion diagram is available. See order form.)

BLUEPRINT PRICE CODE:	B

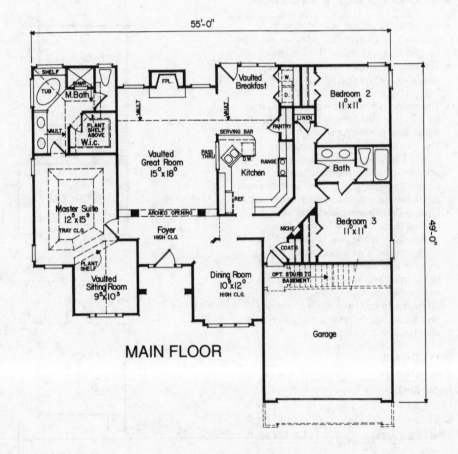

MAIN FLOOR

Fabulous Facade

- Beautiful windows, accented with columns and keystones, blanket the facade of this distinguished home.
- The interior spaces are deceptively spacious, beginning with a two-story-high entry and an open staircase.
- The right side of the home is taken up by a bayed living room that stretches to the formal dining room.
- The casual living area includes an island kitchen with a walk-in pantry and an adjoining morning room with access to a rear patio. The family room has a fireplace and plenty of windows.
- Upstairs, the master bedroom has a ceiling that slopes to 10 feet. The master bath offers two walk-in closets separated by a whirlpool bath, plus a shower and a toilet compartment.
- Walk-in closets are also found in the two remaining bedrooms. The front-facing bedroom boasts a 9-ft. ceiling and an arched window. The game room also has a 9-ft. ceiling.

Plan DD-2460

Bedrooms: 3+	Baths: 2½
Living Area:	
Upper floor	1,407 sq. ft.
Main floor	1,085 sq. ft.
Total Living Area:	**2,492 sq. ft.**
Standard basement	1,085 sq. ft.
Garage	410 sq. ft.
Exterior Wall Framing:	2x4

Foundation Options:

Standard basement

Crawlspace

Slab

(All plans can be built with your choice of foundation and framing. A generic conversion diagram is available. See order form.)

BLUEPRINT PRICE CODE: C

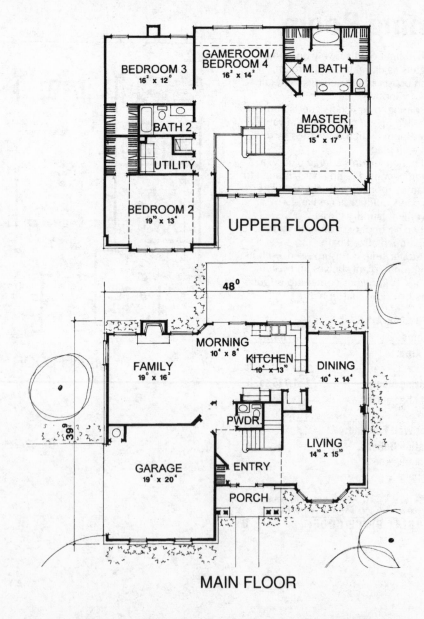

A Chalet for Today

- This new, up-to-date chalet design is ideal for recreational living, whether year-round or part-time. The home's rustic appeal and soaring windows are ideally suited to scenic sites.
- The living and dining rooms are combined to take advantage of the dramatic cathedral ceiling, the view through the spectacular windows and the rugged stone fireplace.
- A quaint balcony adds to the warm country feeling of the living area, which is further expanded by a wrap-around deck. The open, peninsula kitchen includes a breakfast bar that connects it to the living area.
- The first-floor study or den is an added feature rarely found in a home of this size and style.
- A convenient main-floor laundry is adjacent to two bedrooms and a full bath.
- The master bedroom retreat takes up the entire second floor. Cathedral ceilings, sweeping views from the balcony and a private bath with spa tub are highlights here.
- The optional basement plan calls for a tuck-under garage, a large family room, plus utility and storage space.

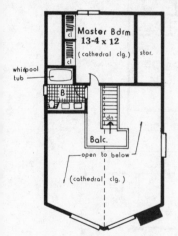

UPPER FLOOR

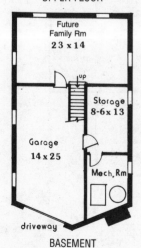

BASEMENT

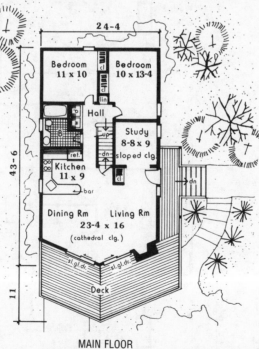

MAIN FLOOR

Plan AHP-9340

Bedrooms: 3-4	Baths: 2
Living Area:	
Upper floor	332 sq. ft.
Main floor	974 sq. ft.
Total Living Area:	**1,306 sq. ft.**
Basement	624 sq. ft.
Garage	350 sq. ft.
Exterior Wall Framing:	2x4 or 2x6

Foundation Options:

Daylight basement
Standard basement
Crawlspace
Slab
(Typical foundation & framing conversion diagram available—see order form.)

BLUEPRINT PRICE CODE: A

Victorian Exterior, Modern Interior

- This classic exterior is built around an interior that offers all the amenities wanted by today's families.
- A Great Room provides ample space for large gatherings and multiple family activities.
- A formal dining room is available for special occasions, and a casual breakfast nook serves everyday dining needs.
- A deluxe main-floor master suite features a cathedral ceiling.
- Upstairs, two secondary bedrooms share a full bath and a balcony overlooking the Great Room below.

Plan DW-2112

Bedrooms: 3	Baths: 2½
Space:	
Upper floor	514 sq. ft.
Main floor	1,598 sq. ft.
Total Living Area	**2,112 sq. ft.**
Basement	1,598 sq. ft.
Exterior Wall Framing	2x4

Foundation options:

Standard Basement

Crawlspace

Slab

(Foundation & framing conversion diagram available—see order form.)

Blueprint Price Code	**C**

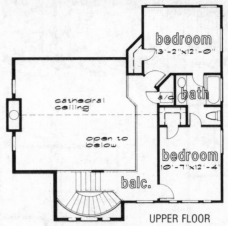

UPPER FLOOR

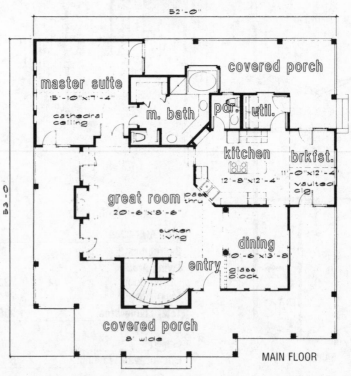

MAIN FLOOR

Angled Solar Design

- This passive solar design with a six-sided core is angled to capture as much sunlight as possible.
- Finished in natural vertical cedar planks and stone veneer, this contemporary three-bedroom requires minimum maintenance.
- Double doors at the entry open into the spacious living and dining areas.
- The formal area features a domed ceiling with skylights, a free-standing fireplace and three sets of sliding glass doors. The central sliders lead to a glass-enclosed sun room.
- The bright U-shaped kitchen is an extension of the den; sliding glass doors lead to one of two large backyard terraces.
- The master bedroom, in a quiet sleeping wing, boasts ample closets, a private terrace and a luxurious bath, complete with a whirlpool tub.

Plan K-534-L

Bedrooms: 3	Baths: 2
Living Area:	
Main floor	1,647 sq. ft.
Total Living Area:	**1,647 sq. ft.**
Standard basement	1,505 sq. ft.
Garage	400 sq. ft.
Exterior Wall Framing:	2x4 or 2x6

Foundation Options:

Standard basement
Slab
(Typical foundation & framing conversion diagram available—see order form.)

BLUEPRINT PRICE CODE:	B

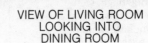

VIEW OF LIVING ROOM
LOOKING INTO
DINING ROOM

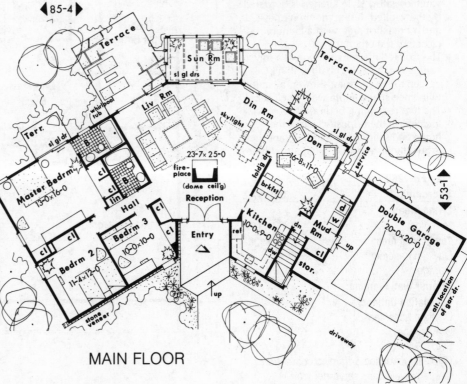

MAIN FLOOR

Eye-Catching Details

- This handsome home features an eye-catching exterior and an exciting floor plan that maximizes square footage.
- A covered porch leads into a vaulted foyer with an angled coat closet. Straight ahead, the vaulted Great Room combines with the dining room and kitchen to create one huge, well-integrated living and entertaining area.
- The Great Room includes a fireplace and access to the backyard. The vaulted, galley-style kitchen is bordered by the vaulted dining room on one side and a breakfast area with a laundry closet on the other.
- The isolated master suite boasts a tray ceiling and a vaulted bath with a garden tub, a separate shower, a vanity with knee space and a walk-in closet.
- The two remaining bedrooms are located on the opposite side of the home and share a full bath. A plant shelf is an attention-getting detail found here.

Plan FB-1289	
Bedrooms: 3	**Baths:** 2
Living Area:	
Main floor	1,289 sq. ft.
Total Living Area:	**1,289 sq. ft.**
Daylight basement	1,289 sq. ft.
Garage	430 sq. ft.
Exterior Wall Framing:	2x4

Foundation Options:
Daylight basement
Crawlspace
Slab
(Typical foundation & framing conversion diagram available – see order form.)

BLUEPRINT PRICE CODE: A

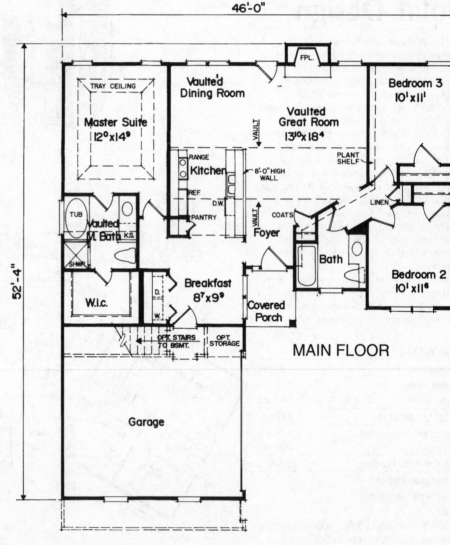

MAIN FLOOR

TO ORDER THIS BLUEPRINT,
CALL TOLL-FREE 1-800-547-5570

Plan FB-1289

PRICES AND DETAILS
ON PAGES 12-15

Extra-Special Ranch-Style

- Repeating gables, wood siding and brick adorn the exterior of this ranch-style home, which offers numerous extras inside.
- The entry leads directly into the vaulted family room, an ideal entertainment area accented by a corner fireplace and a French door to the backyard.
- A serving bar joins the family room to the efficient kitchen, with its walk-in pantry, ample counter space and sunny breakfast room.
- The luxurious master suite boasts a tray ceiling, a large bank of windows and a walk-in closet. The private master bath features a garden tub.
- Two additional bedrooms, one with a vaulted ceiling, share another full bath.
- A two-car garage provides convenient access to the kitchen and laundry area.

Plan FB-1104

Bedrooms: 3	Baths: 2
Living Area:	
Main floor	1,104 sq. ft.
Total Living Area:	**1,104 sq. ft.**
Daylight basement	1,104 sq. ft.
Garage	400 sq. ft.
Exterior Wall Framing:	2x4

Foundation Options:
Daylight basement
Crawlspace
(Typical foundation & framing conversion diagram available—see order form.)

BLUEPRINT PRICE CODE: A

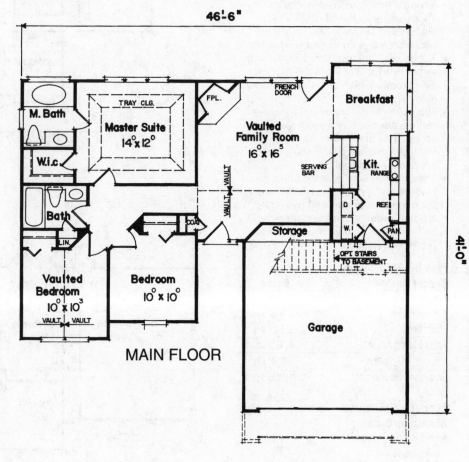

MAIN FLOOR

Tall Two-Story

- This gorgeous two-story is highlighted by a spectacular curved staircase leading to a balcony that overlooks the living room and the foyer.
- Off of the foyer is an open two-story-high library for reading or study.
- A formal dining room opposite the library opens to the fabulous airy kitchen and family area. The island kitchen features an angled serving bar.
- A fireplace flanked by built-in shelving serves as a focal point in the spacious living room, which provides access to a nice patio.
- The master bedroom boasts a gambrel ceiling, a sunny bay window and patio access. The spacious master bath offers his-and-hers walk-in closets, an oval tub and a separate shower.
- A second stairway near the utility room leads to the upper floor, where there are three more bedrooms and two baths.
- A bonus room above the garage could be finished as a game room, a media center or a hobby area.

Plan DD-3125

Bedrooms: 4+	Baths: 3½
Living Area:	
Upper floor	982 sq. ft.
Main floor	2,147 sq. ft.
Total Living Area:	**3,129 sq. ft.**
Unfinished Bonus	196 sq. ft.
Standard basement	1,996 sq. ft.
Garage	771 sq. ft.
Exterior Wall Framing:	2x4

Foundation Options:

Standard basement
Crawlspace
Slab
(Typical foundation & framing conversion diagram available—see order form.)

BLUEPRINT PRICE CODE: E

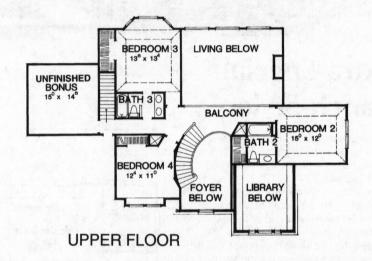

UPPER FLOOR

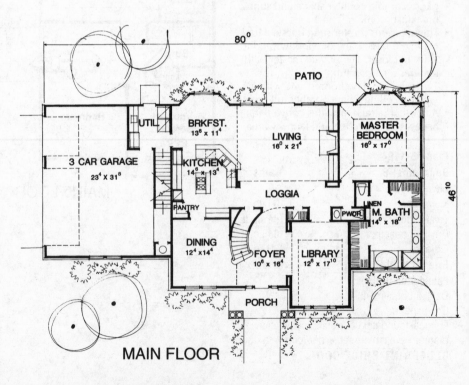

MAIN FLOOR

Full of Surprises

- While dignified and reserved on the outside, this plan presents delightful surprises throughout the interior.
- Interesting angles, vaulted ceilings, surprising spaces and bright windows abound everywhere you look in this home.
- The elegant, vaulted living room is off the expansive foyer, and includes an imposing fireplace and large windows areas.
- The delightful kitchen includes a handy island and large corner windows in front of the sink.
- The nook is brightened not only by large windows, but also by a skylight.
- The vaulted family room includes a corner wood stove area plus easy access to the outdoors.
- A superb master suite includes an exquisite bath with a skylighted dressing area and large walk-in closet.
- Three secondary bedrooms share another full bath, and the large laundry room is conveniently positioned near the bedrooms.

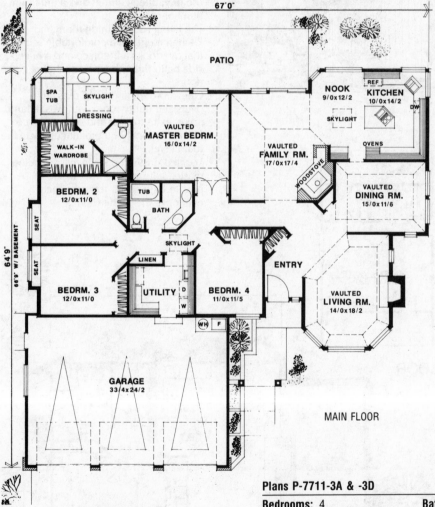

MAIN FLOOR

GARAGE
PLAN P-7711-3D
WITH DAYLIGHT BASEMENT

Plans P-7711-3A & -3D	
Bedrooms: 4	Baths: 2

Space:

Main floor (non-basement version):	2,510 sq. ft.
Main floor (basement version):	2,580 sq. ft.
Basement:	2,635 sq. ft.
Garage:	806 sq. ft.

Exterior Wall Framing:	2x6

Foundation options:
Daylight basement (Plan P-7711-3D).
Crawlspace (Plan P-7711-3A).
(Foundation & framing conversion diagram available — see order form.)

Blueprint Price Code:	D

Unexpected Amenities

- This good-looking design has a casual exterior but an interior filled with amenities you'd expect to find in a much larger and more elegant home.
- Open living areas are created with the use of vaulted ceilings and a minimum number of walls.
- The living room, dining room and kitchen merge in a comfortable setting that overlooks a fireplace and a huge side patio through a pair of sliding glass doors.
- One bedroom and bath, plus an oversized utility room with washer and dryer, extra freezer and storage space for recreational equipment complete the main level.
- Located on the upper level, a spacious master suite with a walk-in closet, private bath and a loft area that overlooks the living room.

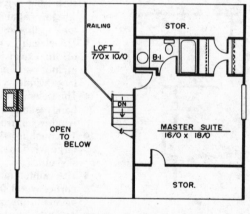

UPPER FLOOR

Plan I-1249-A

Bedrooms: 2	**Baths:** 2
Living Area:	-
Upper floor	297 sq. ft.
Main floor	952 sq. ft.
Total Living Area:	**1,249 sq. ft.**
Standard basement	952 sq. ft.
Exterior Wall Framing:	2x6

Foundation Options:
Standard basement
Crawlspace
(Typical foundation & framing conversion diagram available—see order form.)

BLUEPRINT PRICE CODE: A

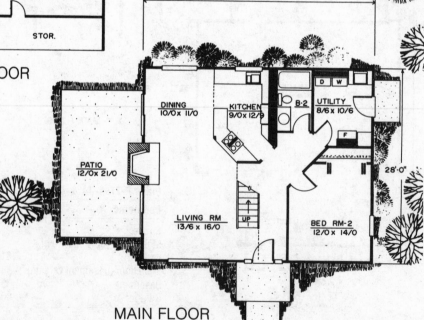

MAIN FLOOR

Plan I-1249-A

Plenty of Presence

- A stucco facade complemented by fieldstone, handsome keystones accenting the interesting window treatments and an imposing roofline give this home lots of presence.
- Inside, a two-story foyer an open stairway with a balcony overlook above provides an impressive welcome. Straight ahead, the huge family room is expanded by a vaulted ceiling, plus a tall window and a French door that frame the fireplace.
- The adjoining dining room flows into the kitchen and breakfast room, which feature an angled serving bar, lots of sunny windows and a French door that opens to a covered patio.
- The main-floor master suite is the pride of the floor plan, offering a tray ceiling, a vaulted spa bath and a spacious walk-in closet brightened by a window.
- The upper floor has two bedrooms, each with a walk-in closet, and a full bath. Abundant attic storage space is easily accessible.

Plan FB-1681

Bedrooms: 3	Baths: 2½
Living Area:	
Upper floor	449 sq. ft.
Main floor	1,232 sq. ft.
Total Living Area:	**1,681 sq. ft.**
Daylight basement	1,232 sq. ft.
Garage	420 sq. ft.
Storage	15 sq. ft.
Exterior Wall Framing:	2x4
Foundation Options:	

Daylight basement
Slab
(Typical foundation & framing conversion diagram available—see order form.)

BLUEPRINT PRICE CODE:	B

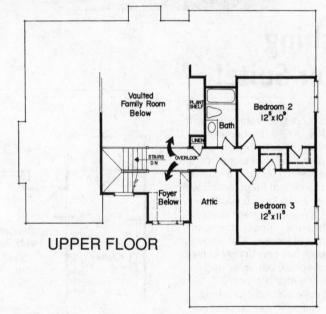

UPPER FLOOR

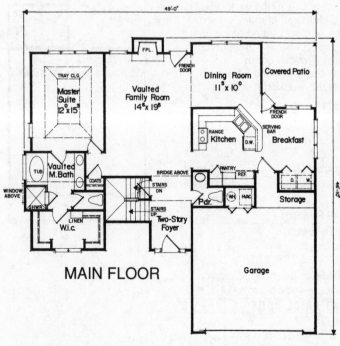

MAIN FLOOR

Smashing Master Suite!

- Corniced gables accented with arched louvers and a covered front porch with striking columns take this one-story design beyond the ordinary.
- The vaulted foyer leads directly into the family room, which also has a vaulted ceiling, plus a central fireplace framed by a window and a French door.
- The angled serving bar/snack counter connects the family room to the sunny dining room and kitchen. The adjoining breakfast room has easy access to the garage, the optional basement and the laundry room with a plant shelf.
- The master suite is simply smashing, with a tray ceiling in the sleeping area and private access to the backyard. The vaulted bath has all of today's finest amenities, while a vaulted sitting area with an angled wall and an optional fireplace is a special bonus.
- Two more bedrooms and a full bath round out this wonderful one-story.

Plan FB-1671

Bedrooms: 3	Baths: 2
Living Area:	
Main floor	1,671 sq. ft.
Total Living Area:	**1,671 sq. ft.**
Daylight basement	1,671 sq. ft.
Garage	240 sq. ft.
Exterior Wall Framing:	2x4

Foundation Options:
Daylight basement
Crawlspace
(Typical foundation & framing conversion diagram available—see order form.)

BLUEPRINT PRICE CODE:	B

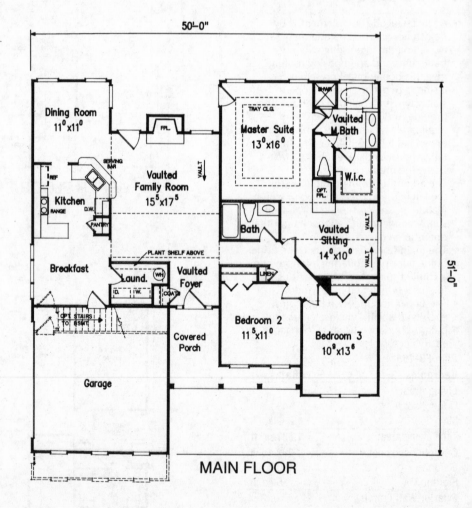

MAIN FLOOR

Plan FB-1671

PRICES AND DETAILS ON PAGES 12-15

Distinctive Inside and Out

- A decorative columned entry, shuttered windows and a facade of stucco and stone offer a distinct look to this economical one-story home.
- The focal point of the interior is the huge, central family room. The room is enhanced with a dramatic corner fireplace, a vaulted ceiling and a neat serving bar that extends from the kitchen and includes a wet bar.
- A decorative plant shelf adorns the entrance to the adjoining breakfast room, which features a lovely bay window. The kitchen offers a pantry and a pass-through to the serving bar.
- The formal dining room is easy to reach from both the kitchen and the family room, and is highlighted by a raised ceiling and a tall window.
- The secluded master suite boasts a vaulted private bath with dual sinks, an oval garden tub, a separate toilet room and a large walk-in closet.
- Two more bedrooms share a second bath at the other end of the home.

Plan FB-5001-SAVA

Bedrooms: 3	Baths: 2
Living Area:	
Main floor	1,429 sq. ft.
Total Living Area:	**1,429 sq. ft.**
Daylight basement	1,429 sq. ft.
Garage	250 sq. ft.
Storage	14 sq. ft.
Exterior Wall Framing:	2x4

Foundation Options:

Daylight basement
Crawlspace
Slab
(Typical foundation & framing conversion diagram available—see order form.)

BLUEPRINT PRICE CODE: A

MAIN FLOOR

Stunning Style

- The stunning detailing of this three-bedroom stucco home includes a stately roofline, round louvers and a sidelighted entry door topped with a half-round transom.
- The open floor plan begins at the foyer, where a decorative column is all that separates the dining room from the living room. Lovely French doors and windows overlook the backyard, while a raised ceiling heightens the effect of this spacious area.

- A sunny breakfast room and a great kitchen with a huge serving bar adjoin a vaulted family room with a fireplace.
- A laundry/mudroom lies between the kitchen and the garage. A nice storage or shop area supplements the garage.
- The opulent master suite has a tray ceiling, a rear window wall and a French door. The master bath includes a long, dual-sink vanity with a sitdown make-up area, a spa tub with a separate shower, a toilet compartment and a spacious walk-in closet.
- Another full bath serves the two remaining bedrooms.

Plan FB-1802	
Bedrooms: 3	**Baths:** 2
Living Area:	
Main floor	1,802 sq. ft.
Total Living Area:	**1,802 sq. ft.**
Garage	452 sq. ft.
Storage	40 sq. ft.
Exterior Wall Framing:	2x4

Foundation Options:
Crawlspace
Slab
(Typical foundation & framing conversion diagram available—see order form.)

BLUEPRINT PRICE CODE:	B

MAIN FLOOR

63'-0"

47'-4"

SHWR

TUB

Master Suite
13⁶x15⁶
TRAY CEILING

FRENCH DR.

M.Bath

LINEN

W.i.c.

LINEN

Bath

FRENCH DOORS

Living Room
14⁹x15⁰
(VOLUME CEILING)

Breakfast
12³x10⁰

SERVING BAR

RANGE

PANTRY

Vaulted
Family Room
13³x17⁴

FPL

D.W.

Kitchen

Laundry

W.

D.

REF.

Storage

DECORATIVE COLUMN

Foyer

COATS

Dining Room
11³x12³

Bedroom 2
11⁰x11⁶

Bedroom 3
11⁰x10⁰

Double Garage

Visual Surprises

- The exterior of this two-story, four-bedroom design is boldly accented with a dramatic roof cavity, while the inside features wall angles that enhance the efficiency of the floor plan and offer visual variety.
- The double-door entry opens into a bright reception area, leading to the sloped-ceilinged living room.
- The efficient kitchen conveniently serves the formal dining room and the cheerful breakfast dinette.
- Off the reception area is a powder room and a large laundry space which could be finished to serve as a hobby room.
- Four bedrooms are isolated on the second level; a connecting balcony is open to the living room below.
- The master suite is fully equipped; sliding glass doors yield access to the open wood deck that is literally carved into the roof.

Plan K-540-L

Bedrooms: 4	Baths: 2½
Space:	
Upper floor:	884 sq. ft.
Main floor:	1,106 sq. ft.
Total living area:	1,990 sq. ft.
Basement:	1,106 sq. ft.
Garage:	400 sq. ft.
Storage, laundry:	254 sq. ft.

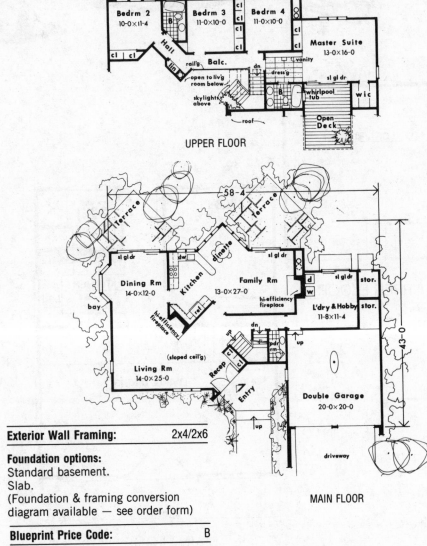

UPPER FLOOR

MAIN FLOOR

Exterior Wall Framing:	2x4/2x6

Foundation options:
Standard basement.
Slab.
(Foundation & framing conversion diagram available — see order form)

Blueprint Price Code:	B

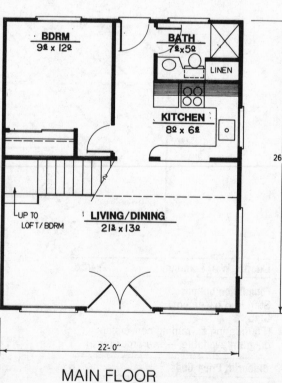

LOFT/BDRM.
308 SQ. FT.

DOWN

UPPER FLOOR

BDRM
9⁹ x 12⁹

BATH
7⁹x5⁹

LINEN

KITCHEN
8⁹ x 6⁹

UP TO
LOFT/BDRM

LIVING/DINING
21⁹ x 13⁹

26'-0''

22'-0''

MAIN FLOOR

Cozy Vacation Retreat

- This cozy cabin is at home in the mountains or on a lake, river or coastline.
- Large enough to provide comfortable living quarters and small enough to fit a modest budget, this is an ideal vacation retreat.
- The openness and minimum number of walls give it a spacious feel. Expanses of glass and a two-story-high ceiling give volume to the living and dining space.
- The kitchen offers a window view and a pass-through to the dining area.
- One bedroom is located on the main level and an optional second bedroom can occupy the loft area above.

Plan I-880-A

Bedrooms: 1-2	Baths: 1
Space:	
Upper floor	308 sq. ft.
Main floor	572 sq. ft.
Total Living Area	**880 sq. ft.**
Exterior Wall Framing	2x6
Foundation options:	
Crawlspace	
(Foundation & framing conversion diagram available—see order form.)	
Blueprint Price Code	A

Large Deck Wraps Home

- A full deck and an abundance of windows surround this exciting two-level contemporary.
- Skywalls brighten the island kitchen and the dining room.
- The brilliant living room boasts a huge fireplace and a cathedral ceiling, plus a stunning prow-shaped window wall.
- The master bedroom offers private access to the deck. The master bath includes a dual-sink vanity, a large tub and a separate shower.
- A generous-sized family room, another bath and two extra bedrooms share the lower level with a two-car garage and a shop area.

Plan NW-579

Bedrooms: 4	Baths: 3
Living Area:	
Main floor	1,707 sq. ft.
Daylight basement	901 sq. ft.
Total Living Area:	**2,608 sq. ft.**
Tuck-under garage	588 sq. ft.
Shop	162 sq. ft.
Exterior Wall Framing:	2x6

Foundation Options:

Daylight basement

(All plans can be built with your choice of foundation and framing. A generic conversion diagram is available. See order form.)

BLUEPRINT PRICE CODE: D

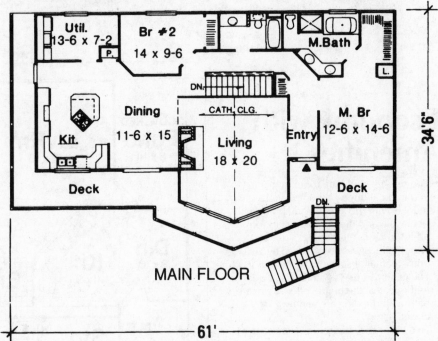

MAIN FLOOR

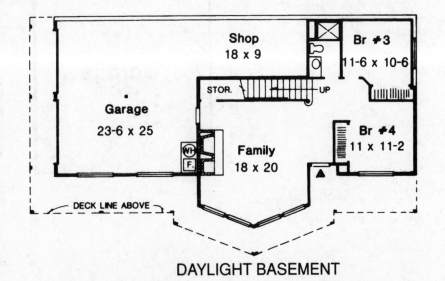

DAYLIGHT BASEMENT

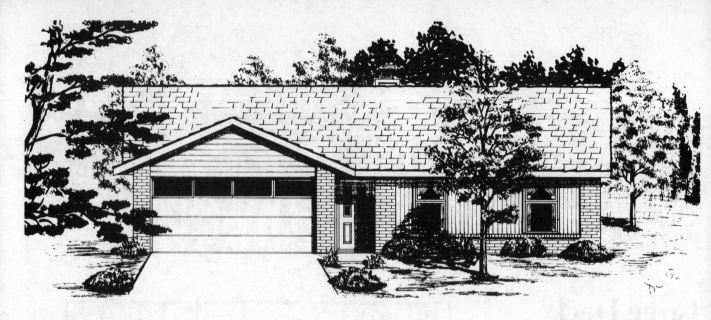

Economy with Amenities

- The rear-facing living room in this economical three-bedroom ranch merges with the kitchen and breakfast peninsula and the dining area to form an informal family setting.
- The spaciousness is enhanced by an entry that allows a view of the rear yard.
- The generous master suite, also oriented to the rear of the home, offers a private bath with dressing area and walk-in closet.
- Two secondary bedrooms have closet space and a nearby second bath.
- A double-car garage has extra storage space; the handy main-floor laundry room is conveniently located near the garage entrance.

Plan SDG-81115	
Bedrooms: 3	**Baths:** 2
Space:	
Main floor	1,296 sq. ft.
Total Living Area	**1,296 sq. ft.**
Garage	400 sq. ft.
Exterior Wall Framing	2x4
Foundation options:	
Slab	
(Foundation & framing conversion diagram available—see order form.)	
Blueprint Price Code	**A**

FRONT VIEW

REAR VIEW

Popular Plan for Any Setting

- City, country, or casual living is possible in this versatile two-story design.
- A spa room and sunning area lie between the master suite and Great Room, all encased in an extended eating and viewing deck.
- U-shaped kitchen, nook, and dining area fulfill your entertaining and dining needs.
- Two additional bedrooms and a balcony hall are located on the second level.
- Daylight basement option provides a fourth bedroom, shop, and recreation area.

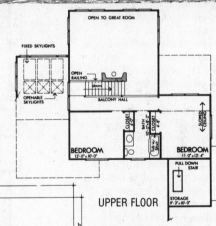

UPPER FLOOR

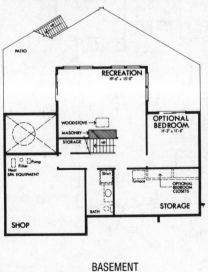

BASEMENT

MAIN FLOOR

Plans H-952-1A &-1B

Bedrooms: 3-4	Baths: 2-3

Space:

Upper floor:	470 sq. ft.
Main floor:	1,207 sq. ft.
Passive spa room:	102 sq. ft.
Total living area:	**1,779 sq. ft.**
Basement:	1,105 sq. ft.
Garage:	496 sq. ft.

Exterior Wall Framing:	**2x6**

Foundation options:
Daylight Basement (Plan H-952-1B).
Crawlspace (Plan H-952-1A).
(Foundation & framing conversion diagram available — see order form.)

Blueprint Price Code:

H-952-1A:	B
H-952-1B:	D

Distinguished Living

- Beautiful arches, sweeping rooflines and a dramatic entry court distinguish this one-story from all the rest.
- Elegant columns outline the main foyer. To the right, the dining room has a 13-ft. coffered ceiling and an ale bar with a wine rack.
- The extraordinary master suite flaunts a 12-ft. ceiling, an exciting three-sided fireplace and a TV niche shared with the private bayed lounge. Veranda access, a luxurious bath and a private library are also featured.
- The centrally located Grand Room can be viewed from the foyer and gallery. French doors and flanking windows alllow a view of the outdoors as well.
- A large island kitchen, a sunny morning room and a casual Gathering Room flow together and offer a big fireplace, a TV niche, bookshelves and a handy snack bar.
- The two smaller bedroom suites have private baths and generous closets.

Plan EOF-62

Bedrooms: 3	Baths: 3½
Living Area:	
Main floor	3,090 sq. ft.
Total Living Area:	**3,090 sq. ft.**
Garage	660 sq. ft.
Exterior Wall Framing:	2x6

Foundation Options:

Slab

(All plans can be built with your choice of foundation and framing. A generic conversion diagram is available. See order form.)

BLUEPRINT PRICE CODE: E

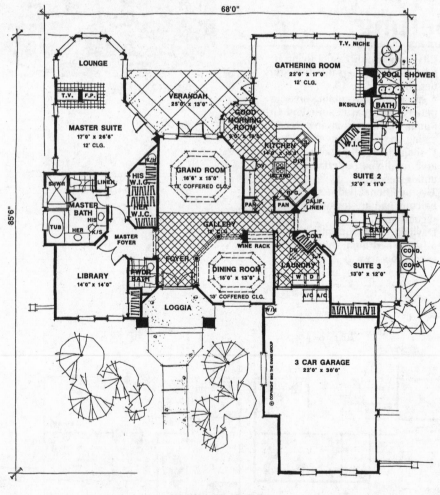

MAIN FLOOR

FRONT VIEW

REAR VIEW

More for Less

- Big in function but small in square footage, this two-story passive-solar plan puts every inch of space to efficient use. It is also designed so that it can be built as a single-family unit or as part of a multiple-unit complex.
- The floor plan flows visually from its open foyer to its high-ceilinged Great Room, ending with a brilliant south-facing sun room that overlooks a backyard patio or terrace.
- The spacious Great Room boasts a high-efficiency fireplace flanked by glass, along with an informal dining area that opens to a side terrace.
- A handy laundry closet and a half-bath are located near the master suite and the entrance from the garage.
- The master bedroom includes a deluxe private bath and two roomy closets.
- Upstairs, a skylighted bath serves two more bedrooms, one with a private, rear-facing balcony.

Plan K-507-S

Bedrooms: 3	Baths: 2½
Living Area:	
Upper floor	397 sq. ft.
Main floor	915 sq. ft.
Sun room	162 sq. ft.
Total Living Area:	**1,474 sq. ft.**
Standard basement	915 sq. ft.
Garage	400 sq. ft.
Exterior Wall Framing:	2x4 or 2x6

Foundation Options:

Standard basement

Slab

(All plans can be built with your choice of foundation and framing. A generic conversion diagram is available. See order form.)

BLUEPRINT PRICE CODE: A

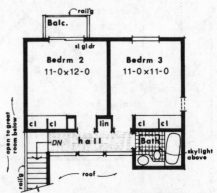

UPPER FLOOR

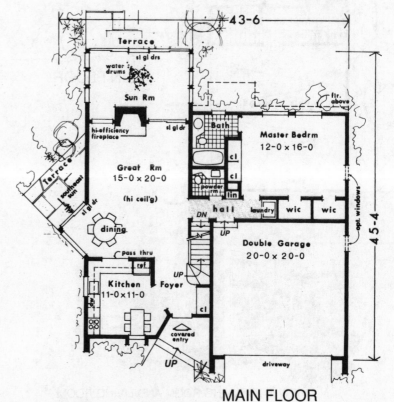

MAIN FLOOR

High-Profile Contemporary

- This design does away with wasted space, putting the emphasis on quality rather than on size.
- The angled floor plan minimizes hall space and creates smooth traffic flow while adding architectural appeal. The roof framing is square, however, to allow for economical construction.
- The spectacular living and dining rooms share a cathedral ceiling and a fireplace. Geared to take advantage of green spaces, both rooms have lots of glass overlooking an angled rear terrace.
- The dining room includes a glass-filled alcove and sliding patio doors topped by transom windows. Tall windows frame the living room fireplace and trace the slope of the ceiling.
- A pass-through joins the dining room to the combination kitchen and family room, which features a snack bar and a clerestory window.
- The sleeping wing provides the option of a den or a third bedroom. The second bedroom offers a sloped ceiling. The super master suite boasts a skylighted dressing area and a luxurious bath.

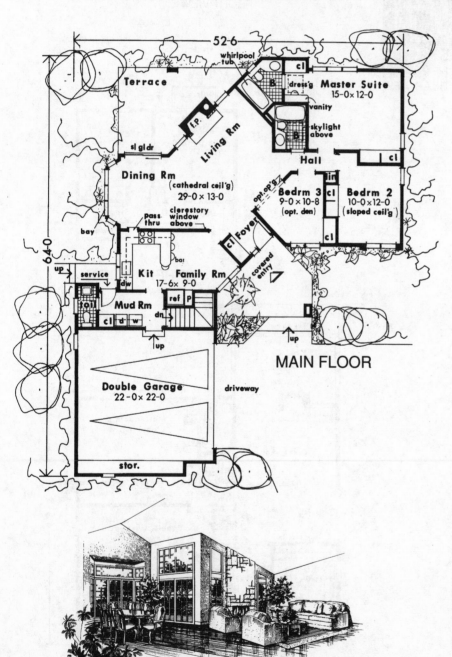

MAIN FLOOR

VIEW INTO DINING ROOM AND LIVING ROOM

Plan K-688-D	
Bedrooms: 2-3	**Baths:** 2½
Living Area:	
Main floor	1,340 sq. ft.
Total Living Area:	**1,340 sq. ft.**
Standard basement	1,235 sq. ft.
Garage	484 sq. ft.
Exterior Wall Framing:	2x4 or 2x6
Foundation Options:	
Standard basement	
Slab	
(Typical foundation & framing conversion diagram available—see order form.)	
BLUEPRINT PRICE CODE:	A

Plan K-688-D

PRICES AND DETAILS
ON PAGES 12-15

Master Suite Fit for a King

- This sprawling one-story has extra-ordinary features.
- All four bedroom suites have private bath access! The isolated master suite stretches from the front of the home to the back and features a stunning two-sided fireplace and an octagonal lounge area with veranda access. His-and-hers closets, separate dressing areas and a garden tub are other amenities.
- The large, central kitchen is nestled between a formal Grand Room and a comfortable Gathering Room with a fireplace, an entertainment center and an ale bar. This exciting core of living spaces offers dramatic views of the outdoors and of the adjoining covered veranda, which is complete with a summer kitchen.
- The private dining room at the front of the home has a 13-ft. coffered ceiling and a niche for a china cabinet.
- An oversized laundry room is conveniently located near the entrance to the three-car garage.

Plan EOF-60

Bedrooms: 4	**Baths:** 3

Living Area:

Main floor	3,002 sq. ft.
Total Living Area:	**3,002 sq. ft.**
Garage	660 sq. ft.
Exterior Wall Framing:	2x6

Foundation Options:

Slab

(Typical foundation & framing conversion diagram available—see order form.)

BLUEPRINT PRICE CODE:	**E**

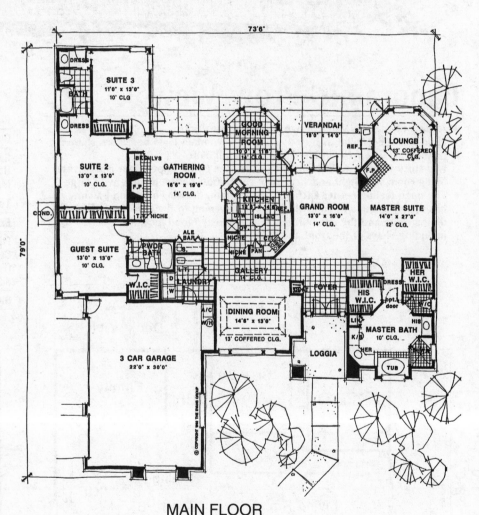

MAIN FLOOR

Panoramic Prow View

- A glass-filled prow gable design is almost as spectacular as the panoramic view from inside. The two-story window-wall floods the living room with light and views.
- The open-feeling corner kitchen has the right angle to enjoy the dining room and the family room, including views of the front and rear decks.
- Two main level bedrooms share a full bath.
- The entire upper floor is a private master bedroom suite with large bath, dressing area and balcony opening to the two-story glass wall, a real "good morning" view.

Plan NW-196

Bedrooms: 3	**Baths:** 2

Space:	
Upper floor	394 sq. ft.
Main floor:	1,317 sq. ft.

Total living area:	1,711 sq. ft.

Exterior Wall Framing:	2x6

Foundation options:
Crawlspace.
(Foundation & framing conversion diagram available — see order form.)

Blueprint Price Code:	B

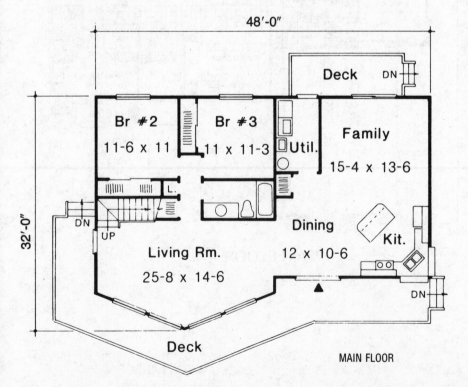

MAIN FLOOR

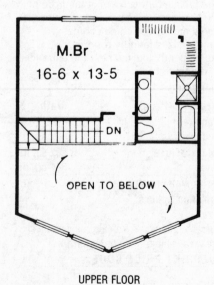

UPPER FLOOR

TO ORDER THIS BLUEPRINT, CALL TOLL-FREE 1-800-547-5570

Plan NW-196

PRICES AND DETAILS ON PAGES 12-15

Creative Spaces

- Here's a home that is not only large, but extremely creative in its use of indoor space.
- A huge area is created by the combination of the vaulted living and dining rooms, which flow together visually but are separated by a railing.
- Another expansive space results from the kitchen/nook/family room arrangement, and their easy access to deck and patio.
- Upstairs, the master suite includes a lavish bath and generous closets.
- Three large secondary bedrooms share another full bath, and each has its own unique design feature.

SKY LIGHT

SH

SUNKEN TUB

DECK

MASTER BATH

SUNKEN **MASTER SUITE**
17/6x13/6

WALK-IN WARDROBE

DN

OPEN TO ENTRY BELOW

LINEN

BEDRM. 2
16/0x11/0

BEDRM. 3
14/0x11/0

SKY LIGHT

TUB

BEDRM. 4
11/4x16/4

WINDOW SEAT

UPPER FLOOR

PANTRY

UP

DN

BASEMENT STAIRWAY LOCATION

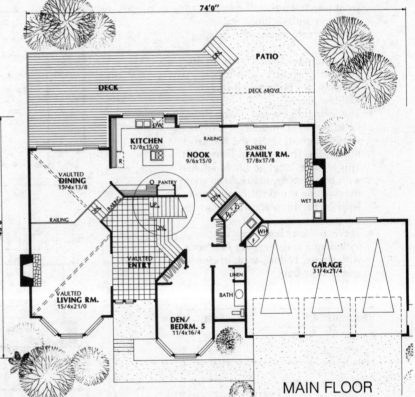

74'0"

PATIO

DECK

DECK ABOVE

45'6"

DW

KITCHEN
12/8x15/0

R

railing

NOOK
9/6x15/0

Sunken **FAMILY RM.**
17/8x17/8

VAULTED **DINING**
15/4x13/8

pantry

UP

WET BAR

railing

DN

W D

F WH

VAULTED ENTRY

LINEN

GARAGE
31/4x21/4

VAULTED **LIVING RM.**
15/4x21/0

BATH

DEN/ BEDRM. 5
11/4x16/4

MAIN FLOOR

Plans P-7664-4A & -4D

Bedrooms: 4 +		Baths: 2½
Living Area:		
Upper floor		1,301 sq. ft.
Main floor		1,853 sq. ft.
Total Living Area:		**3,154 sq. ft.**
Daylight basement		1,486 sq. ft.
Garage		668 sq. ft.

Exterior Wall Framing:	2x4
Foundation Options:	**Plan #**
Daylight basement	P-7664-4D
Crawlspace	P-7664-4A

(Typical foundation & framing conversion diagram available—see order form.)

BLUEPRINT PRICE CODE: E

Nostalgic Exterior Appeal

- Projecting bay windows, a covered front porch, large half-round windows and Victorian gable details create a nostalgic exterior appeal.
- A stunning two-story foyer awaits guests at the entry, with light flooding in from the half-round window above.
- The formal living and dining rooms lie to the right of the entry, while straight ahead, under the balcony bridge, lies the informal living area. This area includes an island kitchen with bay-windowed breakfast room overlooking the skylit family room with corner fireplace and sliders to the patio.
- There are four bedrooms upstairs, including a lavish master bedroom with sloped ceiling, walk-in closet and private bath.

Plan AX-90305

Bedrooms: 4	Baths: 2½

Space:	
Upper floor:	1,278 sq. ft.
Main floor:	1,237 sq. ft.
Total living area:	**2,515 sq. ft.**
Basement:	1,237 sq. ft.
Garage:	400 sq. ft.

Exterior Wall Framing:	2x4

Foundation options:
Standard basement.
Slab.
(Foundation & framing conversion diagram available — see order form.)

Blueprint Price Code:	D

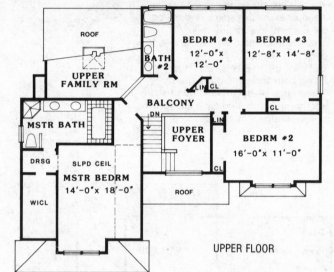

UPPER FLOOR

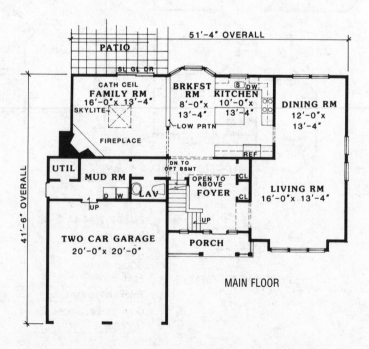

MAIN FLOOR

Plan AX-90305

PRICES AND DETAILS ON PAGES 12-15

FRONT VIEW

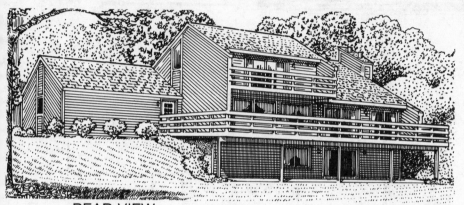

REAR VIEW

Hillside Design
Fits Contours

- The daylight-basement version of this popular plan is perfect for a scenic, sloping lot.
- A large, wraparound deck embraces the rear-oriented living areas, accessed through sliding glass doors.
- The spectacular living room boasts a corner fireplace, a sloped ceiling and outdoor views to the side and rear.
- The secluded master suite upstairs offers a walk-in closet, a private bath and sliders to a sun deck.
- The daylight basement (not shown) includes a fourth bedroom with private bath and walk-in closet, as well as a recreation room with fireplace and sliders to a rear patio.
- The standard basement (not shown) includes a recreation room with fireplace and a room for hobbies or child's play.
- Both basements also have a large unfinished area below the main-floor bedrooms.

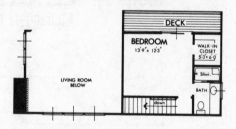

UPPER FLOOR

Plans H-877-4, -4A & -4B	
Bedrooms: 3-4	**Baths: 2-3**
Living Area:	
Upper floor	333 sq. ft.
Main floor	1,200 sq. ft.
Basement (finished portion)	591 sq. ft.
Total Living Area:	**1,533/2,124 sq. ft.**
Basement (unfinished portion)	493 sq. ft.
Garage	480 sq. ft.
Exterior Wall Framing:	2x6
Foundation Options:	**Plan #**
Daylight basement	H-877-4B
Standard basement	H-877-4
Crawlspace	H-877-4A
(Typical foundation & framing conversion diagram available—see order form.)	
BLUEPRINT PRICE CODE:	**B/C**

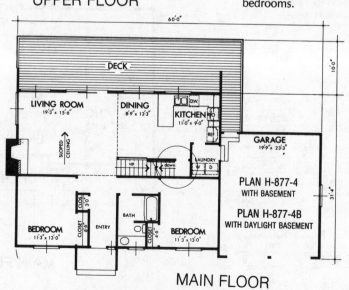

PLAN H-877-4
WITH BASEMENT

PLAN H-877-4B
WITH DAYLIGHT BASEMENT

PLAN H-877-4A
WITHOUT BASEMENT

MAIN FLOOR

TO ORDER THIS BLUEPRINT, CALL TOLL-FREE 1-800-547-5570

PRICES AND DETAILS ON PAGES 12-15

Plans H-877-4, -4A & -4B

Something for Everyone

- This space-efficient traditional's clever floor plan has something special for everyone in its three unique bedrooms.
- Upstairs, the master bedroom includes a walk-in closet and a private bath with a garden tub and a dual-sink vanity.
- The second bedroom features a sunny bay window, while the third bedroom boasts a round-top window, a 10-ft. sloped ceiling and a walk-in closet.
- Past the elegant double-columned brick porch, the inviting entry flows into the spacious living room.
- Warmed by a corner fireplace, the living room is brightened by a large front window. The adjoining formal dining room is close to the kitchen.
- The modern kitchen easily serves the bay-windowed morning room, which has sliding glass doors to a backyard patio. A laundry closet is nearby.

Plan DD-1782

Bedrooms: 3+	Baths: 2½
Living Area:	
Upper floor	1,080 sq. ft.
Main floor	785 sq. ft.
Total Living Area:	**1,865 sq. ft.**
Standard basement	785 sq. ft.
Garage	409 sq. ft.
Exterior Wall Framing:	2x4

Foundation Options:

Standard basement

Crawlspace

Slab

(All plans can be built with your choice of foundation and framing. A generic conversion diagram is available. See order form.)

BLUEPRINT PRICE CODE:	B

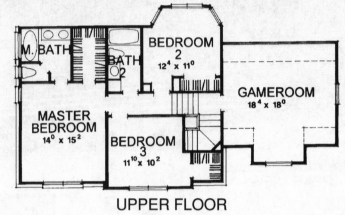

UPPER FLOOR

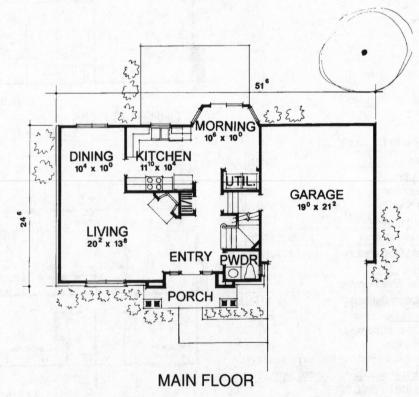

MAIN FLOOR

Plan DD-1782

PRICES AND DETAILS ON PAGES 12-15

Elegant Extras

- Ornate windows set off by stucco and stone give this home an Old World look. Inside, the modern floor plan features many elegant extras.
- The vaulted foyer, brightened by a window above, opens to the living room. This spectacular space is enhanced by a 16-ft. flat ceiling and a rear wall of glass topped by a half-round window.
- An arched opening over a half-wall separates the living room from the sunny breakfast room, which features a French door to the backyard. The fireplace in the adjoining family room is accentuated by tall windows topped by quarter-rounds.
- A serving bar lies between the family room and the gourmet kitchen, which offers a large walk-in pantry and a butler's pantry. An arched opening leads into the formal dining room.
- The bedroom wing is highlighted by a superb master suite with a tray ceiling. The vaulted bath hosts a corner spa tub set beneath an arched window.

Plan FB-5169-HEND

Bedrooms: 3	Baths: 2½
Living Area:	
Main floor	2,177 sq. ft.
Total Living Area:	**2,177 sq. ft.**
Daylight basement	2,177 sq. ft.
Garage and storage	550 sq. ft.
Exterior Wall Framing:	2x4

Foundation Options:

Daylight basement

Crawlspace

(All plans can be built with your choice of foundation and framing. A generic conversion diagram is available. See order form.)

BLUEPRINT PRICE CODE: C

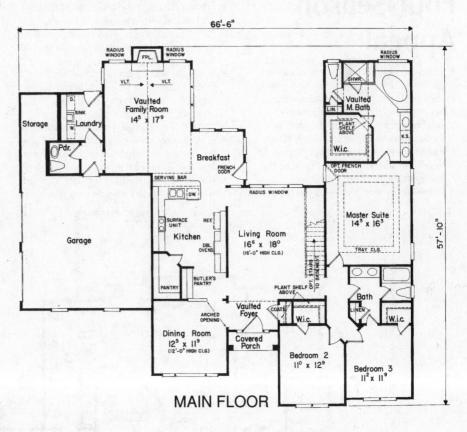

MAIN FLOOR

Four-Season Appeal

- Fantastic easy-living spaces clustered around a delightful four-season porch take center stage in this unique home.
- An intriguing trapezoid window brightens the vaulted foyer, which views into the sunken, vaulted Great Room. Here, an even larger trapezoid window fills the wall overlooking the backyard. A built-in TV cabinet handsomely complements the fireplace.

- French doors in the adjoining dinette and island kitchen open to the inviting four-season porch. This bright, cheerful haven features a vaulted ceiling and three walls of glass.
- A garden sink, a built-in desk and a pocket door to a deluxe laundry room highlight the kitchen. The dinette spreads into a formal dining room, framed by an angled wall and columns.
- A 12-ft. tray-vaulted ceiling embellishes the master bedroom. A whirlpool bath and a walk-in closet are also included.
- The remaining bedroom offers a cozy window seat and easy access to a bath.

Plan PI-92-203	
Bedrooms: 2	**Baths:** 2
Living Area:	
Main floor	1,762 sq. ft.
Four-season porch	224 sq. ft.
Total Living Area:	**1,986 sq. ft.**
Daylight basement	1,744 sq. ft.
Garage	744 sq. ft.
Exterior Wall Framing:	2x6
Foundation Options:	

Daylight basement

(All plans can be built with your choice of foundation and framing. A generic conversion diagram is available. See order form.)

BLUEPRINT PRICE CODE:	B

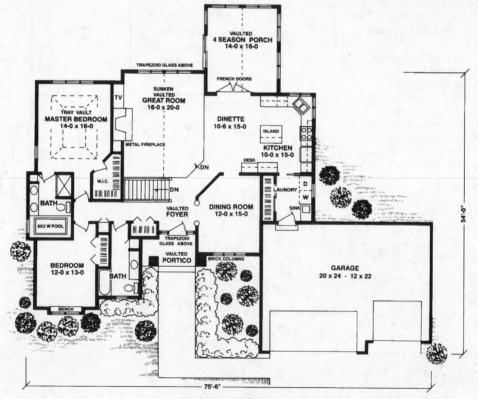

MAIN FLOOR

TO ORDER THIS BLUEPRINT, CALL TOLL-FREE 1-800-547-5570

Plan PI-92-203

PRICES AND DETAILS ON PAGES 12-15

Designed for Quiet, Private Sleeping Area

- This moderate-sized plan presents an impressive facade, with its large and interesting front window arrangement.
- An unusual Great Room plan allows for some separation of the kitchen/breakfast area from the dining/living section, but still makes them all part of one unit.
- The master bedroom includes a private bath with separate tub and shower, and another full bath serves the rest of the home.
- The third bedroom could serve as a den, study, or office if not needed for sleeping.
- The breakfast area offers easy access to an outdoor patio.
- Take special note of the unusual fireplace positioning in the Great Room.
- This plan comes with a full basement, which effectively doubles the space available.

Floor Plan

48'-0"
48'-0"

Mbr 14x12-6 Vaulted Ceiling

Br2 12x10

Patio

Den/Br3 11x9

Kitchen/Brkfst 19x10-8

Dining

Garage 21-4x19-4

Great Room 19x18 Vaulted Ceiling

Dn

Plan B-902

Bedrooms: 2-3	Baths: 2
Total living area:	1,368 sq. ft.
Basement:	1,368 sq. ft.
Garage:	412 sq. ft.
Exterior Wall Framing:	2x4

Foundation options:
Standard basement only.
(Foundation & framing conversion diagram available — see order form.)

Blueprint Price Code: A

TO ORDER THIS BLUEPRINT,
CALL TOLL-FREE 1-800-547-5570

Plan B-902

PRICES AND DETAILS
ON PAGES 12-15

63

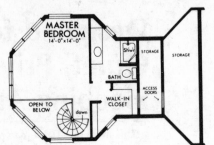

MASTER BEDROOM
14'-0"x14'-0"

Shwr

STORAGE
STORAGE

BATH

ACCESS DOORS

OPEN TO BELOW

down

WALK-IN CLOSET

UPPER FLOOR

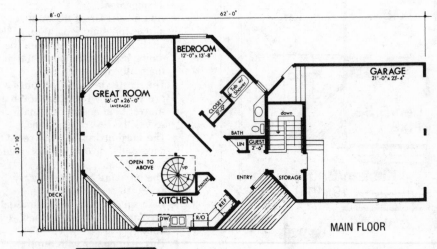

8'-0"

62'-0"

33'-10"

BEDROOM
12'-0" x 13'-8"

GARAGE
21'-0" x 23'-4"

GREAT ROOM
16'-0" x 26'-0"
(AVERAGE)

CLOSET 5'-0"

Tub w/ Shower

down

BATH

LIN

GUEST 2'-6"

OPEN TO ABOVE

up

ENTRY

STORAGE

DECK

PANTRY

KITCHEN

REF

DW

R/O

MAIN FLOOR

BEDROOM
22/0 × 10/0

RECREATION
16/0 × 21/6

CLOSET 4/0
CLOSET 4/0

BATH

up

W D LAUNDRY

LIN

CLOSET 7/6

STORAGE

STOR 3/6

WH

furnace

BASEMENT

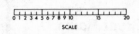

0 1 2 3 4 5 6 7 8 9 10   15   20
SCALE

Octagonal Vacation Retreat

- Octagonal shape offers a view on all sides.
- Living, dining, and meal preparation are combined in a single Great Room, interrupted only by a provocative spiral staircase.
- Winding staircase allows continuous observance of activities below.
- Extraordinary master suite is bordered by glass, a private bath, and dressing room.
- Attached garage has room for boat, camper, or extra automobile.

Plans H-964-1A & -1B

Bedrooms: 2-3	Baths: 2-3
Space:	
Upper floor:	346 sq. ft.
Main floor:	1,067 sq. ft.
Total living area:	**1,413 sq. ft.**
Basement:	approx. 1,045 sq. ft.
Garage:	512 sq. ft.
Storage (2nd floor)	134 sq. ft.
Exterior Wall Framing:	**2x6**

Foundation options:
Daylight basement (Plan H-964-1B).
Crawlspace (Plan H-964-1A).
Foundation & framing conversion diagram available — see order form.)

Blueprint Price Code:

Without basement:	A
With basement:	C

Spectacular Sun-Drenched Home

- Sweeping hip rooflines, stucco siding with interesting quoins and banding, and interesting arched transom windows give this exciting sunbelt design a special flair.
- From an important 1½ story covered entry leading into the foyer, guests are greeted with a stunning view. A bay-window-wall opens the living room, straight ahead, to the covered patio, rear yard, and possible pool. To the left is an open-feeling formal dining room with columns and spectacular receding tray ceiling.
- The island kitchen overlooks the large family room with corner fireplace and breakfast bay.
- The master wing, well separated from the secondary bedrooms, features a coffered ceiling, sitting area with patio access, massive walk-in closet, and sun-drenched garden bath.

Plan HDS-90-814

Bedrooms: 4-5	Baths: 3½
Space:	
Total living area:	3,743 sq. ft.
Garage:	approx. 725 sq. ft.

Exterior Wall Framing:	
	Concrete block & 2x4

Ceiling Heights:	
Main floor:	10', 12' & 14'

Foundation options:	
Slab.	
(Foundation & framing conversion diagram available — see order form.)	

Blueprint Price Code:	F

Handsome Hill-Hugging Haven

- Multiple octagonal rooms allow this dramatic home to take full advantage of surrounding views.
- A dazzling two-story entry greets guests from the three-car garage motor courtyard.
- Once inside the front door, a soaring dome ceiling catches the eye past the octagonal stairway.
- A sunken living and dining room

with cathedral and domed ceiling face out to the rear deck and views.
- The octagonal island kitchen and breakfast nook are sure to please.
- The main floor den features a second fireplace and front-facing window seat.
- The entire second floor houses the master bedroom suite with a sensational master bath.

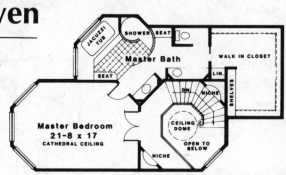

UPPER FLOOR

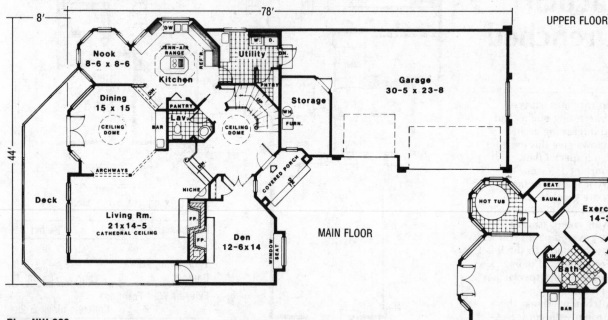

MAIN FLOOR

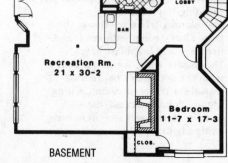

BASEMENT

Plan NW-229

Bedrooms: 2-4	Baths: 2½

Space:

Upper floor:	815 sq. ft.
Main floor:	1,446 sq. ft.
Daylight basement:	1,330 sq. ft.
Total living area:	**3,591 sq. ft.**

Exterior Wall Framing: 2x6

Foundation options:
Daylight basement.
(Foundation & framing conversion diagram available — see order form.)

Blueprint Price Code: F

TO ORDER THIS BLUEPRINT, CALL TOLL-FREE 1-800-547-5570

Plan NW-229

PRICES AND DETAILS ON PAGES 12-15

Large, Dramatic Rooms

- At the center of this stylish brick home is a modern kitchen, Great Room and dining room combination that will please today's close-knit family. A large fireplace, sloped ceiling and a rear window wall with an adjoining patio add to the drama of this intimate setting.
- The opposite end of the kitchen offers a pantry and handy access to the laundry room and garage.
- Separated from the other two bedrooms, the master bedroom is ideally located and spaciously designed. A tray ceiling in the bedroom and a luxurious corner tub in the private bath are a few of its amenities.
- The third bedroom off the foyer could serve as a den or home office; it features lovely double doors and a front bay window.

Plan SDG-91188

Bedrooms: 2-3	Baths: 2
Space:	
Main floor	1,704 sq. ft.
Total Living Area	**1,704 sq. ft.**
Garage	484 sq. ft.
Exterior Wall Framing	**2x4**

Foundation options:

Slab

(Foundation & framing conversion diagram available—see order form.)

Blueprint Price Code	**B**

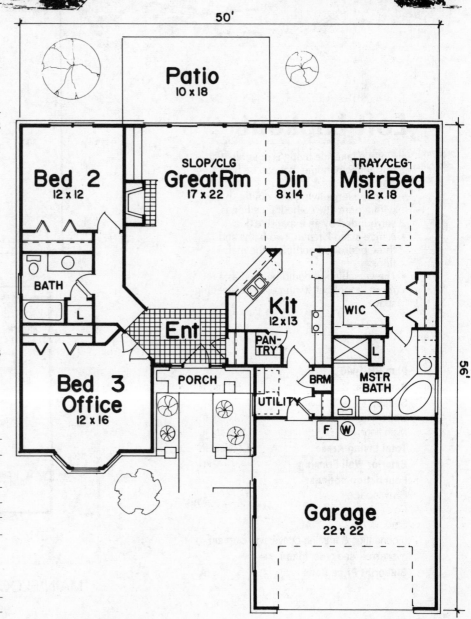

Plan SDG-91188

Loft Lookout

- Unique lakeside living is possible with this getaway home that can be built on posts.
- Inside, a large living and dining space with a dramatic cathedral ceiling is surrounded by an expansive deck.
- A nice-sized kitchen, two baths and three bedrooms complete the main floor.
- The versatile loft could be used as a rec room, a lookout station or extra sleeping space.

Plan PH-1440

Bedrooms: 3	**Baths:** 2

Space:

Upper floor	144 sq. ft.
Main floor	1,296 sq. ft.
Total Living Area	**1,440 sq. ft.**
Exterior Wall Framing	2x6

Foundation options:

Crawlspace

Pole

Slab

(Foundation & framing conversion diagram available—see order form.)

Blueprint Price Code	**A**

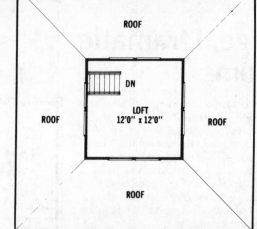

UPPER FLOOR

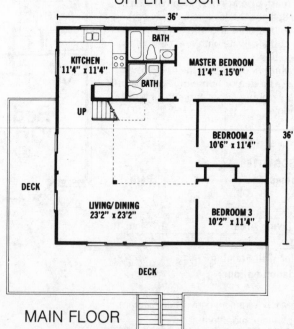

MAIN FLOOR

Low-Cost Comfort

- Designed for the energy-conscious, this passive solar home provides year-round comfort at much lower fuel costs.
- The open, airy interior is a delight. In winter, sunshine penetrates deeply into the living spaces. In summer, wide overhangs shade the interior.
- The family room/breakfast/kitchen combination is roomy and bright for family activities.
- The living/dining areas flow together for more bright, open space.
- The master suite includes a private bath and walk-in closet. Two other bedrooms share another full bath.

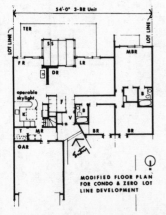

MODIFIED FLOOR PLAN FOR CONDO & ZERO LOT LINE DEVELOPMENT

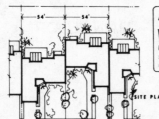

SITE PLAN

ALTERNATIVES – FLEXIBILITY

With minor modifications of the same basic layout, the design is adaptable to attached (condo) or zero lot line development, as shown.

Plan K-392-T	
Bedrooms: 3	**Baths:** 2½
Space	
Main floor	1,592 sq. ft.
Total Living Area	**1,592 sq. ft.**
Basement	634 sq. ft.
Garage	407 sq. ft.
Exterior Wall Framing	2x4/2x6

Foundation options:
Partial Basement
Slab
(Foundation & framing conversion diagram available—see order form.)

Blueprint Price Code	B

Comfortable Ranch Design

- This affordable ranch design offers numerous amenities and is ideally structured for comfortable living, both indoors and out.
- A tiled reception hall leads into the spacious living and dining rooms, which feature a handsome brick fireplace, a high, sloped ceiling and two sets of sliding glass doors to access the rear terrace.
- The adjacent family room, designed for privacy, showcases a large boxed-out window with a built-in seat. The kitchen features an efficient U-shaped counter, an eating bar and a pantry.
- The master suite has its own terrace and a private bath with a whirlpool tub.
- Two additional bedrooms share a second full bath.
- The garage has two separate storage areas—one accessible from the interior and the other from the backyard.

Plan K-518-A

Bedrooms: 3	Baths: 2
Living Area:	
Main floor	1,276 sq. ft.
Total Living Area:	**1,276 sq. ft.**
Standard basement	1,247 sq. ft.
Garage and storage	579 sq. ft.
Exterior Wall Framing:	2x4 or 2x6

Foundation Options:

Standard basement

Slab

(All plans can be built with your choice of foundation and framing. A generic conversion diagram is available. See order form.)

BLUEPRINT PRICE CODE: A

VIEW INTO LIVING ROOM AND DINING ROOM

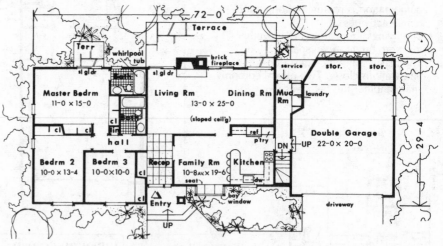

MAIN FLOOR

Plan K-518-A *PRICES AND DETAILS ON PAGES 12-15*

PLAN H-2114-1B FRONT VIEW

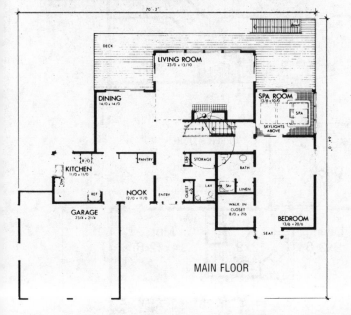

PLAN H-2114-1B REAR VIEW

Designed for Outdoor Living

- Dining room, living room, and spa are oriented toward the full-width deck extending across the rear of the home.
- Floor-to-ceiling windows, vaulted ceilings, and a fireplace are featured in the living room.
- Spa room has tile floor, operable skylights, and private access through connecting master suite.
- Upper level offers two bedrooms, spacious bathroom, and a balcony view of the living room and scenery beyond.

MAIN FLOOR

PLAN H-2114-1A
WITHOUT BASEMENT

PLAN H-2114-1B
WITH DAYLIGHT BASEMENT

UPPER FLOOR

Plans H-2114-1A & -1B

Bedrooms: 3-4	Baths: 2½-3½

Space:

Upper floor:	732 sq. ft.
Main floor:	1,682 sq. ft.
Spa room:	147 sq. ft.

Total living area:	**2,561 sq. ft.**
Basement:	approx. 1,386 sq. ft.
Garage:	547 sq. ft.

Exterior Wall Framing:	2x6

Foundation options:
Daylight basement (Plan H-2114-1B).
Crawlspace (Plan H-2114-1A).
(Foundation & framing conversion diagram available — see order form.)

Blueprint Price Code:

Without basement:	D
With basement:	F

Compact Three-Bedroom Home

- Both openness and privacy are possible in this economical three-bedroom home.
- The vaulted living room with fireplace and corner window combine with the dining area for an open activity and entertaining stretch.
- The modern kitchen and dining area overlook a rear deck.
- A lovely corner window brightens the private master bedroom on the main floor, two additional bedrooms and a bath share the upper loft.

Plan B-101-8501

Bedrooms: 3	Baths: 2

Space:	
Upper floor:	400 sq. ft.
Main floor:	846 sq. ft.
Total living area:	**1,246 sq. ft.**
Garage:	400 sq. ft.

Exterior Wall Framing:	2x4

Foundation options:
Standard basement.
(Foundation & framing conversion diagram available — see order form.)

Blueprint Price Code:	A

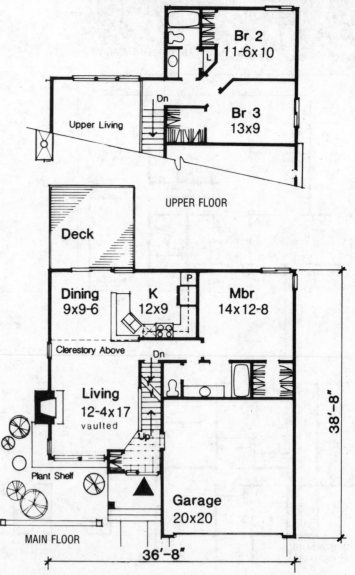

Br 2
11-6x10

Br 3
13x9

Upper Living

Dn

UPPER FLOOR

Deck

Dining
9x9-6

K
12x9

P

Mbr
14x12-8

Clerestory Above

Dn

Living
12-4x17
vaulted

Up

Plant Shelf

Garage
20x20

38'-8"

MAIN FLOOR

36'-8"

Decked Out for Fun

- Spacious deck surrounds this comfortable cabin/chalet.
- Sliding glass doors and windows blanket the living-dining area, indulged with raised hearth and a breathtaking view.
- Dining area and compact kitchen separated by breakfast bar.
- Master bedroom, laundry room and bath complete first floor; two additional bedrooms located on second floor.
- Upper level also features impressive balcony room with exposed beams.

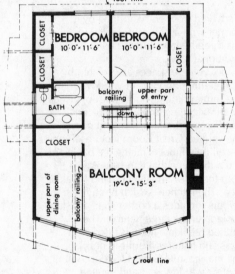

UPPER FLOOR

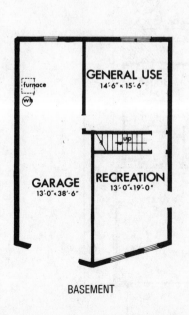

BASEMENT

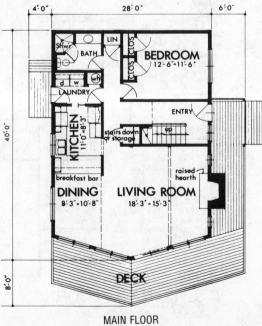

MAIN FLOOR

Plans H-919-1 & -1A

Bedrooms: 3	Baths: 2

Space:

Upper floor:	869 sq. ft.
Main floor:	1,064 sq. ft.
Total living area:	**1,933 sq. ft.**
Basement:	475 sq. ft.
Garage:	501 sq. ft.

Exterior Wall Framing:	2x6

Foundation options:
Daylight basement (Plan H-919-1).
Crawlspace (Plan H-919-1A).
(Foundation & framing conversion diagram available — see order form.)

Blueprint Price Code:

Without basement:	B
With basement:	C

Master Suite Is Hard to Resist

- A covered front entry, topped by a dormer with a half-round window, gives this three-bedroom home an updated traditional look.
- Inside, volume spaces are created by high ceilings and lots of windows.
- The formal dining room is distinguished by a tray ceiling and a large picture window overlooking the front porch.
- The vaulted Great Room features floor-to-ceiling windows facing the backyard and a fireplace that can be enjoyed from the adjoining kitchen and breakfast area. The kitchen, which has a flat ceiling, includes a corner sink, an island cooktop and a large pantry. The vaulted breakfast nook is filled with glass and features a built-in desk.
- The master suite is hard to resist, with its inviting window seat and vaulted ceiling. The luxurious bath is also vaulted and boasts a garden tub in addition to a shower. A walk-in closet is opposite a clever vanity with a sit-down makeup area between the two sinks.
- The two bedrooms upstairs share another full bath.

Plan B-89061

Bedrooms: 3	Baths: 2½
Living Area:	
Upper floor	436 sq. ft.
Main floor	1,490 sq. ft.
Total Living Area:	**1,926 sq. ft.**
Standard basement	1,490 sq. ft.
Garage	400 sq. ft.
Exterior Wall Framing:	2x4
Foundation Options:	

Standard basement
(Typical foundation & framing conversion diagram available—see order form.)

BLUEPRINT PRICE CODE:	B

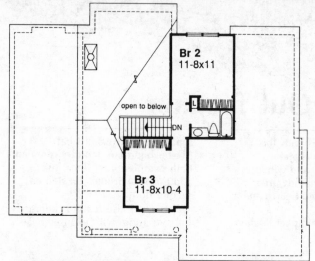

UPPER FLOOR

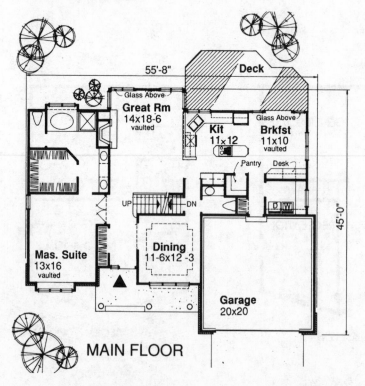

MAIN FLOOR

Plan B-89061

PRICES AND DETAILS ON PAGES 12-15

Light-Filled Interior

- A stylish contemporary exterior and an open, light-filled interior define this two-level home.
- The covered entry leads to a central gallery. A huge living room and dining room combine to generate a spacious ambience that is enhanced by a cathedral ceiling and an energy-saving fireplace.
- Oriented to the rear and overlooking the terrace and backyard landscaping are the informal spaces. The family room, sunny semi-circular dinette and modern kitchen share a snack counter and a private terrace.
- The main-floor master suite boasts a sloped ceiling, a private terrace and a personal bath with a dressing area and a whirlpool tub.
- Two to three extra bedrooms share a skylighted bath on the upper floor.

Plan K-683-D

Bedrooms: 3+	Baths: 2½+
Living Area:	
Upper floor	491 sq. ft.
Main floor	1,475 sq. ft.
Total Living Area:	**1,966 sq. ft.**
Standard basement	1,425 sq. ft.
Garage and storage	487 sq. ft.
Exterior Wall Framing:	2x4 or 2x6

Foundation Options:

Standard basement

Slab

(All plans can be built with your choice of foundation and framing. A generic conversion diagram is available. See order form.)

BLUEPRINT PRICE CODE:	B

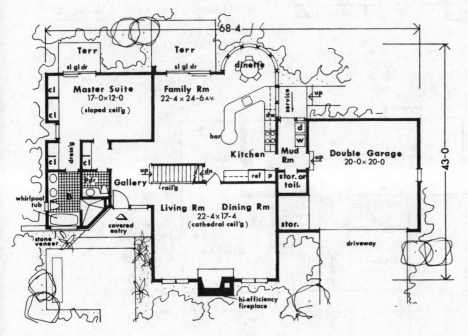

UPPER FLOOR

MAIN FLOOR

PLAN P-7644-2D
WITH DAYLIGHT BASEMENT
BASEMENT LEVEL: 1,286 sq. ft.

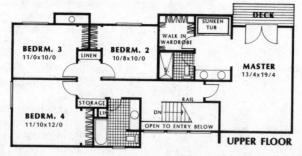

BEDRM. 3
11/0x10/0

BEDRM. 2
10/8x10/0

LINEN

SUNKEN TUB

WALK IN WARDROBE

DECK

MASTER
13/4x19/4

BEDRM. 4
11/10x12/0

STORAGE

DN

RAIL

OPEN TO ENTRY BELOW

UPPER FLOOR

Roomy Four- or Five- Bedroom Plan

First floor:	1,523 sq. ft.
Second floor:	1,101 sq. ft.
Total living area: (Not counting basement or garage)	2,624 sq. ft.

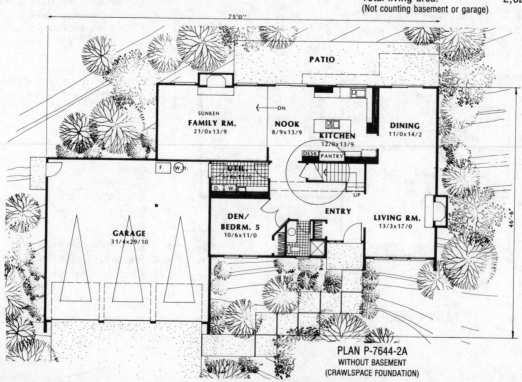

75'0"

46'-6"

PATIO

SUNKEN
FAMILY RM.
21/0x13/9

NOOK
8/9x13/9

KITCHEN
12/0x13/9

DINING
11/0x14/2

DESK PANTRY

UTIL
6/4x11/0

F. W.H.

D. W

DEN/
BEDRM. 5
10/6x11/0

ENTRY

UP

LIVING RM.
13/3x17/0

GARAGE
31/4x29/10

PLAN P-7644-2A
WITHOUT BASEMENT
(CRAWLSPACE FOUNDATION)

Blueprint Price Code D

Affordable Amenities

- An excellent design for a young family or an empty-nest couple.
- This design is an economical, affordable size, but includes the amenities today's homeowners are looking for.
- The large country-style kitchen includes a sunny breakfast nook, garden window over the sink and a pantry.
- The master bedroom includes a private bath and large walk-in closet.
- Living and dining rooms flow together to make an impressive open space for family gatherings or entertaining.
- Living room boasts an impressive fireplace and a vaulted ceiling.
- Optional third bedroom would make a convenient home office.

Plan CDG-1001

Bedrooms: 2-3	Baths: 2
Total living area:	1,199 sq. ft.
Garage:	494 sq. ft.
Exterior Wall Framing:	2x6

Foundation options:
Crawlspace only.
(Foundation & framing conversion diagram available — see order form.)

Blueprint Price Code: A

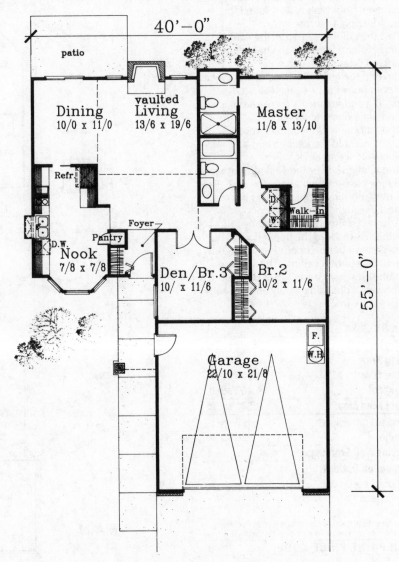

patio

40'-0"

Dining
10/0 x 11/0

vaulted Living
13/6 x 19/6

Master
11/8 X 13/10

Refr.

Walk-in

Foyer

D.W.

Pantry

Nook
7/8 x 7/8

Den/Br.3
10/ x 11/6

Br.2
10/2 x 11/6

F.
W.H.

Garage
22/10 x 21/8

55'-0"

Inside Angles

- This cleverly designed home's space-efficient floor plan is well suited for building on a narrow lot.
- Past the columned porch, the vaulted entry orients guests to the home's angled interior.
- Beyond the entry, the spectacular Great Room boasts a 17-ft.-high vaulted ceiling and features a corner fireplace and glass doors to a patio.
- The adjoining formal dining room is convenient to the kitchen and has access to a rear deck.
- The kitchen serves the Great Room via a handy pass-through above the sink. The sunny morning room accesses the rear deck through sliding glass doors.
- A turned stairway brightened by tall windows leads to the upper floor. The elegant master bedroom is enhanced by a 10-ft. gambrel ceiling. The master bath showcases a spa tub, a separate shower, a dual-sink vanity and his-and-hers walk-in closets.

Plan DD-2594

Bedrooms: 2+	Baths: 2½
Living Area:	
Upper floor	1,127 sq. ft.
Main floor	1,467 sq. ft.
Total Living Area:	**2,594 sq. ft.**
Standard basement	1,467 sq. ft.
Garage	488 sq. ft.
Exterior Wall Framing:	2x4

Foundation Options:

Standard basement
Crawlspace
Slab

(All plans can be built with your choice of foundation and framing. A generic conversion diagram is available. See order form.)

BLUEPRINT PRICE CODE:	D

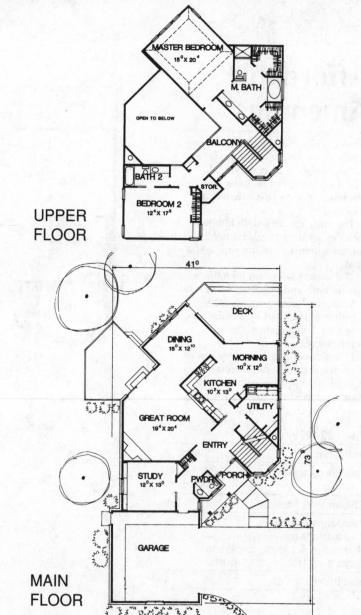

UPPER FLOOR

MAIN FLOOR

Perfectly Planned

- This home's dramatic architecture has many special design features and offers a floor plan that is visually appealing with thoughtful placement of rooms.
- Flanking the elegant foyer are a formal dining room and a den or study, both of which feature volume ceilings.
- Straight ahead is the vaulted living room with its two sets of double doors, one leading to the expansive covered patio and the other leading to the informal region of the home.
- The island kitchen boasts a vaulted ceiling, as well as a nice pantry and a sunny breakfast area. The vaulted family room displays a gorgeous fireplace and convenient built-in shelving.
- Three secondary bedrooms share a full bath and offer handy laundry facilities nearby.
- On the opposite side of the home is the stunning master suite, with its step-up tub, separate shower, his-and-hers walk-in closets and bright solarium.

MAIN FLOOR

Plan HDS-99-171

Bedrooms: 4-5	Baths: 3

Living Area:

Main floor	2,799 sq. ft.
Total Living Area:	**2,799 sq. ft.**
Garage	575 sq. ft.

Exterior Wall Framing:

8-in. concrete block

Foundation Options:

Slab

(Typical foundation & framing conversion diagram available—see order form.)

BLUEPRINT PRICE CODE: D

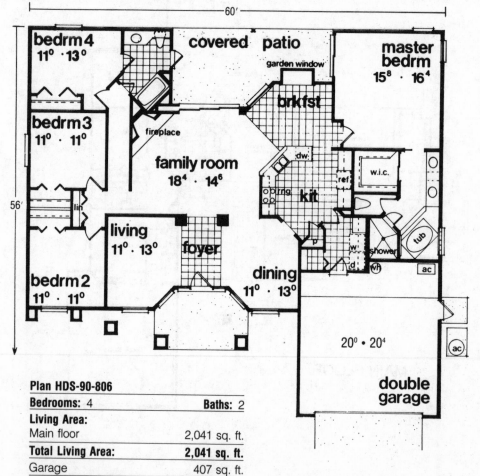

Plan HDS-90-806

Bedrooms: 4	Baths: 2

Living Area:

Main floor	2,041 sq. ft.
Total Living Area:	**2,041 sq. ft.**
Garage	407 sq. ft.

Exterior Wall Framing: Concrete block

Foundation Options:

Slab

(Typical foundation & framing conversion diagram available—see order form.)

BLUEPRINT PRICE CODE: C

Elaborate Entryway

- An important-looking covered entry greets guests with heavy, banded support columns, sunburst transom windows and dual sidelights flanking the front door.
- Once inside, the formal living and dining rooms open up to the left and right of the foyer, while straight ahead, through columns, lies the family room.
- The family room features a vaulted ceiling, fireplace and sliders to the rear covered patio.
- The kitchen overlooks the family room and breakfast eating area which has a garden window focal point.
- The master suite is well-separated on the opposite side of the plan from the three secondary bedrooms. It features sliding-door patio access, a large walk-in closet and private bath with corner platform tub and separate shower.

TO ORDER THIS BLUEPRINT, CALL TOLL-FREE 1-800-547-5570

Plan HDS-90-806

PRICES AND DETAILS ON PAGES 12-15

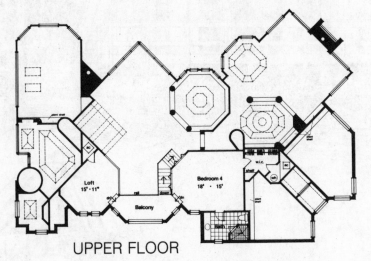

UPPER FLOOR

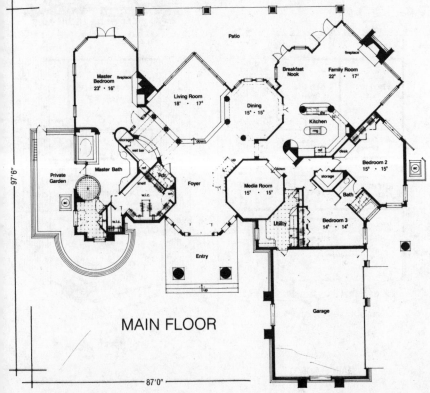

MAIN FLOOR

Grand Style

- The grand style of this luxurious residence exudes elegance and grace.
- The gothic contemporary architecture draws the eye to a stately 2½-story entry portico.
- Equally stunning is the interior with its high, open spaces, interesting angles, coffered ceilings and dramatic columns.
- The formal spaces include an octagonal dining room and a huge sunken living room under corner window walls. A curved wet bar is a nice extra!
- The informal zone consists of an island kitchen with a snack bar, a sunken media room, a bayed breakfast nook and a spacious family room with patio access and an inviting fireplace.
- The elegant master suite is removed from the secondary bedrooms, which share a full bath. The master bedroom boasts a warming fireplace and an oversized bay with outdoor access. The master bath is surrounded by a private garden and features a step-up tub, a circular shower and a toilet room.
- Throughout the home, ceilings are at least 9 ft. high, making every room seem spacious.

Plan HDS-90-819

Bedrooms: 4+	Baths: 3½
Living Area:	
Upper floor	765 sq. ft.
Main floor	3,770 sq. ft.
Total Living Area:	**4,535 sq. ft.**
Garage	750 sq. ft.
Exterior Wall Framing:	2x4

Foundation Options:

Slab

(Typical foundation & framing conversion diagram available—see order form.)

BLUEPRINT PRICE CODE:	**G**

Dramatic Skewed Prow

- This cleverly modified A-frame combines a dramatic exterior with an exciting interior that offers commanding views through its many windows.
- The central foyer opens to a spacious living room and dining room combination with a soaring cathedral ceiling and a massive stone fireplace.
- Directly ahead is the kitchen with sliding glass doors that open to the wraparound deck.
- Two bedrooms are located at the rear near the full bath and the laundry room.
- A third bedroom and a loft area that could sleep overnight guests are found on the upper level.

Plan HFL-1160-CW

Bedrooms: 3	**Baths:** 2

Space:

Upper floor	400 sq. ft.
Main floor	1,016 sq. ft.
Total Living Area	**1,416 sq. ft.**
Exterior Wall Framing	**2x4**

Foundation options:

Crawlspace

(Foundation & framing conversion diagram available—see order form.)

Blueprint Price Code	**A**

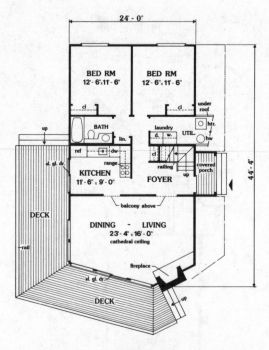

MAIN FLOOR

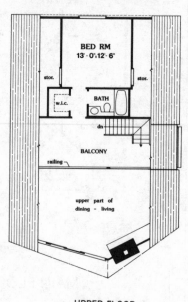

UPPER FLOOR

TO ORDER THIS BLUEPRINT, CALL TOLL-FREE 1-800-547-5570

Plan HFL-1160-CW

PRICES AND DETAILS ON PAGES 12-15

Expandable One-Story

- The hipped roof and covered entry give this well-appointed home a distinguished look.
- Inside, the foyer leads directly into the expansive Great Room, which boasts a vaulted ceiling, a fireplace with a built-in entertainment center, tall windows and access to the full-width deck with a hot tub.
- A half-wall separates the Great Room from the nook, which is open to the U-shaped kitchen. The impressive kitchen includes a snack bar, a walk-in pantry and a greenhouse window.
- The isolated main-floor master suite offers a vaulted ceiling, private access to the deck and the nearby hot tub, and a walk-in closet. The sumptuous master bath has a spa tub backlighted by a glass-block wall.
- Two more bedrooms on the lower level share another full bath. The optional expansion areas provide an additional 730 sq. ft. of space.

Plan S-41792

Bedrooms: 3	Baths: 3
Living Area:	
Main floor	1,450 sq. ft.
Partial daylight basement	590 sq. ft.
Total Living Area:	**2,040 sq. ft.**
Garage	429 sq. ft.
Unfinished expansion areas	730 sq. ft.
Exterior Wall Framing:	2x6

Foundation Options:

Partial daylight basement
(Typical foundation & framing conversion diagram available—see order form.)

BLUEPRINT PRICE CODE:	C

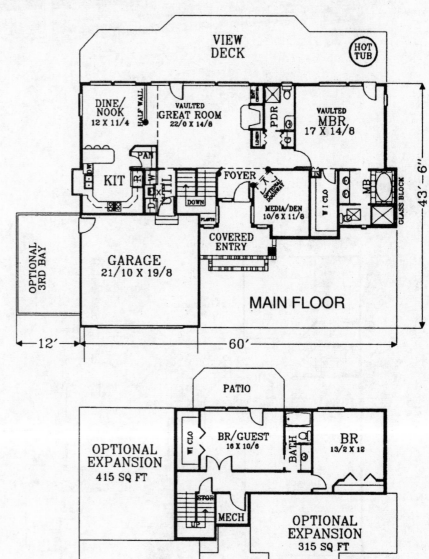

MAIN FLOOR

DAYLIGHT BASEMENT

Plan S-41792

Exciting Interior Angles

- A relatively modest-looking exterior encloses an exciting interior design that's loaded with surprises.
- The Y-shaped entry directs traffic to the more formal living/dining area or to the family room or bedroom wing.
- The family room features an unusual shape, a vaulted ceiling and a fireplace.
- The living room is brightened by a bay window, and also includes a fireplace.
- The dining area, the sun room, the family room and the outdoor patios are grouped around the large kitchen.
- The roomy master suite includes a deluxe bath and a large closet.
- The daylight-basement version adds 1,275 square feet of space.

Plans P-7661-3A & -3D

Bedrooms: 2-3	Baths: 2
Space:	
Main floor	1,693 sq. ft.
Total Living Area	**1,693 sq. ft.**
Basement	1,275 sq. ft.
Garage	462 sq. ft.
Exterior Wall Framing	2x4
Foundation options:	**Plan #**
Daylight Basement	P-7661-3D
Crawlspace	P-7661-3A
(Foundation & framing conversion diagram available—see order form.)	
Blueprint Price Code	**B**

MAIN FLOOR
55'-0"
54'-0"

PATIO

WALK IN WARDROBE

MASTER
13/0x15/6

VAULTED
FAMILY RM.
17/0x13/6

KITCHEN
11/0x10/0

PATIO

LINEN

WOODSTOVE

VAULTED
SUN RM.

PANTRY

BEDRM. 2
10/0x10/0

DEN/
BEDRM. 3
10/0x11/6

ENTRY

DINING
AREA

LIVING RM.
18/4x18/4

GARAGE
21/4x21/8

**MAIN FLOOR
PLAN P-7661-3A
WITH CRAWLSPACE**

MASTER

BAR

DN

**PLAN P-7661-3D
WITH DAYLIGHT BASEMENT**

Design Leaves out Nothing

- This design has it all, from the elegant detailing of the exterior to the exciting, luxurious spaces of the interior.
- High ceilings, large, open rooms and lots of glass are found throughout the home. Nearly all of the main living areas, as well as the master suite, overlook the veranda.
- Unusual features include a built-in ale bar in the formal dining room, an art niche in the Grand Room and a TV niche in the Gathering Room. The Gathering Room also features a fireplace framed by window seats, a wall of windows facing the backyard and a half-wall open to the morning room. The island kitchen is open to all of the main living areas.
- The delicious master suite includes a raised lounge, a three-sided fireplace and French doors that open to the veranda. The spiral stairs nearby lead to the "evening deck" above. The master bath boasts two walk-in closets, a sunken shower and a Roman tub.
- The upper floor hosts two complete suites and a loft, plus a vaulted bonus room reached via a separate stairway.

Plan EOF-61

Bedrooms: 3-5	Baths: 4½
Living Area:	
Upper floor	877 sq. ft.
Main floor	3,094 sq. ft.
Bonus room	280 sq. ft.
Total Living Area:	**4,251 sq. ft.**
Garage	774 sq. ft.
Exterior Wall Framing:	2x6

Foundation Options:

Slab

(Typical foundation & framing conversion diagram available—see order form.)

BLUEPRINT PRICE CODE: G

UPPER FLOOR

MAIN FLOOR

A Welcome Addition to Any Neighborhood

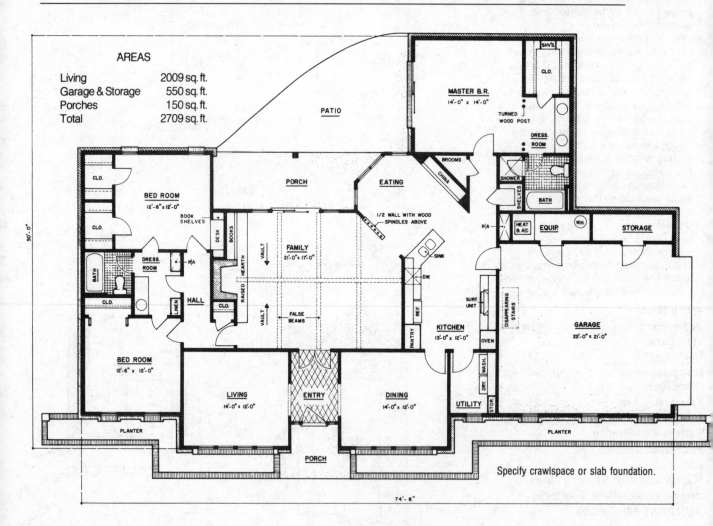

AREAS

Living	2009 sq. ft.
Garage & Storage	550 sq. ft.
Porches	150 sq. ft.
Total	2709 sq. ft.

Specify crawlspace or slab foundation.

TO ORDER THIS BLUEPRINT,
CALL TOLL-FREE 1-800-547-5570

Blueprint Price Code C
Plan E-2000

PRICES AND DETAILS
ON PAGES 12-15

Great Bedroom/Bath Combination

- Dining room has view of entry and living room through surrounding arched openings.
- Living room features 12' ceilings, fireplace, and a view to the outdoor patio.
- Kitchen has attached eating area with sloped ceilings.
- Tray ceiling adorns the master suite; attached bath has skylight and marble enclosed tub.

Plan E-1830

Bedrooms: 3	Baths: 2

Space:

Total living area:	1,868 sq. ft.
Garage and storage:	616 sq. ft.
Porch:	68 sq. ft.

Exterior Wall Framing:	2x6

Foundation options:
Crawlspace.
Slab.
(Foundation & framing conversion diagram available — see order form.)

Blueprint Price Code:	B

Design Excellence

- This stunning one-story offers dramatics and function.
- The brick exterior and exciting window treatments beautifully conceal an equally spectacular interior design.
- Twelve-foot ceilings throughout the formal areas and the family room, decorative niches and transom windows are some of its dramatic highlights.
- Other features include a three-way fireplace and a built-in entertainment center in the family room, an octagonal breakfast room with adjoining porch, a sunken living room with a second fireplace, and an amazing master suite with private sitting area and luxurious bath.

Plan KLF-922

Bedrooms: 3-4	Baths: 3 ½
Space:	
Main floor	3,450 sq. ft.
Total Living Area	**3,450 sq. ft.**
Garage and Workshop	698 sq. ft.
Exterior Wall Framing	2x4
Foundation options:	
Slab	
(Foundation & framing conversion diagram available—see order form.)	
Blueprint Price Code	E

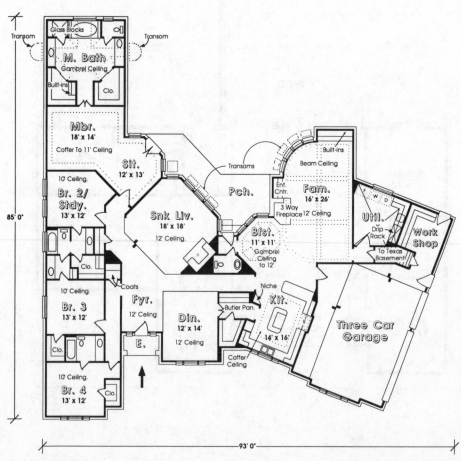

Exciting Great Room Featured

- A brick and wood exterior accented by multiple gables and ornate windows gives this smart-looking one-story lots of curb appeal.
- The amenity-filled interior is just as exciting. The vaulted foyer leads immediately into the spacious Great Room that features a vaulted ceiling and a fireplace flanked by windows.
- The adjoining dining room flows nicely into the breakfast area and the kitchen. The impressive kitchen offers an angled serving bar and a convenient pantry, while the sunny breakfast area has a French door to the backyard.
- The master suite boasts a tray ceiling, a walk-in closet with a plant shelf and a vaulted bath with a garden tub.
- The two remaining bedrooms are serviced by another full bath.

Plan FB-1359

Bedrooms: 3	Baths: 2
Living Area:	
Main floor	1,359 sq. ft.
Total Living Area:	**1,359 sq. ft.**
Garage	407 sq. ft.
Exterior Wall Framing:	2x4

Foundation Options:

Crawlspace
Slab
(Typical foundation & framing conversion diagram available—see order form.)

BLUEPRINT PRICE CODE: A

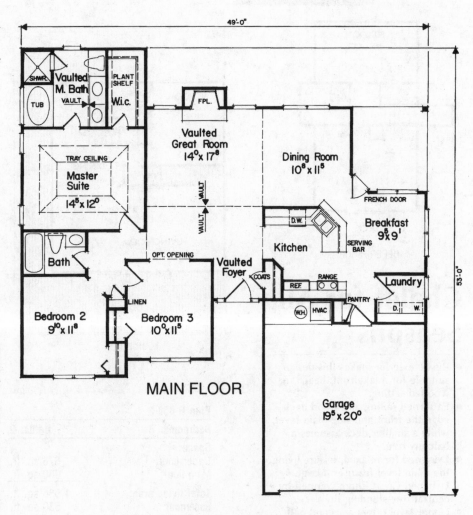

MAIN FLOOR

BEDROOM
17'6" x 9'9"

WALK-IN
CLOSET
6'0"
down

Shwr
BATH

CLOSET
5'6"

BEDROOM
17'6" x 13'9"

DECK

UPPER FLOOR

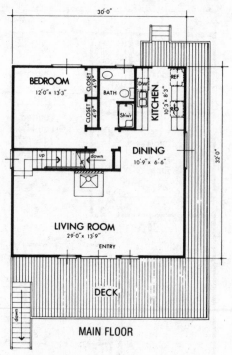

30'-0"

BEDROOM
12'0" x 13'3"

CLOSET 4'9"
CLOSET 4'9"

BATH
Shwr

DW
KITCHEN 10'3" x 8'3"
REF
R.O.

32'-0"

up
down

DINING
10'9" x 6'6"

LIVING ROOM
29'0" x 13'9"

ENTRY

DECK

down

MAIN FLOOR

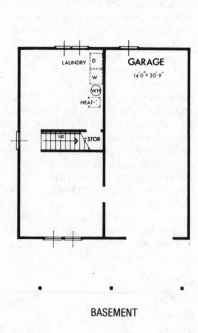

LAUNDRY
D
W
WH
HEAT

GARAGE
14'0" x 30'9"

up
STOR

BASEMENT

Chalet for All Seasons

- Rustic exterior makes this design suitable for a lakefront, beach, or wooded setting.
- Patterned railing and wood deck edge the front and side main level, while a smaller deck assumes a balcony role.
- Designed for relaxed, leisure living, the main level features a large L-shaped Great Room warmed by a central free-standing fireplace.
- Upper level offers a second bath and added sleeping accommodations.

Plan H-858-2

Bedrooms: 3	Baths: 2

Space:
Upper floor:	576 sq. ft.
Main floor:	960 sq. ft.

Total living area:	1,536 sq. ft.
Basement:	530 sq. ft.
Garage:	430 sq. ft.

Exterior Wall Framing: 2x6

Foundation options:
Daylight basement.
(Foundation & framing conversion diagram available — see order form.)

Blueprint Price Code: B

TO ORDER THIS BLUEPRINT, CALL TOLL-FREE 1-800-547-5570

Plan H-858-2

PRICES AND DETAILS ON PAGES 12-15

Compact Home Offers Soaring Living Room Ceiling

Main floor: 780 sq. ft.
Upper floor: 317 sq. ft.

Total living area: 1,097 sq. ft.
(Not counting basement or garage)
Basement level: 780 sq. ft.

PLAN P-6543-2A
WITHOUT BASEMENT
(CRAWLSPACE FOUNDATION)

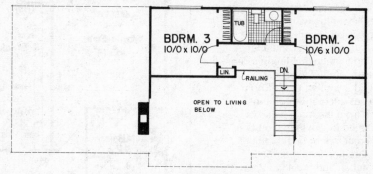

UPPER FLOOR

PLAN P-6543-2D
WITH DAYLIGHT BASEMENT

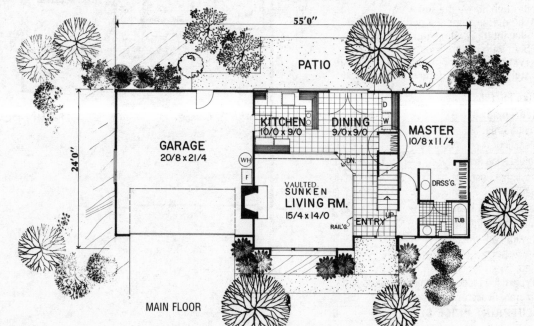

MAIN FLOOR

Blueprint Price Code A

One-Story with Impact

- Striking gables, a brick facade and an elegant sidelighted entry door with a half-round transom give this one-story lots of impact.
- The interior spaces are just as impressive, beginning with the raised ceiling in the foyer. To the left of the foyer, decorative columns and a large picture window grace the dining room.
- The wonderful family living spaces center around a vaulted Great Room, which also has decorative columns separating it from the main hall. A fireplace framed by a window on one side and a French door on the other provides a stunning focal point.
- The open kitchen and breakfast area features a built-in desk and a pass-through above the sink.
- The master suite is superb, with its elegant tray ceiling and vaulted spa bath with a plant shelf.
- Two more bedrooms and a full bath are at the other end of the home.

Plan FB-1553

Bedrooms: 3	**Baths:** 2
Living Area:	
Main floor	1,553 sq. ft.
Total Living Area:	**1,553 sq. ft.**
Daylight basement	1,553 sq. ft.
Garage	410 sq. ft.
Exterior Wall Framing:	2x4

Foundation Options:

Daylight basement
Crawlspace
Slab
(Typical foundation & framing conversion diagram available—see order form.)

BLUEPRINT PRICE CODE: B

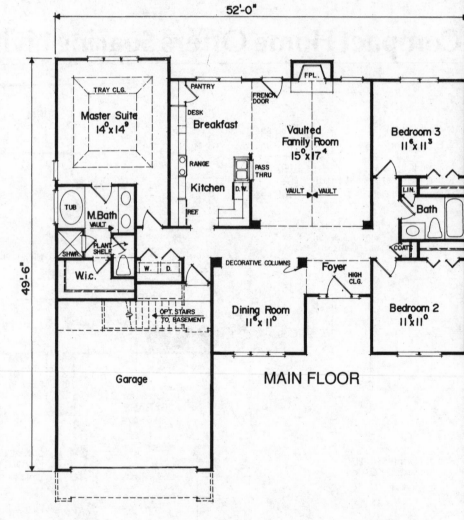

MAIN FLOOR

Plan FB-1553

PRICES AND DETAILS ON PAGES 12-15

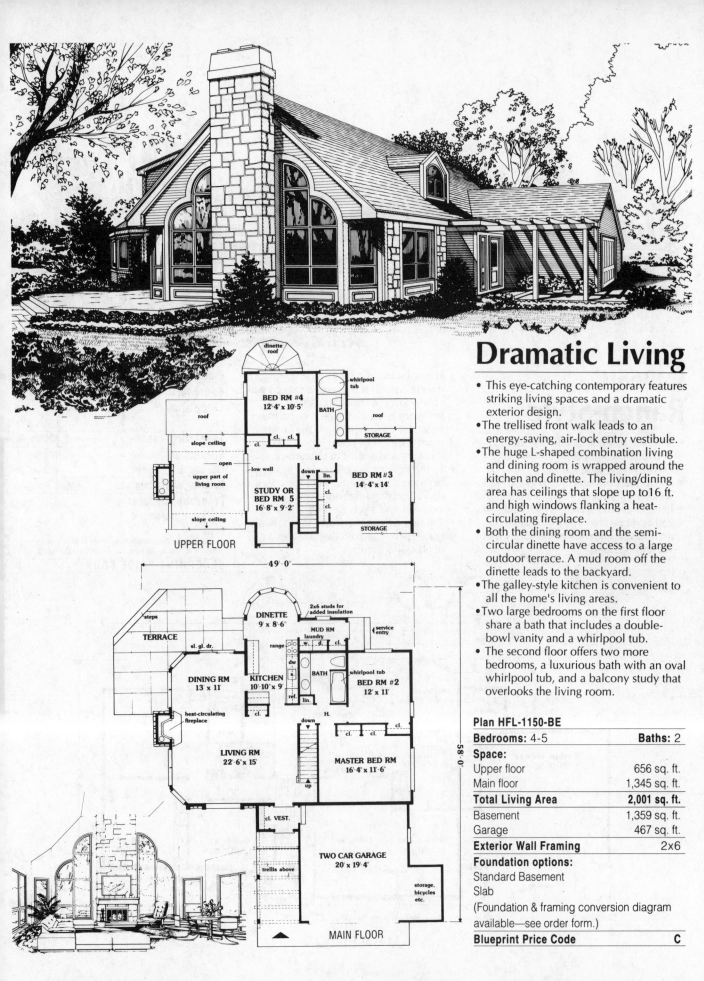

BED RM #4
12'-4" x 10'-5"

BATH

whirlpool tub

roof

STORAGE

roof

slope ceiling

open

low wall

upper part of living room

down

lin.

H.

BED RM #3
14'-4" x 14'

STUDY OR BED RM 5
16'-8" x 9'-2"

slope ceiling

STORAGE

cl. cl.

UPPER FLOOR

dinette roof

49'-0"

steps

TERRACE

sl. gl. dr.

DINETTE
9' x 8'-6"

2x6 studs for added insulation

MUD RM
laundry

service entry

DINING RM
13' x 11'

KITCHEN
10'-10" x 9'

range

dw

ref.

BATH

lin.

lin.

whirlpool tub

BED RM #2
12' x 11'

heat-circulating fireplace

cl.

down

H.

cl.

cl.

cl.

LIVING RM
22'-6" x 15'

MASTER BED RM
16'-4" x 11'-6"

up

58'-0"

cl. VEST.

TWO CAR GARAGE
20' x 19'-4"

trellis above

storage, bicycles etc.

MAIN FLOOR

Dramatic Living

- This eye-catching contemporary features striking living spaces and a dramatic exterior design.
- The trellised front walk leads to an energy-saving, air-lock entry vestibule.
- The huge L-shaped combination living and dining room is wrapped around the kitchen and dinette. The living/dining area has ceilings that slope up to16 ft. and high windows flanking a heat-circulating fireplace.
- Both the dining room and the semi-circular dinette have access to a large outdoor terrace. A mud room off the dinette leads to the backyard.
- The galley-style kitchen is convenient to all the home's living areas.
- Two large bedrooms on the first floor share a bath that includes a double-bowl vanity and a whirlpool tub.
- The second floor offers two more bedrooms, a luxurious bath with an oval whirlpool tub, and a balcony study that overlooks the living room.

Plan HFL-1150-BE	
Bedrooms: 4-5	**Baths:** 2
Space:	
Upper floor	656 sq. ft.
Main floor	1,345 sq. ft.
Total Living Area	**2,001 sq. ft.**
Basement	1,359 sq. ft.
Garage	467 sq. ft.
Exterior Wall Framing	2x6
Foundation options:	
Standard Basement	
Slab	
(Foundation & framing conversion diagram available—see order form.)	
Blueprint Price Code	C

Classic Ranch-Style

- A classic exterior facade of stone and unpainted wood distinguishes this classic ranch-style home.
- A covered front entry leads guests into a welcoming gallery. At the left is the living and dining area, with its elegant cathedral ceiling. The living room has an optional entrance to the family room via folding doors.

- The open kitchen offers an adjoining dinette, which showcases a curved wall of windows overlooking the huge backyard terrace. A screen or partition separates the dinette from the family room. The family room boasts a built-in fireplace and access to the terrace.
- To the right of the gallery lie the three bedrooms. The master suite features a skylighted dressing/vanity area, a walk-in closet and a private bath.
- The two remaining bedrooms share a convenient hall bath that features a double-sink vanity.

Plan K-162-J

Bedrooms: 3	**Baths:** 2
Living Area:	
Main floor	1,721 sq. ft.
Total Living Area:	**1,721 sq. ft.**
Standard basement	1,672 sq. ft.
Garage and storage	496 sq. ft.
Exterior Wall Framing:	2x4 or 2x6

Foundation Options:

Standard basement
Slab
(All plans can be built with your choice of foundation and framing. A generic conversion diagram is available. See order form.)

BLUEPRINT PRICE CODE: B

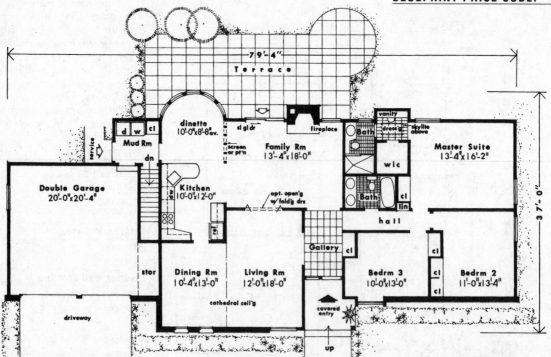

MAIN FLOOR

Plan K-162-J

PRICES AND DETAILS ON PAGES 12-15

Open Living Room and Dining Area

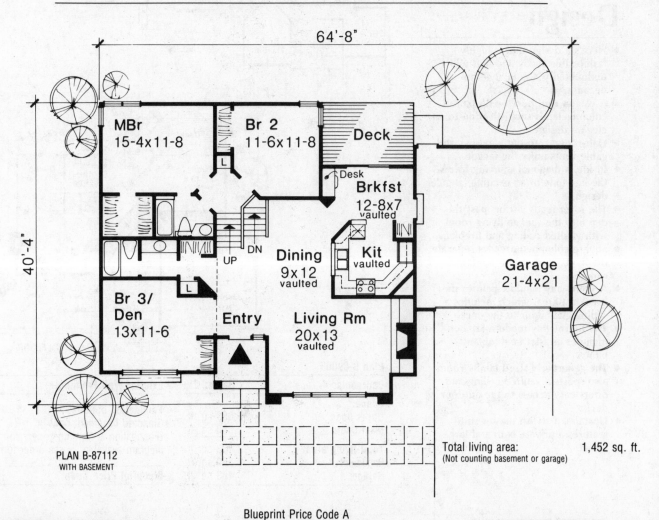

64'-8"

40'-4"

MBr
15-4x11-8

Br 2
11-6x11-8

Deck

Desk

Brkfst
12-8x7
vaulted

Kit
vaulted

Garage
21-4x21

Dining
9x12
vaulted

UP   DN

Br 3/
Den
13x11-6

Entry

Living Rm
20x13
vaulted

PLAN B-87112
WITH BASEMENT

Total living area: 1,452 sq. ft.
(Not counting basement or garage)

Blueprint Price Code A
Plan B-87112

PRICES AND DETAILS
ON PAGES 12-15

Elegant Post-Modern Design

- Here's a design that is highly fashionable today and that will undoubtedly stay in style for decades.
- A wagon roof porch with paired columns lends sophistication to an elegant design.
- Half-round transom windows and gable vents unify the facade.
- Inside, a diagonal stairway forms the keystone of an exciting, angular design.
- The foyer leads visitors past the den into the sunken living room with vaulted ceiling and fireplace.
- Square columned arcades separate the living room from the dining room.
- A sunny bay window defines the breakfast area, which includes a sliding glass door to the deck.
- The thoroughly modern kitchen includes an islet cooktop and pantry.
- The generously sized family room also sports a vaulted ceiling and offers easy access to the outdoor deck.
- Upstairs, a stylish master suite features a private bath and large closet.

UPPER FLOOR

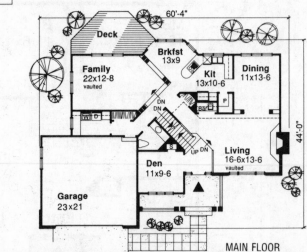

MAIN FLOOR

Plan B-89005

Bedrooms: 4	Baths: 2½

Space:

Upper floor:	1,083 sq. ft.
Main floor:	1,380 sq. ft.
Total living area:	2,463 sq. ft.
Basement:	1,380 sq. ft.
Garage:	483 sq. ft.

Exterior Wall Framing: 2x4

Foundation options:
Standard basement only.
(Foundation & framing conversion diagram available — see order form.)

Blueprint Price Code: C

Plan B-89005

PRICES AND DETAILS ON PAGES 12-15

Refined One-Story

- A symmetrical roofline and stucco walls with corner quoins and keystone accents add a refined look to this elegant one-story.
- The eye-catching entry leads into a surprisingly spacious interior, beginning with a family room that features a high ceiling and an inviting fireplace flanked by windows.
- The kitchen showcases an angled serving bar that faces the sunny breakfast room. A French door between the breakfast room and the formal dining room opens to a covered patio for more dining and entertaining space.
- The fantastic master suite features a tray ceiling and a superb private bath with a vaulted ceiling, an overhead plant shelf, a garden tub and a walk-in closet.
- The two front-facing bedrooms share a hall bath that includes a vanity with knee space.

Plan FB-1531

Bedrooms: 3	Baths: 2

Living Area:

Main floor	1,531 sq. ft.
Total Living Area:	**1,531 sq. ft.**
Garage	440 sq. ft.
Exterior Wall Framing:	2x4

Foundation Options:

Crawlspace
Slab
(Typical foundation & framing conversion diagram available—see order form.)

BLUEPRINT PRICE CODE: B

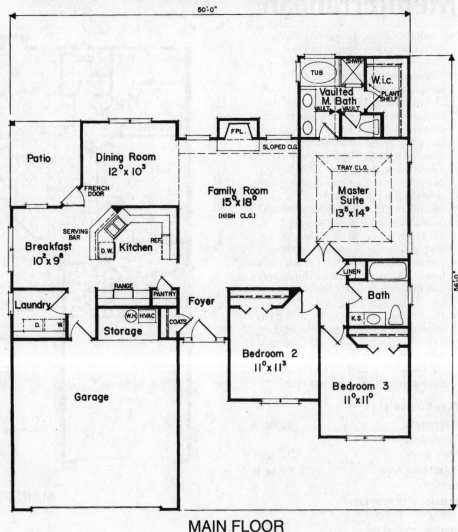

MAIN FLOOR

TO ORDER THIS BLUEPRINT, CALL TOLL-FREE 1-800-547-5570

PRICES AND DETAILS ON PAGES 12-15

Ultra-Modern Mediterranean

- Soaring ceilings, a luxurious master suite and a clean stucco exterior with stylish arched windows give this nouveau-Mediterranean home its unique appeal.

- The magnificent living room and the elegant dining room combine to form one large, open area. The dining room has a tall, arched window and a 12-ft. coffered ceiling. The living room boasts a flat ceiling that is over 12 ft. high, a convenient wet bar and sliding glass doors to the covered patio.

- The informal family room is warmed by a fireplace and shares a soaring 12-ft. flat ceiling with the sunny breakfast area and the large, modern kitchen.

- The kitchen is easily accessible from the family area and the formal dining room, and features an eating bar and a spacious pantry.

- The luxurious master suite offers patio access and is enhanced by an elegant 11-ft., 6-in. tray ceiling and his-and-hers walk-in closets. The huge master bath features a dual-sink vanity, a large tiled shower and a whirlpool tub.

Plan HDS-99-158

Bedrooms: 4	Baths: 3

Living Area:	
Main floor	2,352 sq. ft.
Total Living Area:	**2,352 sq. ft.**
Garage	440 sq. ft.

Exterior Wall Framing:
8-in. concrete block and 2x4

Foundation Options:

Slab
(All plans can be built with your choice of foundation and framing. A generic conversion diagram is available. See order form.)

BLUEPRINT PRICE CODE: C

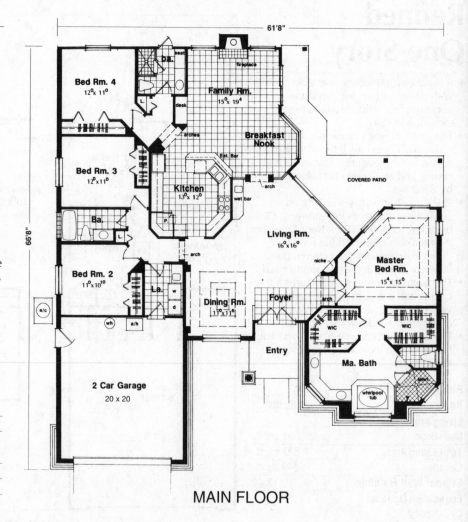

MAIN FLOOR

TO ORDER THIS BLUEPRINT, CALL TOLL-FREE 1-800-547-5570

Plan HDS-99-158

PRICES AND DETAILS ON PAGES 12-15

Room for Large Family

- An expansive home, this plan puts a heap of living space for a big, busy family all on one floor.
- The formal entertaining zone, consisting of a large, bright living room and a dining room, is located at the front, to the left as guests enter the large foyer.
- The more casual areas include a huge family room with a massive fireplace, and wet bar, a huge, open kitchen and sunny breakfast area.
- The magnificent master suite is fit for royalty, with its double-door entry, corner fireplace, incredible bath and large closet.
- Bedroom 2 has a private bath, while bedrooms 3 and 4 share a compartmentalized walk-through bath with private lavatory/dressing areas.
- Note the covered porch and double-doored entry at the front, plus the covered patio at the rear.

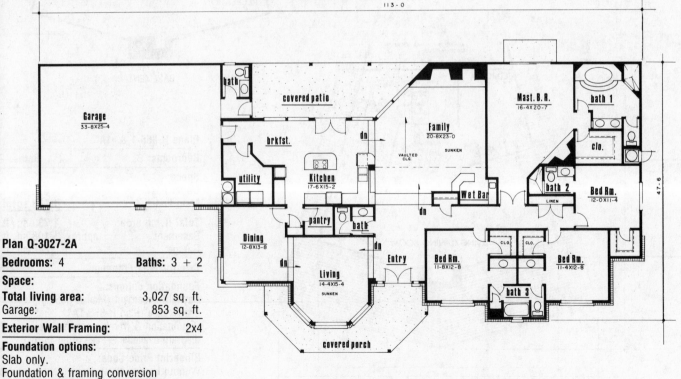

Plan Q-3027-2A

Bedrooms: 4	**Baths:** 3 + 2

Space:

Total living area:	3,027 sq. ft.
Garage:	853 sq. ft.

Exterior Wall Framing: 2x4

Foundation options:
Slab only.
Foundation & framing conversion diagram available — see order form.)

Blueprint Price Code: E

Panoramic View Embraces Outdoors

- This geometric design takes full advantage of scenic sites.
- Living area faces a glass-filled wall and wrap-around deck.
- Open dining/living room arrangement is complemented by vaulted ceilings, an overhead balcony, and a 5-ft-wide fireplace.
- 12′ deep main deck offers generous space for outdoor dining and entertaining.

PLAN H-855-1A
WITHOUT BASEMENT

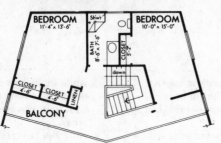

UPPER FLOOR

SCALE

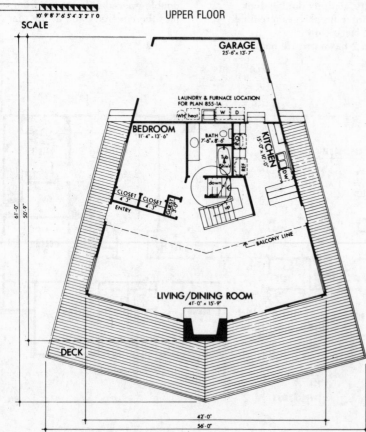

MAIN FLOOR

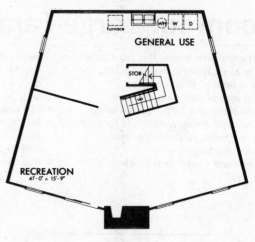

BASEMENT

Plans H-855-1 & -1A

Bedrooms: 3	Baths: 2

Space:	
Upper floor:	625 sq. ft.
Main floor:	1,108 sq. ft.

Total living area:	1,733 sq. ft.
Basement:	approx. 1,108 sq. ft.
Garage:	346 sq. ft.

Exterior Wall Framing:	2x6

Foundation options:
Daylight basement (Plan H-855-1).
Crawlspace (Plan H-855-1A).
(Foundation & framing conversion diagram available — see order form.)

Blueprint Price Code:

Without basement	B
With basement	D

TO ORDER THIS BLUEPRINT, CALL TOLL-FREE 1-800-547-5570

Plans H-855-1 & -1A

PRICES AND DETAILS ON PAGES 12-15

Design Exudes Warmth and Comfort

- This plan represents a return to traditional styling with the open-concept interior so much in demand today.
- A vaulted entry and living room with an adjacent dining room make up the formal portion of this plan.
- A spacious hall leads to the large informal entertaining area composed of the kitchen, nook and family room.

- The second floor offers a large master suite and two additional bedrooms with a bonus room that can be left unfinished until needed.
- Exterior rooflines are all gabled for ease of construction and lower framing costs. The brick veneer garage face echoes the brick columns supporting the covered entry.

Plan S-8389	
Bedrooms: 3-4	**Baths:** 2½
Living Area:	
Upper floor	932 sq. ft.
Main floor	1,290 sq. ft.
Bonus room	228 sq. ft.
Total Living Area:	**2,450 sq. ft.**
Standard basement	1,290 sq. ft.
Garage	429 sq. ft.
Exterior Wall Framing:	2x6

Foundation Options:
Standard basement
Crawlspace
Slab
(Typical foundation & framing conversion diagram available—see order form.)

BLUEPRINT PRICE CODE:	C

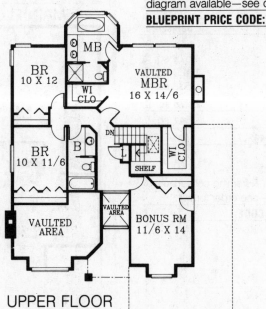

MAIN FLOOR

UPPER FLOOR

Chalet Style for Town or Country

- The exterior features exposed beams, board siding and viewing decks with cut-out railings to give this home the look of a mountain chalet.
- Inside, the design lends itself equally well to year-round family living or part-time recreational enjoyment.
- An expansive Great Room features an impressive fireplace and includes a dining area next to the well-planned kitchen.
- The upstairs offers the possibility of an adult retreat, with a fine master bedroom with private bath and large closets, plus a loft area available for many uses.
- Two secondary bedrooms are on the main floor, and share another bath.
- The daylight basement level includes a garage and a large recreation room with a fireplace and a half-bath.

Plan P-531-2D

Bedrooms: 3	Baths: 2½
Living Area:	
Upper floor	573 sq. ft.
Main floor	1,120 sq. ft.
Daylight basement	532 sq. ft.
Total Living Area:	**2,225 sq. ft.**
Garage	541 sq. ft.
Exterior Wall Framing:	2x6
Foundation Options:	
Daylight basement (Typical foundation & framing conversion diagram available—see order form.)	
BLUEPRINT PRICE CODE:	C

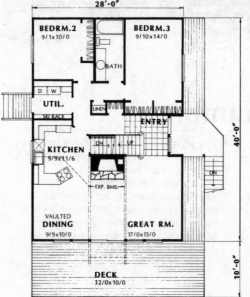

MAIN FLOOR

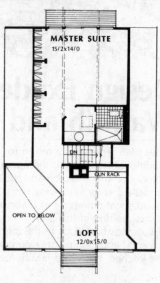

UPPER FLOOR

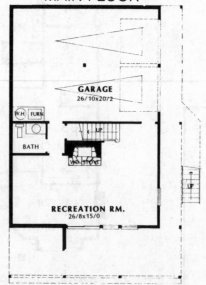

DAYLIGHT BASEMENT

Plan P-531-2D

PRICES AND DETAILS ON PAGES 12-15

Casual Flexibility

- This beautifully designed vacation or year-round home is spacious and flexible.
- The interior is brightened by an abundance of windows.
- The open, vaulted living room boasts a central fireplace that makes a great conversation place or a cozy spot for spending cold winter evenings.
- The kitchen opens to the dining room and the scenery beyond through the dramatic window wall with half-round transom.
- The sleeping room and loft upstairs can easily accommodate several guests or could be used as multi-purpose space.

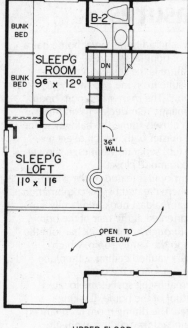

UPPER FLOOR

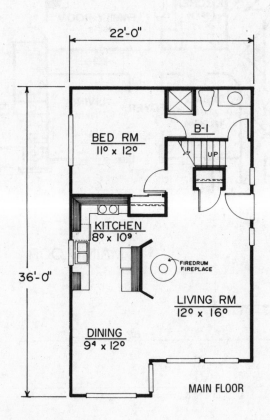

MAIN FLOOR

Plan I-1032-A

Bedrooms: 2-3	Baths: 1½
Living Area:	
Upper floor	288 sq. ft.
Main floor	744 sq. ft.
Total Living Area:	**1,032 sq. ft.**
Exterior Wall Framing:	2x6

Foundation Options:
Crawlspace
(Typical foundation & framing conversion diagram available—see order form.)

BLUEPRINT PRICE CODE: A

A Palette of Pleasures

- This stylish traditional brick home has a palette of popular features.
- One feature is the separation of the master suite from the two secondary bedrooms. The master bedroom opens to a romantic rear deck. His-and-hers walk-in closets frame the hallway to the private master bath, which offers a garden tub, separate vanities, a shower and a commode closet.
- Another popular feature is the warm atmosphere created by the combination kitchen, breakfast nook and family room, oriented at the rear of the home. A pass-through and a snack bar join the kitchen to the family room, which features a vaulted ceiling, a fireplace and patio doors to the deck.
- The formal living spaces are located at the front of the home, flanking the foyer. The dining room is enhanced by an elegant tray ceiling, while the living room boasts a cathedral ceiling.

Plan APS-2309

Bedrooms: 3	Baths: 2
Living Area:	
Main floor	2,275 sq. ft.
Total Living Area:	**2,275 sq. ft.**
Standard basement	2,356 sq. ft.
Garage	418 sq. ft.
Exterior Wall Framing:	2x4

Foundation Options:

Standard basement

(All plans can be built with your choice of foundation and framing. A generic conversion diagram is available. See order form.)

BLUEPRINT PRICE CODE:	C

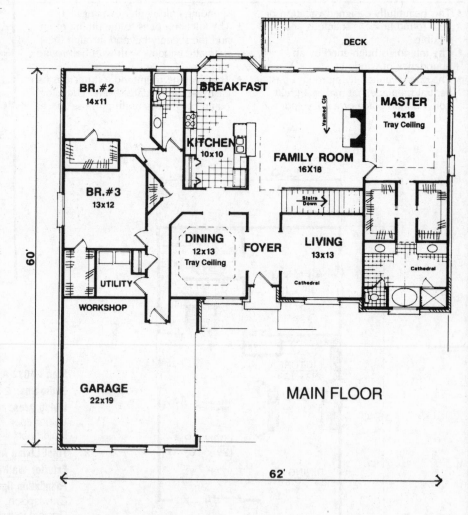

MAIN FLOOR

Comfortable, Open Plan

- A central Great Room features a cathedral ceiling and is visually separated from the dining area by a huge fireplace.
- A wing on the left includes two secondary bedrooms which share a bath.
- In the right wing, you'll find a spacious master bedroom with private bath and walk-in closet.
- The kitchen is roomy and well-planned,

with a utility room in the garage entry area.
- A house-spanning front deck adds an extra welcoming touch to the plan.

Plan C-8160		
Bedrooms: 3		**Baths:** 2
Space:		
Main floor		1,669 sq. ft.
Total Living Area		**1,669 sq. ft.**
Basement	(approx.)	1,660 sq. ft.
Carport		413 sq. ft.
Storage	(approx.)	85 sq. ft.
Exterior Wall Framing		2x4

Foundation options:

Standard Basement
Crawlspace
Slab
(Foundation & framing conversion diagram available—see order form.)

Blueprint Price Code	B

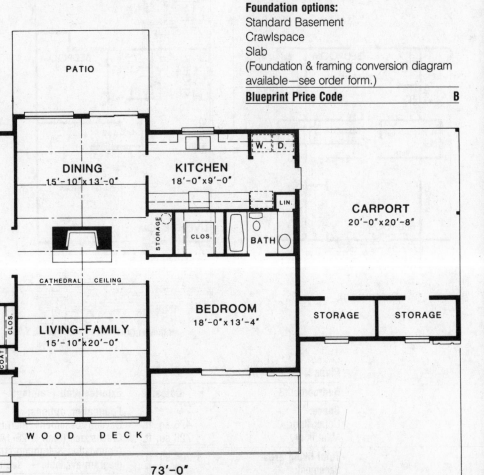

TO ORDER THIS BLUEPRINT,
CALL TOLL-FREE 1-800-547-5570

Plan C-8160

PRICES AND DETAILS
ON PAGES 12-15

105

Simple and Economical Chalet

- This home away from home is relatively simple to construct; it is also an enjoyable reason to spend your weekends in the mountains or at the beach.
- The main level is largely devoted to open living space, other than the kitchen and master bedroom, which could also be used as a study or hobby room.
- Second-floor bedrooms are larger and share a full bath and large storage areas.

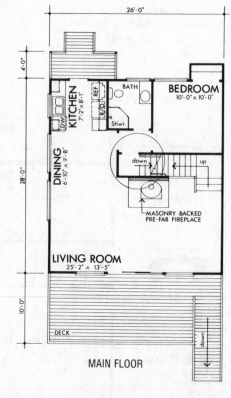

UPPER FLOOR

MAIN FLOOR

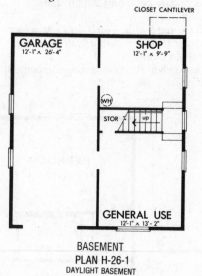

BASEMENT
PLAN H-26-1
DAYLIGHT BASEMENT

PLAN H-26-1A
WITHOUT BASEMENT

Plans H-26-1 & -1A		
Bedrooms: 3	**Baths:** 2	
Space:		
Upper floor:	476 sq. ft.	
Main floor:	728 sq. ft.	
Total living area:	1,204 sq. ft.	
Basement:	410 sq. ft.	
Garage:	318 sq. ft.	

Exterior Wall Framing: 2x4

Foundation options:
Daylight basement (Plan H-26-1).
Crawlspace (Plan H-26-1A).
(Foundation & framing conversion diagram available — see order form.)

Blueprint Price Code: A

Gracious One-Floor Living

- An impressive roofscape, stately brick with soldier coursing, and an imposing entry grace the exterior of this exciting single-story home.
- The free-flowing interior spaces are well zoned into formal, informal, and sleeping areas.
- The entry opens into the formal living and dining areas, with an interesting angled den for an additional

entertaining area, guest room or home office.
- The informal family room with fireplace extends from the octagonal island kitchen/breakfast room.
- Three secondary bedrooms are zoned to the right of the plan.
- The lavish master suite with fireplace and state-of-the-art bath is privately situated in the left wing.

Plan DD-3076	
Bedrooms: 4	**Baths: 3**
Space:	
Main floor	3,076 sq. ft.
Total Living Area	**3,076 sq. ft.**
Basement	3,076 sq. ft.
Garage	648 sq. ft.
Exterior Wall Framing	2x4
Ceiling Heights	9'
Foundation options:	
Standard Basement	
Crawlspace	
Slab	
(Foundation & framing conversion diagram available—see order form.)	
Blueprint Price Code	E

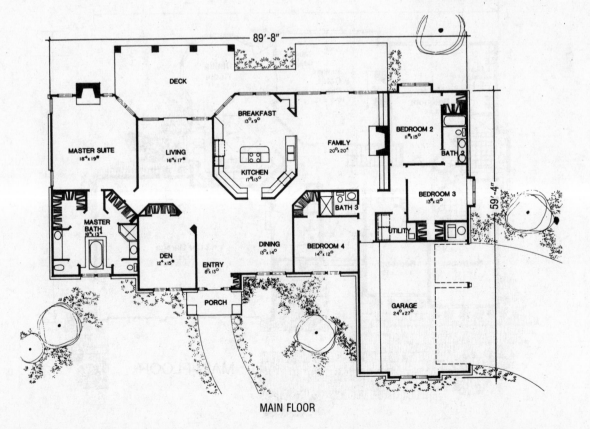

MAIN FLOOR

Playful Floor Plan

- High, hipped roofs and a recessed entry give this home a smart-looking exterior. A dynamic floor plan – punctuated with angled walls, high ceilings and playful window treatments – gives the home an exciting interior.
- The sunken and vaulted Great Room, the circular dining room and the angled island kitchen are the heartbeat of the home. The Great Room offers a fireplace, a built-in corner entertainment center and tall arched windows overlooking the backyard.

- An angled railing separates the Great Room from the open kitchen and dining room. An atrium door next to the glassed-in dining area opens to the backyard. The kitchen includes an island snack bar and a garden window.
- The master bedroom is nestled into one corner for quiet and privacy. This deluxe suite features two walk-in closets and a whirlpool bath. The two smaller bedrooms share another full bath.
- An extra-large laundry area, complete with a clothes-folding counter and a coat closet, is accessible from the three-car garage.
- The home is visually expanded by 9-ft. ceilings throughout, with the exception of the vaulted Great Room.

Plan PI-90-435

Bedrooms: 3	**Baths:** 2

Living Area:	
Main floor	1,896 sq. ft.
Total Living Area:	**1,896 sq. ft.**
Basement	1,889 sq. ft.
Garage	667 sq. ft.
Exterior Wall Framing:	2x6

Foundation Options:
Daylight basement
Standard basement
(Typical foundation & framing conversion diagram available—see order form.)

BLUEPRINT PRICE CODE:	B

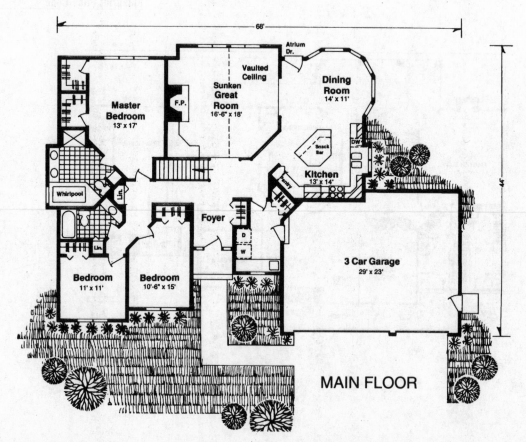

MAIN FLOOR

TO ORDER THIS BLUEPRINT, CALL TOLL-FREE 1-800-547-5570

Plan PI-90-435

PRICES AND DETAILS ON PAGES 12-15

A Pillar of Success

- A stunning two-story entry porch with heavy support pillars creates a look of success for this exciting new design.
- Once inside the entry, there is a wide-open view ahead into the vaulted Great Room, with dramatic angled, two-story window-walls. The Great Room also features a fireplace and TV niche.
- The galley kitchen has a cooktop island with snack counter and overlooks the dining bay and view deck beyond ample windows.
- The main-floor master suite has a trayed ceiling, angled windows, private deck access, dressing area, and a private bath with separate tub and shower.
- A main-floor den/guest room has a vaulted ceiling, private deck access, and is just steps away from a full bath. Two more bedrooms, a full bath, and a hobby area are upstairs.

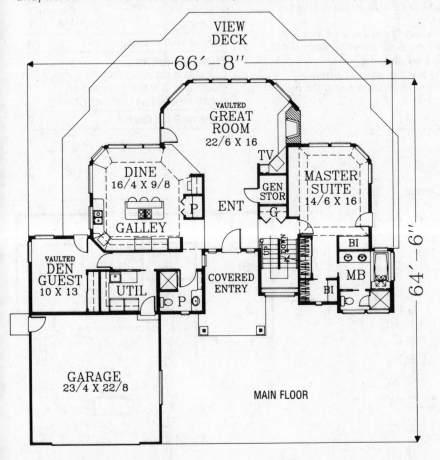

MAIN FLOOR

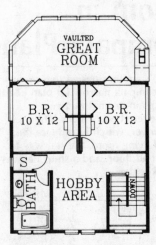

UPPER FLOOR

Plan LRD-32190

Bedrooms: 3-4	Baths: 3
Space:	
Upper floor	606 sq. ft.
Main floor	1,865 sq. ft.
Total Living Area	**2,471 sq. ft.**
Basement	1,865 sq. ft.
Garage	529 sq. ft.
Exterior Wall Framing	2x6

Foundation options:
Standard basement
Crawlspace
Slab
(Foundation & framing conversion diagram available—see order form.)

Blueprint Price Code	C

Vaulted Living Room in Compact Plan

- Here's another design that proves that a compact narrow lot plan need not be plain or unattractive.
- A sheltered entry leads into a raised foyer, which introduces the vaulted living room, the stairway to the second floor, and a short hallway to the kitchen.

- A cozy breakfast nook is included in the efficient, open-design kitchen.
- Also note the convenient half-bath and storage closet between the kitchen and garage entry.
- Upstairs, the master suite includes a private bath and large walk-in closet.
- Bedroom 2 also includes a large closet.
- Bedroom 3 can be used as a loft, library, exercise room or study if not needed for sleeping.
- The upstairs hallway offers a balcony looking down into the living room below.

Plan B-224-8512

Bedrooms: 2-3	Baths: 2½

Space:

Upper floor:	691 sq. ft.
Main floor:	668 sq. ft.

Total living area:	**1,359 sq. ft.**
Basement:	+/– 668 sq. ft.
Garage:	458 sq. ft.

Exterior Wall Framing:	2x4

Foundation options:
Standard basement only.
(Foundation & framing conversion diagram available — see order form.)

Blueprint Price Code:	A

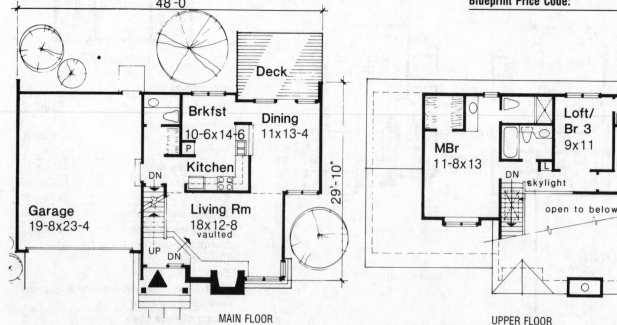

MAIN FLOOR

UPPER FLOOR

TO ORDER THIS BLUEPRINT, CALL TOLL-FREE 1-800-547-5570

Plan B-224-8512

PRICES AND DETAILS ON PAGES 12-15

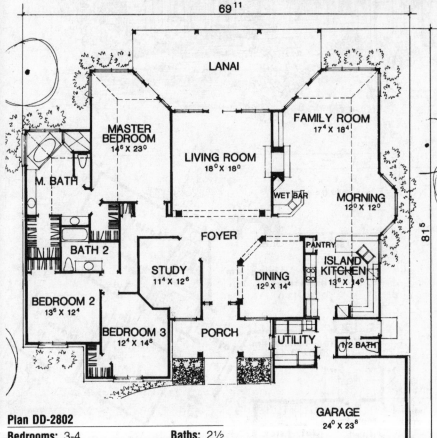

69¹¹ → 69^{11}

81⁵ → 81^5

LANAI

MASTER BEDROOM
14^6 X 23^0

LIVING ROOM
18^0 X 18^0

FAMILY ROOM
17^4 X 18^4

M. BATH

WET BAR

MORNING
12^0 X 12^0

BATH 2

FOYER

PANTRY

ISLAND KITCHEN
13^6 X 14^0

STUDY
11^4 X 12^6

DINING
12^0 X 14^0

BEDROOM 2
13^6 X 12^4

BEDROOM 3
12^4 X 14^8

PORCH

UTILITY

1/2 BATH

GARAGE
24^0 X 23^8

Plan DD-2802

Bedrooms: 3-4	Baths: 2½
Space:	
Main floor	2,899 sq. ft.
Total Living Area	**2,899 sq. ft.**
Basement	2,899 sq. ft.
Garage	568 sq. ft.
Exterior Wall Framing	2x4

Foundation options:
Basement
Crawlspace
Slab
(Foundation & framing conversion diagram available—see order form.)

Blueprint Price Code	**D**

Unique Inside and Out

- This plan gives new dimension to one-story living. The exterior features graceful arched windows and a sweeping roofline The interior is marked by unusual angles and curves.
- The living areas are clustered around a large "lanai," or covered porch. French doors in the master bedroom and the family room angle toward the porch.
- Extras include the two-way fireplace, warming both the family room and the living room. The home's expansiveness is enhanced by ceilings that slope up to 10 feet. Columns frame both the living room and the formal dining room, echoing the columns of the porches.
- The island kitchen and the morning room are open to the family room, which features a wet bar. The living room is highlighted by French doors and arched transom windows.
- The formal dining room and the study are stationed near the front of the home, away from the major activity areas.
- The master bedroom includes an irresistible bath with a spa tub, dual vanities, two walk-in closets and a separate shower.
- Two more good-sized bedrooms share another full bath.
- A large utility room and a half-bath are conveniently located between the kitchen and the garage.

TO ORDER THIS BLUEPRINT,
CALL TOLL-FREE 1-800-547-5570

Plan DD-2802

PRICES AND DETAILS
ON PAGES 12-15

111

Small Home Has Big Impact

- Small in area but big on function, this angled, three-bedroom ranch glows with charm.
- The central foyer neatly channels traffic to the bedroom wing, the formal areas to the rear and the kitchen and family room to the left.
- Highlighted by a sloped ceiling and a stone fireplace, the living and dining rooms combine for a dramatic setting that overlooks a backyard terrace.
- The family room and kitchen also flow together smoothly for a casual family atmosphere.
- Two skylighted bathrooms and three bedrooms are secluded to the right of the home.

Plan K-696-T

Bedrooms: 3	Baths: 2½
Living Area:	
Main floor	1,272 sq. ft.
Total Living Area:	**1,272 sq. ft.**
Standard basement	1,232 sq. ft.
Garage	509 sq. ft.
Exterior Wall Framing:	2x4 or 2x6

Foundation Options:
Standard basement
Slab
(Typical foundation & framing conversion diagram available—see order form.)

BLUEPRINT PRICE CODE: A

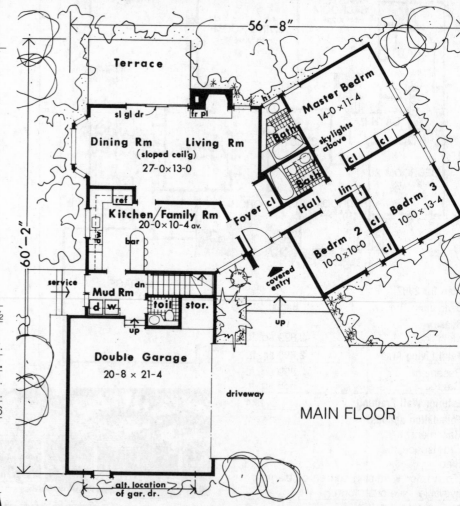

MAIN FLOOR

Plan K-696-T

Designed for Maximum Livability

- An elegant French Provincial design, this home represents an impressive facade to visitors, family and passers-by.
- Interior is designed for maximum flexibility for the busy family that entertains frequently.

- The optional fourth bedroom is located so it can easily serve as a library, den, office or music room.
- A living/sitting room with a 12' ceiling may serve as a formal living room or a master suite sitting room.
- The large, high-ceilinged family room blends into the sunny morning room and spacious kitchen.
- The master suite includes a huge, luxurious master bath with two large walk-in closets and two vanity sinks.
- A sunny atrium leads to a game room for family or party guests.

Plan E-2704

Bedrooms: 3-4	**Baths:** 2

Space:

Total living area:	2,791 sq. ft.
Garage:	682 sq. ft.
Porches, etc.:	543 sq. ft.

Exterior Wall Framing:	2x4

Foundation options:
Crawlspace.
Slab.
(Foundation & framing conversion diagram available — see order form.)

Blueprint Price Code:	D

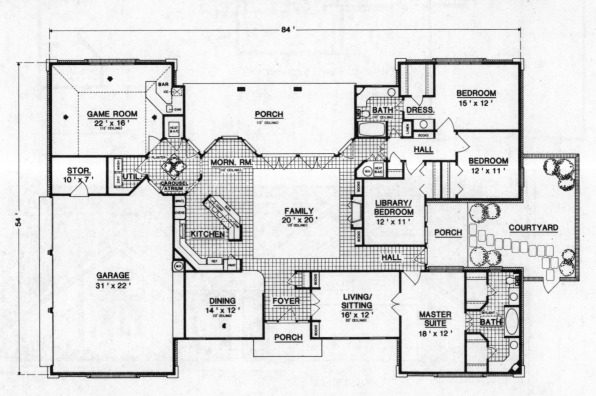

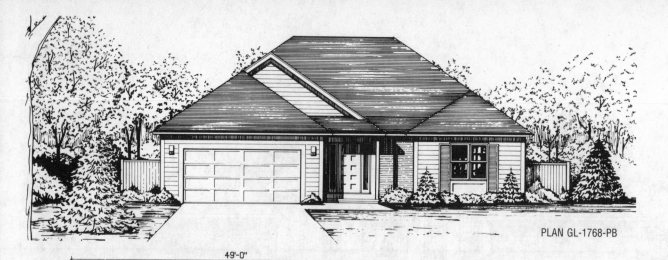

PLAN GL-1768-PB

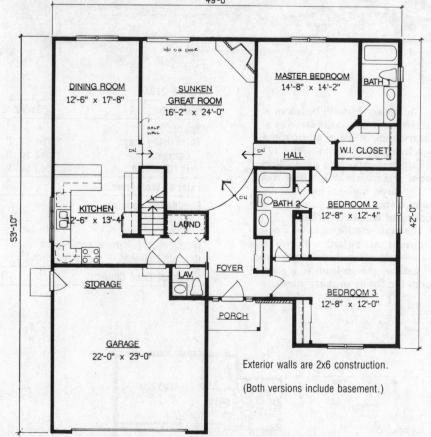

DINING ROOM
12'-6" x 17'-8"

SUNKEN
GREAT ROOM
16'-2" x 24'-0"

MASTER BEDROOM
14'-8" x 14'-2"

BATH

W.I. CLOSET

HALF
WALL

HALL

KITCHEN
12'-6" x 13'-4"

LAUND

BATH 2

BEDROOM 2
12'-8" x 12'-4"

STORAGE

LAV.

FOYER

PORCH

BEDROOM 3
12'-8" x 12'-0"

GARAGE
22'-0" x 23'-0"

49'-0"

53'-10"

42'-0"

Exterior walls are 2x6 construction.

(Both versions include basement.)

Choice of Exterior Treatments for Same Floor Plan

Total living area: 1,768 sq. ft.
(Not counting basement or garage)

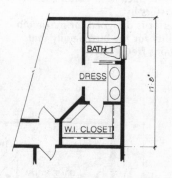

BATH

DRESS

W.I. CLOSET

17'-8"

OPT. MASTER BATH

PLAN GL-1768-PA

Blueprint Price Code B

Plans GL-1768-PA & -PB

PRICES AND DETAILS ON PAGES 12-15

An Array Of Luxuries

- This luxury home would ideally be built into a hill to allow full use of the home's basement.
- A panoramic view is captured from every primary room, including a deck that stretches along the rear of the home.
- Luxurious amenities inside include an island kitchen with separate walk-in pantry, window-enclosed nook, a huge family room with wood stove and rear window wall, a formal dining room with window seat, and a formal sunken living room.
- Other extras are the master bedroom with step-down onto the deck, roomy walk-in closet and a private bath with bayed step-up spa tub, separate shower and work area.
- Downstairs you'll find an exciting recreation room with wood stove and eye-catching bar, plus room for two additional bedrooms, a full bath and storage space.

Plan NW-744

Bedrooms: 4	Baths: 3½

Space:	
Main floor:	2,539 sq. ft.
Daylight basement:	1,461 sq. ft.
Total living area:	**4,000 sq. ft.**
Storage rooms:	948 sq. ft.
Garage:	904 sq. ft.

Exterior Wall Framing:	2x6

Foundation options:
Daylight basement.
(Foundation & framing conversion diagram available — see order form.)

Blueprint Price Code:	G

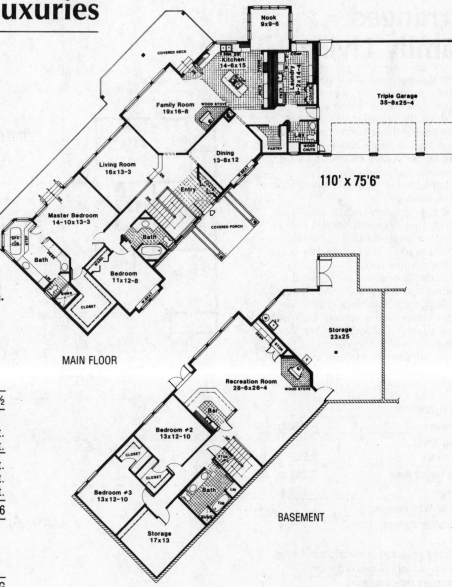

110' x 75'6"

MAIN FLOOR

BASEMENT

Neatly Arranged Family Living

- This distinguished ranch home has a neatly arranged floor plan with a large activity area at the center and a strategically placed master bedroom.
- The double-doored entry opens to the large sunken family room with cathedral ceiling, decorative columned bridge, fireplace and patio view.
- A formal living room and dining room flank the foyer.
- The huge modern kitchen offers a handy snack counter, open to the adjacent family room. The bayed breakfast room has French-door access to the covered patio.
- Secluded to one end of the home is a deluxe master bedroom with a cathedral ceiling, a spacious walk-in closet, a private patio and a personal bath with dual vanities and additional outdoor access.
- Three additional bedrooms and two more baths are located at the opposite end of the home.

Plan Q-2266-1A

Bedrooms: 4	Baths: 3

Living Area:	
Main floor	2,266 sq. ft.

Total Living Area:	**2,266 sq. ft.**
Garage	592 sq. ft.

Exterior Wall Framing:	2x4

Foundation Options:
Slab
(Typical foundation & framing conversion diagram available—see order form.)

BLUEPRINT PRICE CODE:	**C**

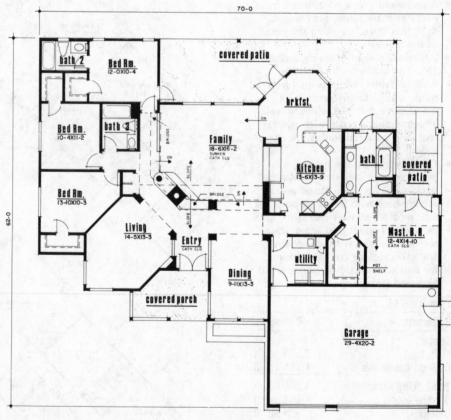

MAIN FLOOR

TO ORDER THIS BLUEPRINT, CALL TOLL-FREE 1-800-547-5570

Plan Q-2266-1A

PRICES AND DETAILS ON PAGES 12-15

Garden Home

- This thoroughly modern plan exhibits beautiful traditional touches in its exterior design.
- A gracious courtyard-like area leads visitors to a side door with a vaulted entry.
- A delightful kitchen/nook area is just to the right of the entry, and includes abundant window space and a convenient utility room.
- The vaulted living and dining areas join together to create an impressive space for entertaining and family living.
- The master suite boasts a large closet and a private bath.
- The daylight-basement option adds almost 1,500 square feet of space to the home.

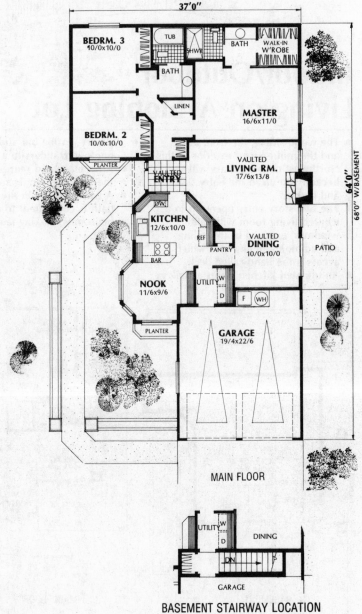

MAIN FLOOR

BASEMENT STAIRWAY LOCATION

Plans P-6598-2A & -2D

Bedrooms: 3	Baths: 2
Living Area:	
Main floor (without basement)	1,375 sq. ft.
Main floor (with basement)	1,470 sq. ft.
Total Living Area:	**1,375/1,470 sq. ft.**
Daylight basement	1,470 sq. ft.
Garage	435 sq. ft.
Exterior Wall Framing:	2x4
Foundation Options:	Plan #
Daylight basement	P-6598-2D
Crawlspace	P-6598-2A
(Typical foundation & framing conversion diagram available—see order form.)	
BLUEPRINT PRICE CODE:	A

TO ORDER THIS BLUEPRINT,
CALL TOLL-FREE 1-800-547-5570

Plans P-6598-2A & -2D

PRICES AND DETAILS
ON PAGES 12-15

117

Indoor/Outdoor Living on A Sloping Lot

- The wood siding, the front deck, and the multi-paned exterior of this Northwest contemporary will beckon you up to the entry stairs and inside.
- The two-story entry opens up to a vaulted living room with tall windows, exposed beam ceiling and adjoining dining area which accesses the hand-railed deck.
- An updated kitchen offers a walk-in pantry, eating bar and breakfast nook with sliders to a rear deck.
- A fireplace and rear patio highlight the attached family room.
- A washer/dryer in the upper level bath is convenient to all three bedrooms, making laundry a breeze.

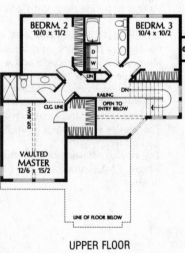

UPPER FLOOR

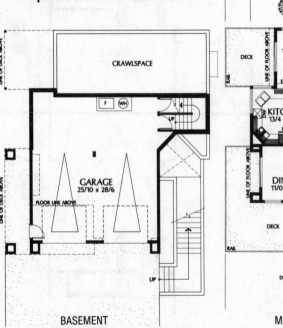

BASEMENT

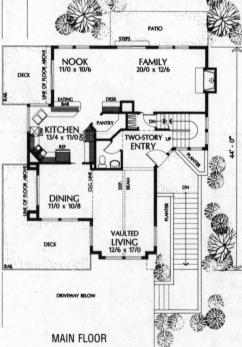

MAIN FLOOR

Plan P-7737-4D	
Bedrooms: 3	**Baths: 2½**
Space:	
Upper floor:	802 sq. ft.
Main floor:	1,158 sq. ft.
Total living area:	1,960 sq. ft.
Garage/basement:	736 sq. ft.
Exterior Wall Framing:	2x6
Foundation options: Crawlspace. (Foundation & framing conversion diagram available — see order form.)	
Blueprint Price Code:	B

TO ORDER THIS BLUEPRINT, CALL TOLL-FREE 1-800-547-5570

Plan P-7737-4D

PRICES AND DETAILS ON PAGES 12-15

Super Southern Home

- Super indoor/outdoor living features are the main ingredients in this sprawling one-story home.
- A spectacular vaulted family room sits at the center of the floor plan and extends to the outdoor living spaces. A huge fireplace flanked with storage space adds further excitement.
- The adjoining island kitchen and vaulted breakfast nook also open to the patio.
- The master suite is intended to offer the ultimate in comfort. Double entry doors and a tray ceiling are featured in the master bedroom, which opens to the adjoining patio. A see-through fireplace opens to the garden tub in the private bath.
- Three secondary bedrooms share two full baths at the opposite end of the home.

Plan HDS-99-164

Bedrooms: 4	Baths: 3

Living Area:

Main floor	2,962 sq. ft.
Total Living Area:	**2,962 sq. ft.**
Garage	567 sq. ft.

Exterior Wall Framing:

Combination concrete block and 2x4

Foundation Options:

Slab

(Typical foundation & framing conversion diagram available—see order form.)

BLUEPRINT PRICE CODE: D

MAIN FLOOR

Octagonal Home with Lofty View

- There's no better way to avoid the ordinary than by building an octagonal home and escaping from square corners and rigid rooms.
- The roomy main floor offers plenty of space for full-time family living or for a comfortable second-home retreat.
- The vaulted entry hall leads to the bedrooms on the right or down the hall to the Great Room.
- Warmed by a woodstove, the Great Room offers a panoramic view of the surrounding scenery.
- The center core of the main floor houses two baths, one of which contains a spa tub and is private to the master bedroom.
- This plan also includes a roomy kitchen and handy utility area.
- A large loft is planned as a recreation room, also with a woodstove.
- The daylight basement version adds another bedroom, a bath, a garage and a large storage area.

FRONT VIEW

Plans P-532-3A & -3D

Bedrooms: 3-4	Baths: 2-3
Living Area:	
Upper floor	355 sq. ft.
Main floor	1,567 sq. ft.
Daylight basement	430 sq. ft.
Total Living Area:	**1,922/2,352 sq. ft.**
Garage and storage	1,137 sq. ft.
Exterior Wall Framing:	2x6
Foundation Options:	**Plan #**
Daylight basement	P-532-3D
Crawlspace	P-532-3A

(Typical foundation & framing conversion diagram available—see order form.)

BLUEPRINT PRICE CODE:	**B/C**

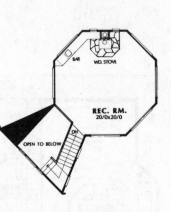

UPPER FLOOR

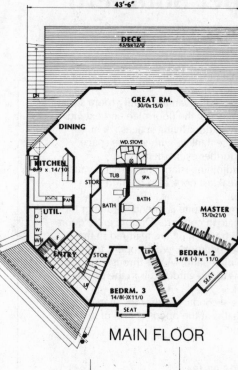

MAIN FLOOR

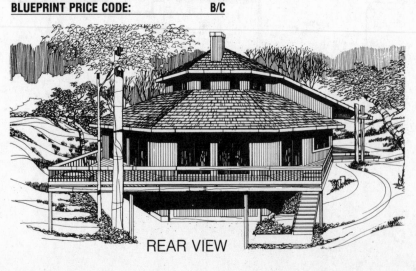

REAR VIEW

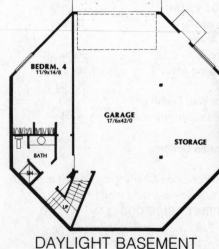

DAYLIGHT BASEMENT

TO ORDER THIS BLUEPRINT, CALL TOLL-FREE 1-800-547-5570 Plans P-532-3A & -3D **PRICES AND DETAILS ON PAGES 12-15**

Patio Living

- A well-executed floor plan sets this impeccable design apart from the ordinary. Rooms of various shapes are arranged to maintain openness and to take advantage of the wonderful patio.
- The granite-paved foyer is open to the large living room, which provides a terrific view of the covered patio.
- An octagonal dining room and den/study flank the foyer and also face the living room.
- The uniquely shaped family room, with a fireplace centered between a wall of built-ins, has a dynamic view of the outdoors and is open to the kitchen.
- The spacious kitchen has an island range, a pantry, an octagonal nook and a convenient laundry room near the entrance to the garage.
- Two nicely placed bedrooms allow privacy. They have ample closet space and share a full bath, which is also accessible from the patio.
- The master suite is a wing in itself. The bedroom boasts a romantic fireplace and glass walls at the front and back. The superb private bath has a large whirlpool tub, an oversized corner shower and separate dressing areas.

Plan HDS-99-137	
Bedrooms: 3	**Baths:** 2½
Living Area:	
Main floor	2,656 sq. ft.
Total Living Area:	**2,656 sq. ft.**
Garage	503 sq. ft.
Exterior Wall Framing:	2x4 & 8-in. block

Foundation Options:

Slab
(Typical foundation & framing conversion diagram available—see order form.)

BLUEPRINT PRICE CODE:	D

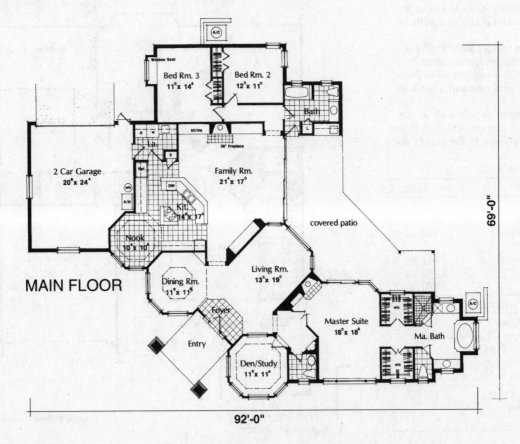

MAIN FLOOR

Plan HDS-99-137

Spacious Vaulted Great Room

- Behind an unpretentious facade lies an exciting and highly livable floor plan.
- A vaulted entry leads visitors to an impressive vaulted Great Room with exposed-beam ceiling.
- The roomy kitchen also boasts a vaulted ceiling, and skylights as well.
- The sunny nook looks out onto a large patio, and includes a built-in desk.
- A first-class master suite includes a large dressing area, enormous walk-in closet and sumptuous bath.
- Bedroom 2 also contains a walk-in closet.
- Also note other details such as the pantry, linen storage and convenient washer/dryer area in the garage entry.

Plans P-6577-3A & -3D

Bedrooms: 3	Baths: 2

Space:

Main floor (crawlspace version):	1,978 sq. ft.
Main floor (basement version):	2,047 sq. ft.
Basement:	1,982 sq. ft.
Garage:	438 sq. ft.

Exterior Wall Framing:	2x4

Foundation options:
Daylight basement (Plan P-6577-3D).
Crawlspace (Plan P-6577-3A).
(Foundation & framing conversion diagram available — see order form.)

Blueprint Price Code:

Without basement:	B
With basement:	C

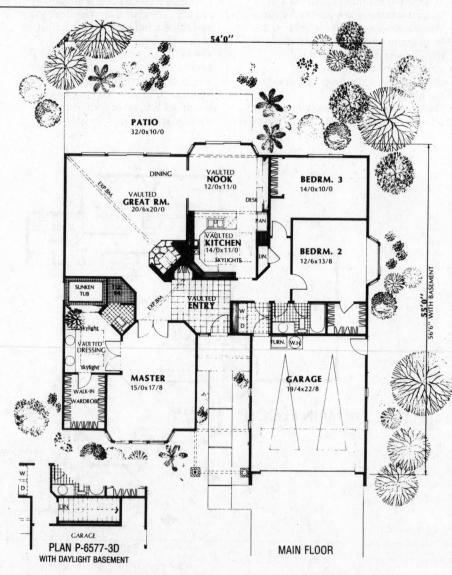

PLAN P-6577-3D
WITH DAYLIGHT BASEMENT

MAIN FLOOR

TO ORDER THIS BLUEPRINT, CALL TOLL-FREE 1-800-547-5570

Plans P-6577-3A & -3D

PRICES AND DETAILS ON PAGES 12-15

Attractive, Open Interior

- Multiple rooflines and an articulate facade generate an attractive curb appeal.
- Inside, sloped ceilings and jutting bays heighten the open, airy atmosphere.
- The formal living and dining rooms are highlighted by an angled fireplace.
- The informal living areas at the rear of the home include a modern, open kitchen flanked by a cozy family room with fireplace and a bright dinette.
- A den or fourth bedroom and a main-floor laundry room complete this level.
- An angled stairway leads to the three additional bedrooms on the upper level.

Plan K-684-D

Bedrooms: 3-4	Baths: 3
Space:	
Upper floor	702 sq. ft.
Main floor	1,273 sq. ft.
Total Living Area	**1,975 sq. ft.**
Basement	1,225 sq. ft.
Garage	440 sq. ft.
Exterior Wall Framing	2x4 or 2x6

Foundation options:

Standard Basement
Slab
(Foundation & framing conversion diagram available—see order form.)

Blueprint Price Code	**B**

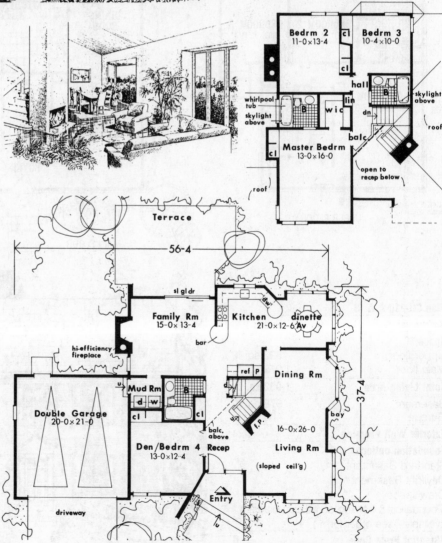

CH-210-B

Alternate Exteriors

- Timeless exterior detailing and a functional, cost-effective interior are found in this traditional home.
- The kitchen, bayed breakfast room and vaulted family room with skylights and fireplace flow together to form the heart of the home.
- Lots of light filters into the front-facing formal living room.
- Upstairs, the master suite boasts a vaulted ceiling, large walk-in closet and private luxury bath.
- For the flavor of a full, covered front porch, Plan CH-210-B should be your choice.

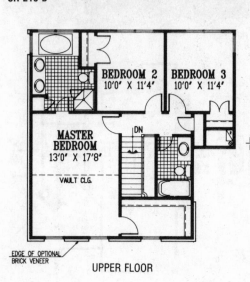

BEDROOM 2
10'0" X 11'4"

BEDROOM 3
10'0" X 11'4"

MASTER BEDROOM
13'0" X 17'8"

DN

VAULT CLG.

EDGE OF OPTIONAL BRICK VENEER

UPPER FLOOR

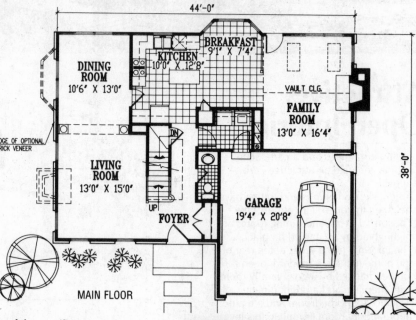

44'-0"

DINING ROOM
10'6" X 13'0"

KITCHEN
10'0" X 12'8"

BREAKFAST
9'1" X 7'4"

VAULT CLG.

FAMILY ROOM
13'0" X 16'4"

EDGE OF OPTIONAL BRICK VENEER

LIVING ROOM
13'0" X 15'0"

DN

UP

FOYER

GARAGE
19'4" X 20'8"

38'-0"

MAIN FLOOR

CH-210-A

Plan CH-210-A & -B	
Bedrooms: 3	**Baths:** 2½
Space:	
Upper floor	823 sq. ft.
Main floor	1,079 sq. ft.
Total Living Area	**1,902 sq. ft.**
Basement	978 sq. ft.
Garage	400 sq. ft.
Exterior Wall Framing	2x4

Foundation options:
Standard Basement
Daylight Basement
Crawlspace
(Foundation & framing conversion diagram available—see order form.)

Blueprint Price Code	**B**

TO ORDER THIS BLUEPRINT, CALL TOLL-FREE 1-800-547-5570

Plans CH-210-A & -B

PRICES AND DETAILS ON PAGES 12-15

Proven Plan Features Passive Sun Room

- A passive sun room, energy-efficient wood stove, and a panorama of windows make this design highly economical.
- Open living/dining room features attractive balcony railing, stone hearth, and adjoining sun room with durable stone floor.
- Well-equipped kitchen is separated from dining area by a convenient breakfast bar.
- Second level sleeping areas border a hallway and balcony.
- Optional basement plan provides extra space for entertaining or work.

Plans H-855-3A & -3B

Bedrooms: 3	Baths: 2-3

Space:	
Upper floor:	586 sq. ft.
Main floor:	1,192 sq. ft.
Sun room:	132 sq. ft.
Total living area:	**1,910 sq. ft.**
Basement:	approx. 1,192 sq. ft.
Garage:	520 sq. ft.

Exterior Wall Framing:	2x6

Foundation options:
Daylight basement (Plan H-855-3B).
Crawlspace (Plan H-855-3A).
(Foundation & framing conversion diagram available — see order form.)

Blueprint Price Code:

Without basement	B
With basement	E

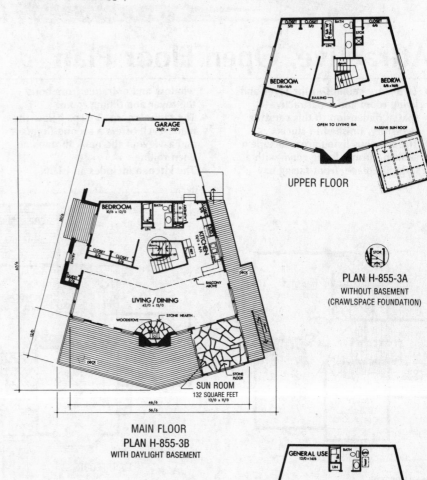

UPPER FLOOR

MAIN FLOOR
PLAN H-855-3B
WITH DAYLIGHT BASEMENT

PLAN H-855-3A
WITHOUT BASEMENT
(CRAWLSPACE FOUNDATION)

BASEMENT

TO ORDER THIS BLUEPRINT,
CALL TOLL-FREE 1-800-547-5570

Plans H-855-3A & -3B

PRICES AND DETAILS
ON PAGES 12-15

125

Attractive, Open Floor Plan

- Two-story ceilings in the foyer and living room add an attractive spatial dimension to this versatile two-story, finished in stucco.
- The spacious living areas include a sunken, formal living room with a large fireplace, front-facing bay window and entrance from both the foyer and dining room.
- The family room, 3 steps below the main level, offers a second fireplace and a view of the nook through an open railing.
- The kitchen includes an island work area, corner window, pantry and sliding doors to the attached deck.
- The home accommodates a master bedroom and two secondary bedrooms on the second floor and a single bedroom on the main level.

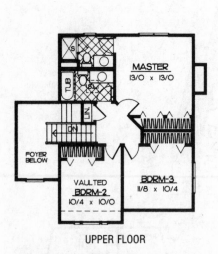

UPPER FLOOR

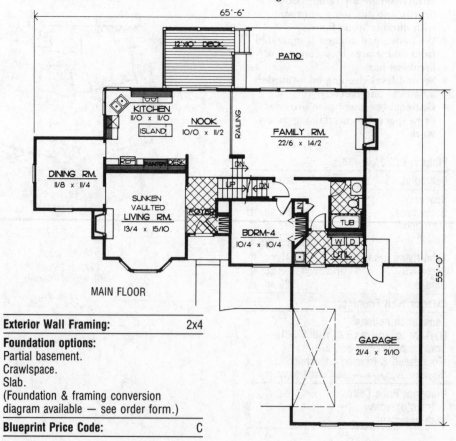

MAIN FLOOR

Plan U-89-403

Bedrooms: 4	Baths: 3

Space:

Upper floor:	656 sq. ft.
Main floor:	1,385 sq. ft.
Total living area:	**2,041 sq. ft.**
Basement:	704 sq. ft.
Garage:	466 sq. ft.

Exterior Wall Framing:	2x4

Foundation options:
Partial basement.
Crawlspace.
Slab.
(Foundation & framing conversion diagram available — see order form.)

Blueprint Price Code:	C

Vaulted Ceiling in Spacious Family Room

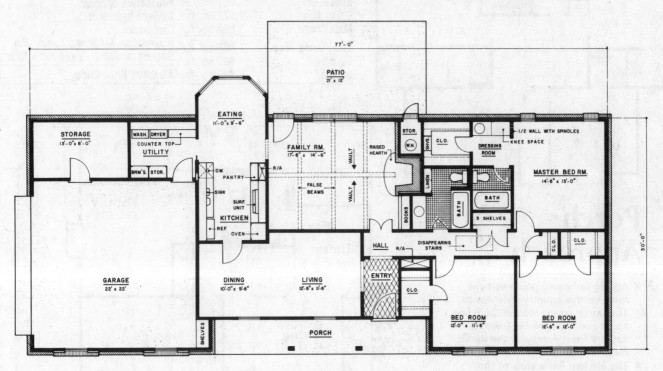

PLAN E-1601
WITHOUT BASEMENT

Specify crawlspace or slab foundation.

AREAS

Living	1630 sq. ft.
Garage & Storage	610 sq. ft.
Porch	116 sq. ft.
Total	2356 sq. ft.

TO ORDER THIS BLUEPRINT,
CALL TOLL-FREE 1-800-547-5570

Blueprint Price Code B
Plan E-1601

PRICES AND DETAILS
ON PAGES 12-15

127

Br.2
10/8 x 12/0

Walk-in Wardrobe

Lin.

Master
14/8 x 11/6

dn

Open

Spa

Br.4
12/4 x 11/8

Entry Below

W. D.

Br.3
10/8 x 11/8

UPPER FLOOR

Plan CDG-2002

Bedrooms: 4	Baths: 2½

Space:

Upper floor:	1,077 sq. ft.
Main floor:	888 sq. ft.
Total living area:	1,965 sq. ft.
Basement:	682 sq. ft.
Garage:	420 sq. ft.

Exterior Wall Framing: 2x4

Foundation options:
Daylight basement.
Crawlspace.
(Foundation & framing conversion diagram available — see order form.)

Blueprint Price Code: B

Porch Approach

- An old-fashioned porch sets the tone for this country-style design. The porch wraps around the living room and is accessible from the vaulted front entry and the dining room.

- The kitchen has a view of the breakfast nook and beyond to the family room with fireplace and rear sliders to the deck.

- There are four bedrooms upstairs, each with spacious walk-in closets.

- The master suite includes a private bath with luxurious spa tub under glass, double vanities and a compartmented toilet/shower.

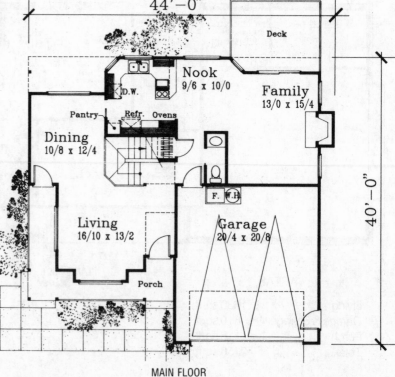

44'-0"

Deck

Nook
9/6 x 10/0

Family
13/0 x 15/4

D.W.

Pantry

Refr. Ovens

Dining
10/8 x 12/4

F. W.H

40'-0"

Living
16/10 x 13/2

Garage
20/4 x 20/8

Porch

MAIN FLOOR

Plan CDG-2002

PRICES AND DETAILS
ON PAGES 12-15

Bright and Airy

- Soaring ceilings, elegant transom windows and an open floor plan give this home a bright and airy feel.
- Past the inviting entry, a decorative arch introduces the Great Room, which boasts a spectacular 22-ft.-high vaulted ceiling and a built-in media center flanked by bookshelves. Surrounded by glass, an efficient gas fireplace adds warmth to the room. A French door opens to a backyard deck.
- The adjacent island kitchen includes a serving bar and a sunny eating area. A half-bath and a laundry/utility room with garage access are nearby.
- The deluxe master bedroom boasts an 11-ft. ceiling and access to the deck. The master bath features a spa tub, a separate shower and a dual-sink vanity.
- Two additional bedrooms share a second full bath. Unless otherwise specified, all main-floor rooms have 9-ft. ceilings.
- Upstairs, an open railing in the loft/bonus room overlooks the Great Room below. A French door accesses a covered balcony over the front porch.

Plan NW-322-S

Bedrooms: 3+	**Baths:** 2½

Living Area:	
Upper floor	200 sq. ft.
Main floor	1,941 sq. ft.
Total Living Area:	**2,141 sq. ft.**
Daylight basement	1,592 sq. ft.
Garage	720 sq. ft.
Exterior Wall Framing:	2x6

Foundation Options:

Daylight basement
Crawlspace
(All plans can be built with your choice of foundation and framing. A generic conversion diagram is available. See order form.)

BLUEPRINT PRICE CODE: C

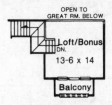

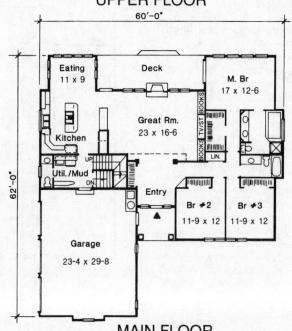

UPPER FLOOR

MAIN FLOOR

REAR VIEW

Elaborate Outdoor Spaces

- Sleek lines and rich brick distinguish this exciting indoor/outdoor home.
- Decorative brick walls embrace an elaborate entry courtyard that dresses up the facade. The wide entry hall inside offers two coat closets and unfolds to the living room.
- The sunken living room showcases a regal freestanding fireplace that rises to meet the 17-ft. sloped ceiling. A dramatic window wall frames the adjoining covered terrace.
- The stunning formal dining room is surrounded by glass and flanked by covered terraces, accessed through sliding glass doors.
- The cozy breakfast area and the island kitchen merge to the right of the living room. A convenient serving counter extends to the adjoining terrace, while a laundry room with extra freezer space is just around the corner.
- The sleeping wing includes three bedrooms and two baths. The master bedroom opens to the main terrace and has its own bath with a separate dressing area. The secondary bedrooms share another compartmentalized bath.

Plan DD-1973

Bedrooms: 3	Baths: 2
Living Area:	
Main floor	2,047 sq. ft.
Total Living Area:	**2,047 sq. ft.**
Standard basement	2,047 sq. ft.
Garage and storage	485 sq. ft.
Exterior Wall Framing:	2x4

Foundation Options:

Standard basement

Crawlspace

Slab

(All plans can be built with your choice of foundation and framing. A generic conversion diagram is available. See order form.)

BLUEPRINT PRICE CODE: C

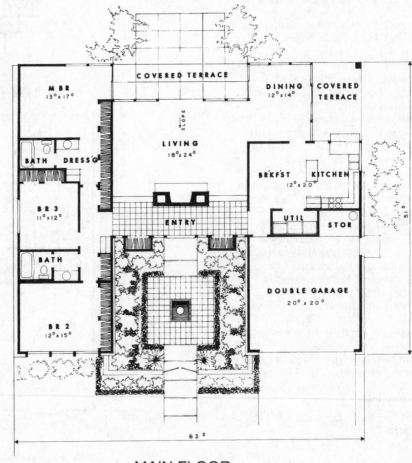

MAIN FLOOR

REAR VIEW

Cozy and Efficient

- This cozy and attractive vacation home is designed for efficiency.
- Functional benches flank the home's front porch, offering a perfect spot for relaxing conversation.
- Straight ahead, in the skylighted living areas, a 20-ft., 9-in. cathedral ceiling embraces a dramatic wall of glass. Double French doors open to a sizable backyard deck.
- The living room features an inviting inglenook: a nook that is warmed by a large, open fireplace.
- The bright dining area is large enough for any occasion.
- Columns set off both the L-shaped island kitchen and the convenient laundry area.
- The secluded main-floor bedroom is serviced by a spacious bath with a double-sink vanity.
- An 11-ft., 9-in. vaulted ceiling presides over the upstairs loft, which provides a stunning view of the living areas below and the outdoors beyond. The loft could serve as a playroom, a home office or additional sleeping quarters.

Plan U-93-201

Bedrooms: 1+	Baths: 1
Living Area:	
Upper floor	484 sq. ft.
Main floor	942 sq. ft.
Total Living Area:	**1,426 sq. ft.**
Exterior Wall Framing:	2x6

Foundation Options:

Crawlspace
(All plans can be built with your choice of foundation and framing. A generic conversion diagram is available. See order form.)

BLUEPRINT PRICE CODE: A

UPPER FLOOR

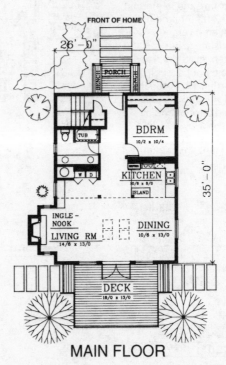

MAIN FLOOR

Award Winner

- Filled with innovative features, this elegant one-story stucco home has won numerous national design awards.
- Accented by an overhead plant shelf, the marble-floored, 12-ft.-high foyer flows into the spacious Grand Room.
- Boasting a soaring 18-ft., 8-in. ceiling, the Grand Room offers an ale bar, a stunning two-way fireplace and glass doors to a backyard pool and spa area.
- The formal dining room, which also enjoys pool access, shares the Grand Room's high ceiling, fireplace and ale bar. A built-in buffet across the gallery overlooks a decorative fountain garden.
- The island kitchen's handy snack bar serves the sunny morning and gathering rooms, each with a 12-ft., 8-in. ceiling and a view of the covered veranda.
- The luxurious master suite features a 12-ft. ceiling, a sunken, glass-enclosed sitting area and private pool access. The master bath has a garden tub, a separate shower, a laundry closet and his-and-hers amenities. A media room and a pool bath complete the wing.
- Two more bedrooms boast 10-ft. ceilings and share a large dual-vanity bath with a 12-ft. ceiling.

Plan EOF-72

Bedrooms: 3	Baths: 3

Living Area:.

Main floor	3,600 sq. ft.
Total Living Area:	**3,600 sq. ft.**
Garage and golf cart storage	672 sq. ft.

Exterior Wall Framing: 8-in. concrete block

Foundation Options:

Slab
(All plans can be built with your choice of foundation and framing. A generic conversion diagram is available. See order form.)

BLUEPRINT PRICE CODE: F

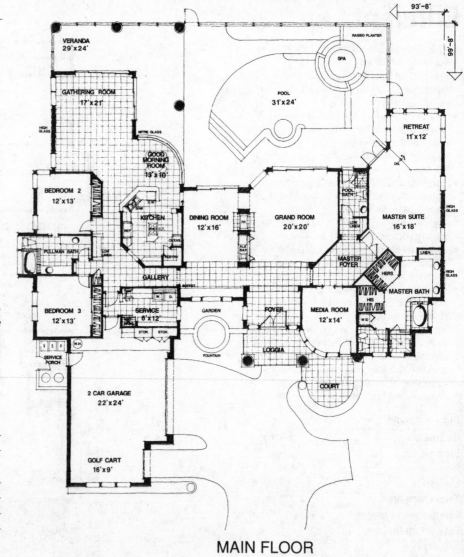

MAIN FLOOR

Fabulous Facade

- A decorative railing atop the roof and a columned entry with an arched transom window introduce this fabulous home.
- French doors open from the arched entry to the foyer, where a 12-ft., 8-in. ceiling directs light to the expansive Great Room beyond. All other areas are enhanced by 10-ft. ceilings.
- To the left of the foyer, the dining room has views to the front yard and is easily serviced from the kitchen.
- The spacious Great Room is highlighted by a striking corner fireplace, a media center and sliding glass doors to a covered backyard patio.
- An angled snack bar in the gourmet kitchen serves both the Great Room and the sunny breakfast area. A pantry closet and a utility/laundry room with garage access are nearby.
- A step from the breakfast room, the master suite has private patio access and a large bath with a garden shower, a dual-sink vanity and a walk-in closet.
- Across the home, two additional bedrooms share another full bath.

Plan HDS-99-173

Bedrooms: 3	Baths: 2

Living Area:

Main floor	1,550 sq. ft.
Total Living Area:	**1,550 sq. ft.**
Garage	387 sq. ft.
Exterior Wall Framing:	2x4

Foundation Options:

Slab

(All plans can be built with your choice of foundation and framing. A generic conversion diagram is available. See order form.)

BLUEPRINT PRICE CODE:	B

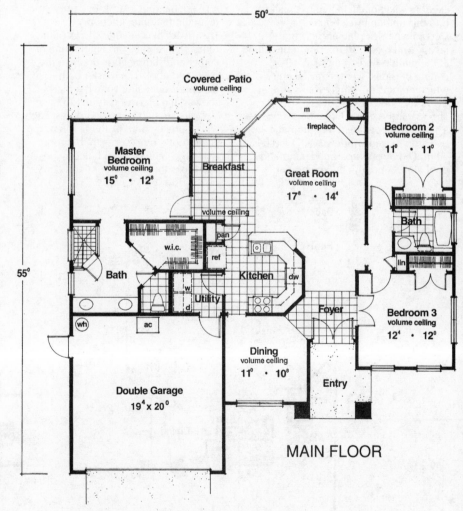

MAIN FLOOR

Vacation Living!

- Exciting vacation-style living is packed into this unique brick home.
- Decorative brick planters accent the facade and create an interior impression at the marble-floored entry. A 19-ft. ceiling presides over the raised entry, which adjoins the dining room and overlooks the Great Room.
- The spacious central Great Room boasts a 19-ft., 4-in. ceiling and a dramatic two-story bayed window wall, which is embraced by a wraparound patio and pool area. A built-in entertainment

center, a brick fireplace and a hardwood floor add to the ambience.
- A snack bar and a walk-in pantry highlight the open kitchen.
- The dream master suite shows off a romantic fireplace, an entertainment center and sliding glass doors to the patio and pool. The master bath features a dual-sink vanity, a marble shower and an oval garden tub.
- Upstairs are two more bedrooms, each with a private bath. A living room, game room, office or extra bedroom sits at the center, and a balcony overlooks the Great Room and entry.

Plan SDG-20928	
Bedrooms: 3+	**Baths:** 3½
Living Area:	
Upper floor	869 sq. ft.
Main floor	1,897 sq. ft.
Wine cellar	120 sq. ft.
Total Living Area:	**2,886 sq. ft.**
Garage	608 sq. ft.
Exterior Wall Framing:	2x4
Foundation Options:	
Slab	

(All plans can be built with your choice of foundation and framing. A generic conversion diagram is available. See order form.)

BLUEPRINT PRICE CODE:	**D**

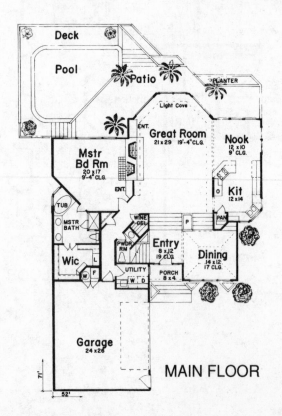

MAIN FLOOR

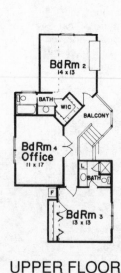

UPPER FLOOR

Plan SDG-20928

PRICES AND DETAILS ON PAGES 12-15

Dramatic Angled Ranch

- A rustic cedar and stone veneer exterior distinguishes this dramatic angled ranch, while passive-solar features add energy efficiency.
- Double front doors open into an inviting reception area, which flows directly into the bright and airy living room. Warmed by a window-flanked fireplace, the living room merges with the formal dining room, where sliding glass doors open to a backyard terrace.

- The skylighted kitchen includes a nice dinette and shares an 11-ft., 4-in.-high cathedral ceiling with the family room. The nearby mudroom/laundry room includes a pantry, a service entrance and access to the garage.
- The family room features a handsome fireplace and sliding doors to a second terrace. A passive-solar sunroof with adjustable shades allows the winter sun in but keeps the summer sun out.
- The spacious master bedroom enjoys a private backyard terrace. The master bath offers a whirlpool tub.
- Two additional bedrooms are serviced by a second full bath.

Plan K-536-L	
Bedrooms: 3	**Baths:** 2
Living Area:	
Main floor	1,595 sq. ft.
Total Living Area:	**1,595 sq. ft.**
Daylight basement	1,554 sq. ft.
Garage	507 sq. ft.
Exterior Wall Framing:	2x4 or 2x6
Foundation Options:	
Daylight basement	
Slab	

(All plans can be built with your choice of foundation and framing. A generic conversion diagram is available. See order form.)

BLUEPRINT PRICE CODE:	B

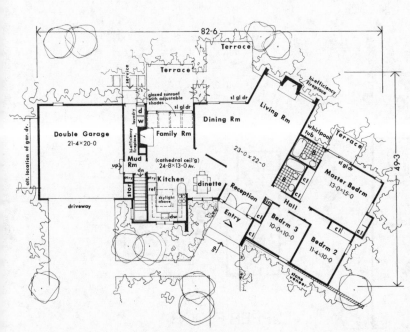

MAIN FLOOR

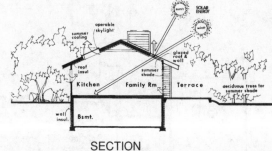

SECTION

VIEW INTO DINING ROOM AND LIVING ROOM

High-Caliber Contemporary

- Bold and statuesque, this striking stucco home is sure to catch the eye!
- The columned entrance opens to an airy foyer brightened by the entry's sidelights and transom window.
- Beyond is the elegant formal dining room, which features an 11-ft. vaulted ceiling, decorative columns and a handy buffet.
- Also close to the foyer is a powder room, convenient for arriving guests.
- The large island kitchen adjoins a sunny bayed breakfast nook at the center of the main floor. A pantry and lots of counter space make storage and cooking a breeze. Casual dining can be extended to the backyard patio.
- The kitchen extends a serving counter to the adjoining family room, which boasts a warm fireplace and shares the kitchen's 10½-ft. ceiling.
- The removed master suite features a 10½-ft. ceiling and a delectable see-through fireplace open to the master bath's oval tub! The plush skylighted bath also flaunts dual vanities and revolving his-and-hers closets.
- Upstairs are two more bedrooms and another skylighted bath. The main-floor study has a 9-ft. ceiling and may serve as an extra bedroom.

Plan DW-2149

Bedrooms: 3+	Baths: 2½
Living Area:	
Upper floor	433 sq. ft.
Main floor	1,798 sq. ft.
Total Living Area:	**2,231 sq. ft.**
Standard basement	1,798 sq. ft.
Garage	528 sq. ft.
Exterior Wall Framing:	2x4

Foundation Options:

Standard basement
Crawlspace
Slab
(All plans can be built with your choice of foundation and framing. A generic conversion diagram is available. See order form.)

BLUEPRINT PRICE CODE: C

◄ 61'-0" ►

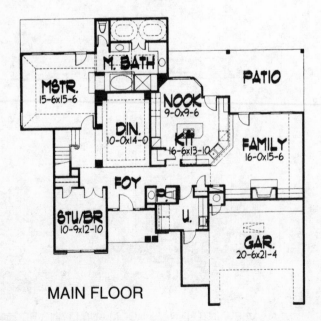

MAIN FLOOR

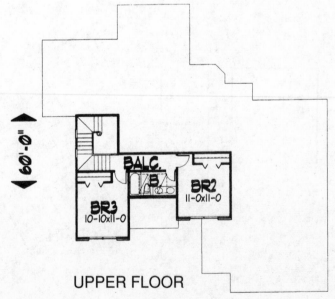

UPPER FLOOR

Prairie Home

- This stone prairie-style home is unique in its design and symmetry.
- The sidelighted entrance opens to an attractive, tiled entry foyer.
- The adjoining living and dining rooms share a dramatic window wall and make an impressive entertaining area.
- Brightened by recessed fluorescent lighting, the open kitchen is just steps away from a walk-in pantry, a home office, a laundry/utility room and the three-car garage. A snack bar extends to the breakfast nook, which boasts a built-in pantry or china closet.
- Visible over a wrought-iron railing, the sunken family room is magnificent! Its highlights include a rear deck, three sets of sliding glass doors, a soaring stone fireplace and an exposed-beam cathedral ceiling that rises to 12 feet.
- Closet space is abundant in the main-floor bedroom wing. The master bedroom boasts a dressing area with a sit-down makeup table and built-in storage space. Two wardrobe closets and a private bath round out the master suite. The front-facing bedroom is served by the adjoining powder room.
- Upstairs, two good-sized bedrooms share a hall bath with two sinks.

Plan DD-3186

Bedrooms: 4	**Baths:** 2½

Living Area:

Upper floor	618 sq. ft.
Main floor	2,689 sq. ft.
Total Living Area:	**3,307 sq. ft.**
Garage	706 sq. ft.
Exterior Wall Framing:	2x4

Foundation Options:

Slab
(All plans can be built with your choice of foundation and framing. A generic conversion diagram is available. See order form.)

BLUEPRINT PRICE CODE: E

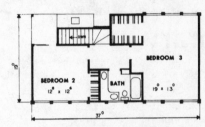

UPPER FLOOR

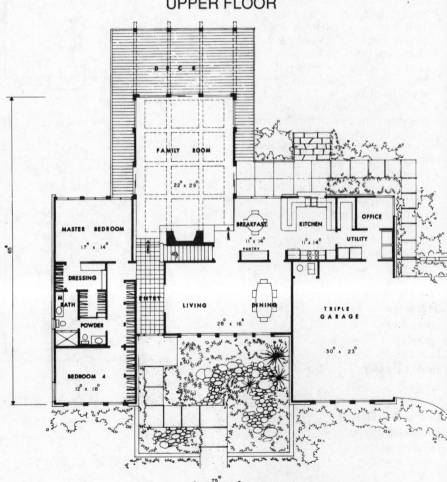

MAIN FLOOR

Contemporary Dimensions

- Vertical siding and stylish rounded corners add a striking contemporary dimension to this two-story home.
- Double doors introduce a dramatic 20-ft.-high skylighted foyer, which unfolds to each of the living areas.
- The formal living and dining area is large and bright as it extends to a backyard terrace. Windows flank a warm fireplace.
- The central kitchen is efficiently designed with a snack bar and a nearby pantry. Casual meals may be enjoyed in the attached dinette or outside on the dinette's private terrace.
- Informal activities can be entertained in the adjoining family room, with its built-in media center.
- Four bedrooms and two baths are neatly arranged around the upper-floor balcony. The master bedroom has its own private bath, along with a separate dressing area and a big walk-in closet.

Plan AHP-8030

Bedrooms: 4	Baths: 2½
Living Area:	
Upper floor	1,009 sq. ft.
Main floor	1,082 sq. ft.
Total Living Area:	**2,091 sq. ft.**
Standard basement	922 sq. ft.
Garage	430 sq. ft.
Exterior Wall Framing:	2x4 or 2x6

Foundation Options:

Standard basement
Crawlspace
Slab

(All plans can be built with your choice of foundation and framing. A generic conversion diagram is available. See order form.)

BLUEPRINT PRICE CODE: C

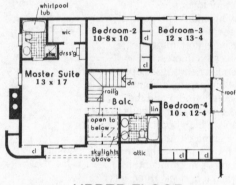

UPPER FLOOR

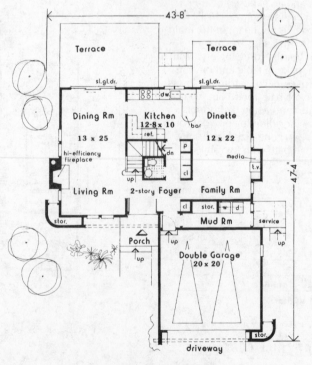

MAIN FLOOR

TO ORDER THIS BLUEPRINT, CALL TOLL-FREE 1-800-547-5570

Plan AHP-8030

PRICES AND DETAILS ON PAGES 12-15

Work at Home!

- Furnished with a large office, this attractive one-story is ideal for families who want to spend more time at home.
- Decorative columns off the entry introduce the formal living and dining rooms, which feature a built-in buffet and can be closed off from the informal spaces with a pocket door.
- The skylighted kitchen includes an island cooktop and a pantry. The adjoining breakfast nook enjoys a sunny bay window, while the spacious family room boasts a handsome corner

fireplace flanked by built-in shelves. Sliding glass doors open the area to an expansive backyard deck.
- Double doors lead into the master bedroom, which is set off from the skylighted master bath by an arched opening. The bath flaunts a spa tub, a separate shower and a dual-sink vanity.
- A second bath and a convenient laundry room service the second bedroom and the den or third bedroom.
- In addition to the functional home office, the partial daylight basement offers a hobby room and a half-bath. A French door accesses a wide patio.

Plan CDG-1017	
Bedrooms: 2+	**Baths:** 2½
Living Area:	
Main floor	1,948 sq. ft.
Partial daylight basement	952 sq. ft.
Total Living Area:	**2,900 sq. ft.**
Garage	529 sq. ft.
Exterior Wall Framing:	2x6

Foundation Options:

Partial daylight basement
(All plans can be built with your choice of foundation and framing. A generic conversion diagram is available. See order form.)

BLUEPRINT PRICE CODE:	D

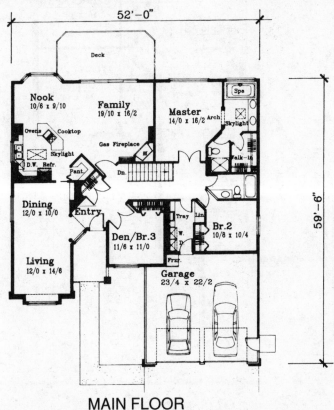

MAIN FLOOR

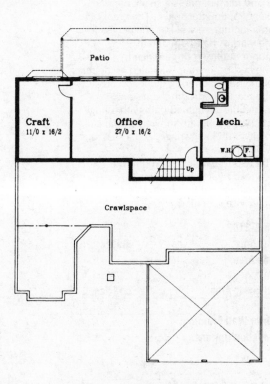

DAYLIGHT BASEMENT

TO ORDER THIS BLUEPRINT,
CALL TOLL-FREE 1-800-547-5570

Plan CDG-1017

PRICES AND DETAILS
ON PAGES 12-15

139

Designed for Narrow Lots

- This stately brick home is masterfully designed to fit narrow lots, while still providing maximum privacy.
- Inside, the foyer is flanked by the formal areas of the home. The living room boasts a fireplace and outdoor access. Located close to the kitchen, the dining room is convenient yet private.
- The kitchen and breakfast room are expanded by a 13-ft.-high ceiling, tall windows and skylights. The sunny island kitchen offers a snack bar and plenty of counter space. The breakfast area includes a wet bar and access to the yard. A half-bath and a laundry/utility room are nearby.
- The bedroom wing is located at the rear of the home, offering quiet and privacy.
- The master bedroom flaunts an incredible skylighted bath with a huge spa tub, a separate shower, a dual-sink vanity with knee space, and a spacious walk-in closet.
- The two remaining bedrooms are serviced by a second full bath.
- All ceilings are 9 ft. high unless otherwise specified.

Plan E-2102

Bedrooms: 3	**Baths:** 2½
Living Area:	
Main floor	2,194 sq. ft.
Total Living Area:	**2,194 sq. ft.**
Garage	615 sq. ft.
Exterior Wall Framing:	2x6

Foundation Options:

Slab

(All plans can be built with your choice of foundation and framing. A generic conversion diagram is available. See order form.)

BLUEPRINT PRICE CODE: **C**

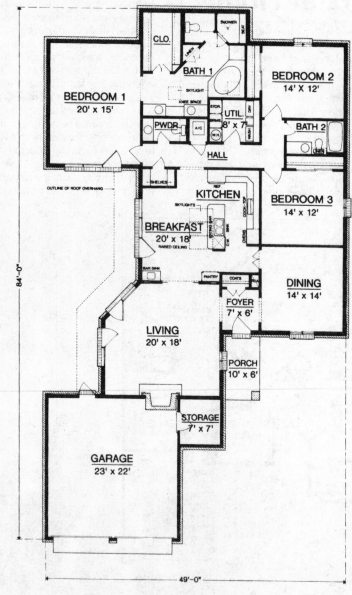

MAIN FLOOR

Plan E-2102

PRICES AND DETAILS ON PAGES 12-15

Charm and Warmth

- With its narrow wood siding and attractive window treatments, this inviting home reflects New England charm and warmth.
- At the center of the floor plan, the living room is warmed by an inspiring fireplace. French doors open to a wide backyard terrace.
- The adjoining formal dining room also offers terrace access.

- The kitchen has an opening to the family room over a 3½-ft.-high wall. The bayed dinette is a nice spot for casual dining.
- The spacious master bedroom boasts a dressing alcove, two closets and a private bath with a whirlpool tub, a separate shower and a dual-sink vanity.
- Two front-facing secondary bedrooms share a hall bath. The larger bedroom features a 12-ft.-high cathedral ceiling.
- Adjacent to the two-car garage is the service area, which includes a covered porch, a laundry/mudroom and a convenient powder room.

Plan HFL-1720-CE	
Bedrooms: 3	**Baths:** 2½
Living Area:	
Main floor	1,686 sq. ft.
Total Living Area:	**1,686 sq. ft.**
Standard basement	1,609 sq. ft.
Garage and storage	430 sq. ft.
Exterior Wall Framing:	2x6
Foundation Options:	
Standard basement	
Slab	

(All plans can be built with your choice of foundation and framing. A generic conversion diagram is available. See order form.)

BLUEPRINT PRICE CODE:	B

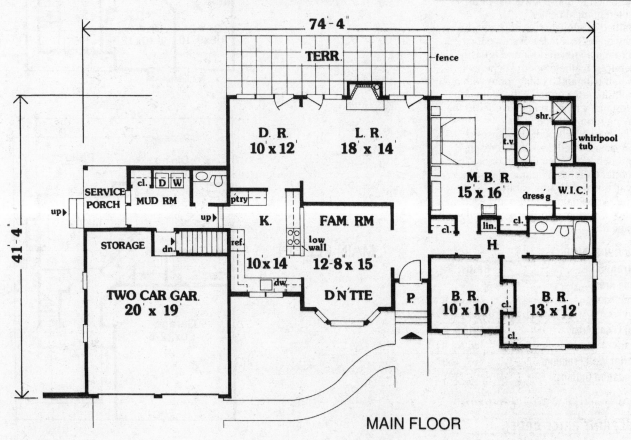

MAIN FLOOR

Open Plan for Narrow Lot

- This home's smart floor plan provides plenty of open spaces while fitting nicely on a narrow lot.
- The two-story foyer welcomes guests and provides a nice view through the living area and into the backyard.
- The sunken living room features a 16-ft. ceiling, a gas fireplace framed by windows and a corner niche that is designed to house a wet bar or an entertainment center.
- Bathed in sunlight, the adjacent dining bay opens to a rear covered patio through a French door and is easily serviced by the modern kitchen.
- A half-bath and a utility room with a built-in desk complete the main floor.
- Upstairs, a railed bridge overlooks the living room and the foyer.
- The master bedroom showcases a private covered deck that is reached through an elegant French door. The master bath has a unique glass-block wall and a dual-sink vanity.
- The two remaining bedrooms each have a custom window seat. A full bath is nearby.

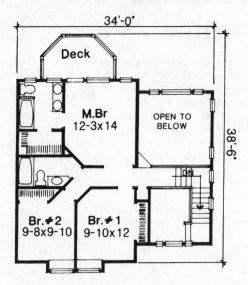

UPPER FLOOR

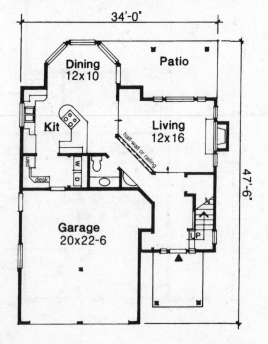

MAIN FLOOR

Plan NW-366-ND

Bedrooms: 3	Baths: 2½
Living Area:	
Upper floor	703 sq. ft.
Main floor	788 sq. ft.
Total Living Area:	**1,491 sq. ft.**
Garage	485 sq. ft.
Exterior Wall Framing:	2x6

Foundation Options:

Crawlspace
(All plans can be built with your choice of foundation and framing. A generic conversion diagram is available. See order form.)

BLUEPRINT PRICE CODE: A

Plan NW-366-ND

PRICES AND DETAILS ON PAGES 12-15

Fit for a King!

- Filled with luxurious features, this majestic Mediterranean-style home is designed with livability in mind.
- Double doors open from the covered porch entrance into the two-story-high foyer. A decorative arch introduces the sunken living room, which features a window-flanked fireplace. A second arch leads into the formal dining room. Both rooms boast 12-ft. ceilings.
- The spacious island kitchen includes an eating bar and a walk-in pantry. Sliding glass doors in the adjoining breakfast nook open to a covered patio.
- The sunken family room is enhanced by an 18-ft. ceiling and offers a fireplace, a wet bar and built-in shelving.
- A powder room and an oversized utility room are located near the entrance to the expansive four-car garage.
- Unless otherwise specified, all rooms on the main floor have 9-ft. ceilings.
- Upstairs, railed balconies overlook the foyer and the family room. Double doors open into the master suite, with its 12-ft. vaulted ceiling and corner fireplace. The master bath has a spa tub, a glass-block shower and two vanities.
- A second bedroom and a bonus room share a hall bath. The remaining bedroom offers a private bath.

Plan U-93-212

Bedrooms: 3+	**Baths:** 3½

Living Area:

Upper floor	1,653 sq. ft.
Main floor	2,415 sq. ft.
Total Living Area:	**4,068 sq. ft.**
Garage	1,019 sq. ft.
Exterior Wall Framing:	2x6

Foundation Options:

Crawlspace

(All plans can be built with your choice of foundation and framing. A generic conversion diagram is available. See order form.)

BLUEPRINT PRICE CODE: G

UPPER FLOOR

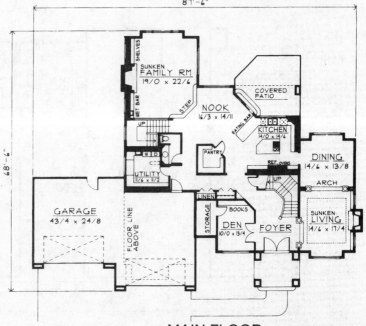

MAIN FLOOR

Private Patio Home

- Privacy and security are important features of this narrow, zero-lot-line patio home.
- An iron gate opens to a courtyard that leads to the home's main entrance.
- The sidelighted entry reveals the large, open format of the family room and dining room, each set off by decorative columns. The skylighted family room is enhanced by a fireplace, a 10-ft.

gambrel ceiling and views of an exciting interior atrium.
- The efficient kitchen offers a handy snack counter, a windowed sink and a sizable walk-in pantry. The sunny breakfast nook extends to the atrium through sliding glass doors.
- The gorgeous master bedroom has a 10-ft. gambrel ceiling and a huge walk-in closet. The private master bath boasts an oval tub, a separate shower and a dual-sink vanity with knee space.
- Two additional bedrooms share a hall bath at the opposite end of the home.
- The garage includes a neat work space.

Plan KLF-9224	
Bedrooms: 3	Baths: 2
Living Area:	
Main floor	1,996 sq. ft.
Total Living Area:	**1,996 sq. ft.**
Garage	484 sq. ft.
Exterior Wall Framing:	2x4
Foundation Options:	

Slab
(All plans can be built with your choice of foundation and framing. A generic conversion diagram is available. See order form.)

BLUEPRINT PRICE CODE:	B

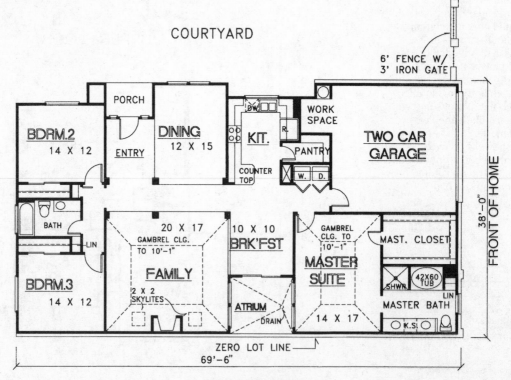

MAIN FLOOR

Plan KLF-9224

Zesty Southwestern!

- Elegant arches and a bright stucco exterior add a zesty southwestern flavor to this beautiful one-story home.
- Past the columned front porch, the angled entry is flanked by the living room and the dining room, both of which feature 9½-ft. tray ceilings and lovely bay windows.
- The skylighted island kitchen offers a windowed sink, a built-in planning desk and a sunny breakfast nook.
- The adjacent family room boasts a tray ceiling and a corner fireplace. A French door opens to a covered patio.
- Double doors introduce the luxurious master bedroom, which enjoys patio access and a 9-ft.-high tray ceiling. The skylighted master bath includes a garden spa tub, a separate shower, a walk-in closet and a dual-sink vanity.
- Two additional bedrooms have built-in window seats and share a second skylighted bath. A den off the entry could easily be used as an extra bedroom or as a home office.

Plans P-7752-3A & -3D

Bedrooms: 3+	Baths: 2

Living Area:

Main floor (crawlspace version)	2,503 sq. ft.
Main floor (basement version)	2,575 sq. ft.
Total Living Area:	**2,503/2,575 sq. ft.**
Daylight basement	2,578 sq. ft.
Garage	962 sq. ft.
Exterior Wall Framing:	**2x6**

Foundation Options:	Plan #
Daylight basement	P-7752-3D
Crawlspace	P-7752-3A

(All plans can be built with your choice of foundation and framing. A generic conversion diagram is available. See order form.)

BLUEPRINT PRICE CODE:	**D**

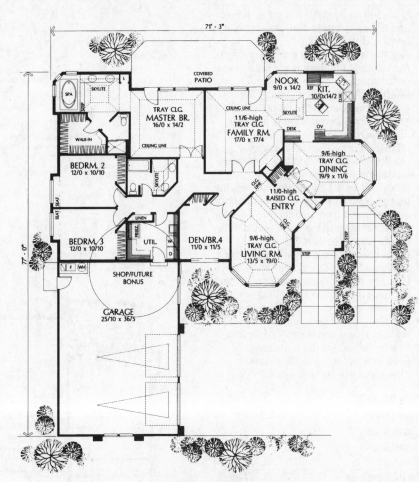

MAIN FLOOR

BASEMENT STAIRWAY LOCATION

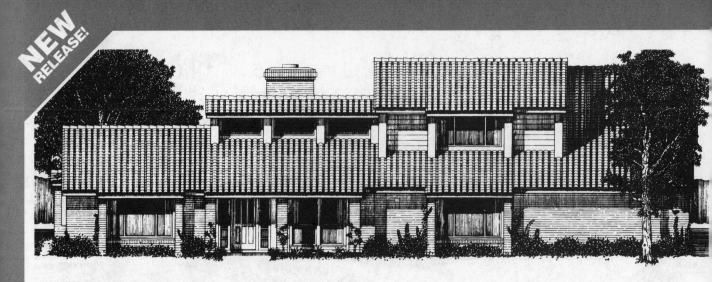

Distinct Style

- A unique facade of brick, glass, siding and tile gives this stylish contemporary home a distinct look.
- Past the wide, inviting entry, a gorgeous freestanding fireplace is the focal point of the spacious living room, which boasts an 18-ft. sloped ceiling. Sliding glass doors open to the outdoors.
- The adjoining formal dining room is conveniently close to the island kitchen, where a bayed breakfast area overlooks a patio. Garage access and a laundry/utility room are nearby.
- Enhanced by a 12-ft. sloped ceiling, the master bedroom enjoys private outdoor access. The master bath boasts a garden tub, a separate shower and a dual-sink vanity with knee space.
- Perfect for a guest room, the study off the entry has private bathroom access.
- Upstairs, the multipurpose game room includes a 13-ft. sloped ceiling and a half-wall overlooking the living room.
- The front-facing bedroom includes a walk-in closet and is serviced by a nearby half-bath. The remaining bedroom features a deck, a walk-in closet and private bathroom access.

Plan DD-3633

Bedrooms: 3+	**Baths:** 3½
Living Area:	
Upper floor	1,187 sq. ft.
Main floor	2,490 sq. ft.
Total Living Area:	**3,677 sq. ft.**
Standard basement	2,135 sq. ft.
Garage and golf cart storage	619 sq. ft.
Exterior Wall Framing:	2x4

Foundation Options:

Standard basement
Crawlspace
Slab
(All plans can be built with your choice of foundation and framing. A generic conversion diagram is available. See order form.)

BLUEPRINT PRICE CODE: F

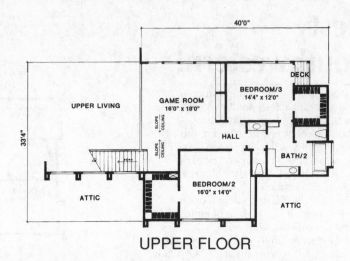

UPPER FLOOR

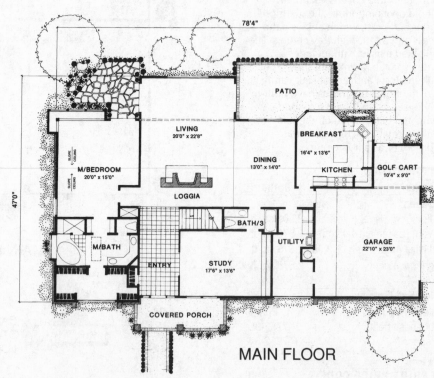

MAIN FLOOR

TO ORDER THIS BLUEPRINT, CALL TOLL-FREE 1-800-547-5570

Plan DD-3633

PRICES AND DETAILS ON PAGES 12-15

Sunny Spaces

- Graced by skylights and clerestory windows, this bright and airy home is filled with sunny spaces.
- The skylighted foyer boasts a 12-ft. sloped ceiling and showcases a sunstreaked open-railed stairway.
- Off the foyer, the intimate sunken living room features a 16-ft. cathedral ceiling and tall corner windows. Defined by columns and rails, the adjacent formal dining room is enhanced by an elegant 12-ft. stepped ceiling.
- The skylighted island kitchen includes a sunny breakfast space, which is separated from the family room by a half-wall. Expanded by a skylighted 16-ft. cathedral ceiling, the family room offers a handsome fireplace and access to a sunken rear sun room.
- The deluxe master suite is graced by a stepped ceiling, a bayed sitting room and a private bath. Sliding glass doors open to the sun room, which boasts an 11-ft., 7-in. vaulted ceiling.
- Two more bedrooms, a study alcove and a full bath are found upstairs.

Plan AX-91314

Bedrooms: 3+	Baths: 3
Living Area:	
Upper floor	544 sq. ft.
Main floor	1,959 sq. ft.
Sun room	202 sq. ft.
Total Living Area:	**2,705 sq. ft.**
Standard basement	1,833 sq. ft.
Garage	482 sq. ft.
Exterior Wall Framing:	2x4

Foundation Options:

Standard basement

Crawlspace

Slab

(All plans can be built with your choice of foundation and framing. A generic conversion diagram is available. See order form.)

BLUEPRINT PRICE CODE: D

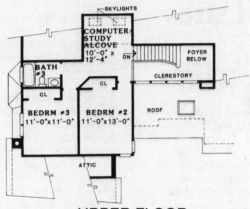

UPPER FLOOR

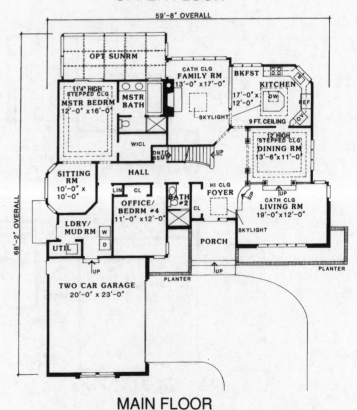

MAIN FLOOR

Exciting Extras

- Exciting extras give this ranch-style home lots of appeal.
- The quaint columned porch opens to the sidelighted foyer, which includes a handy coat closet.
- The sunken Great Room has an 11-ft., 9-in. cathedral ceiling and a fabulous two-way fireplace that is shared with a dramatic sun room. Half-walls add definition to the Great Room, but maintain a spacious, open ambience.
- The skylighted sun room is ideal for reading or relaxing and extends to a large backyard deck through sliding glass doors.
- The open kitchen offers a work island/snack bar, a pantry closet and a nice-sized laundry room. Skylights brighten the kitchen and the adjoining dining area, which opens to the deck.
- The bedroom wing houses two bedrooms and two baths. The quiet master suite boasts a walk-in closet and its own bath. The second bedroom has private access to the hall bath.
- The attached two-car garage is neatly entered from the side, keeping the front yard stylish and uncluttered.

Plan GL-1404	
Bedrooms: 2	**Baths: 2**
Living Area:	
Main floor	1,404 sq. ft.
Sun room	172 sq. ft.
Total Living Area:	**1,576 sq. ft.**
Standard basement	1,571 sq. ft.
Garage	449 sq. ft.
Exterior Wall Framing:	2x6

Foundation Options:

Standard basement
(All plans can be built with your choice of foundation and framing. A generic conversion diagram is available. See order form.)

BLUEPRINT PRICE CODE: B

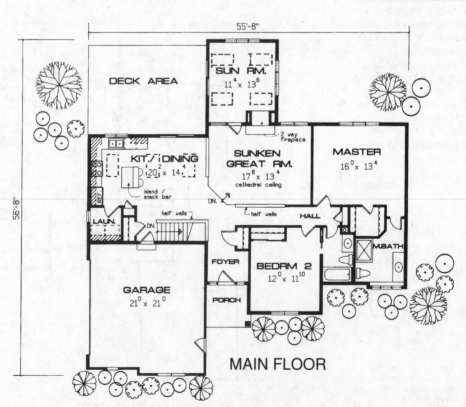

MAIN FLOOR

Sweeping Rooflines

- Sweeping rooflines, vertical cedar siding and natural stone accent this contemporary three-bedroom ranch.
- Double doors lead to a reception hall with a lovely view through the formal areas and into the backyard.
- The dining room and living room are highlighted by a 15-ft.-high ceiling, a stone fireplace and a boxed-out solar bay opening to a rear terrace.
- The adjacent family room boasts a second fireplace flanked by tall windows.
- The U-shaped kitchen serves the formal dining room and the bright dinette. Sliding glass doors in the dinette open to a corner terrace. A half-bath and a utility room are conveniently nearby.
- Tucked into the sleeping wing are three bedrooms. The master bedroom features a 10-ft.-high sloped ceiling, a private terrace and a skylighted whirlpool bath.
- The two remaining bedrooms share the second full bath.

Plan K-658-UA

Bedrooms: 3	Baths: 2½
Living Area:	
Main floor	1,618 sq. ft.
Total Living Area:	**1,618 sq. ft.**
Daylight basement	1,588 sq. ft.
Garage	478 sq. ft.
Exterior Wall Framing:	2x4 or 2x6

Foundation Options:

Daylight basement

Slab

(All plans can be built with your choice of foundation and framing. A generic conversion diagram is available. See order form.)

BLUEPRINT PRICE CODE: B

VIEW INTO DINING ROOM AND LIVING ROOM

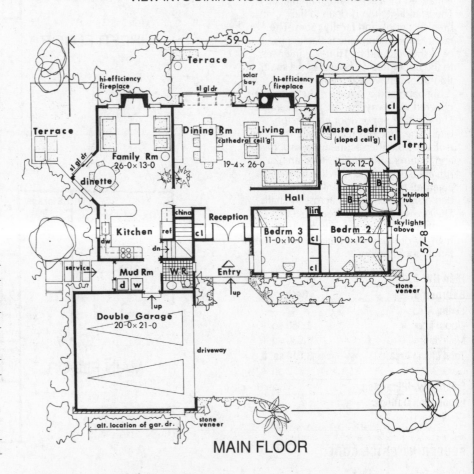

MAIN FLOOR

Natural Innovation

- Rustic cedar-shingle siding and a durable concrete tile roof make this home a nice complement to nature. The hardwood floors inside add to the naturalness of the home.
- Off the entry, the Gathering Room and the breakfast nook incorporate seating and storage space into their curved window walls for unique style and function. The two rooms are further enhanced by a see-through fireplace.
- The island kitchen is open to the breakfast nook and family room. The family room's fireplace is flanked by bookshelves, and its 16-ft. ceiling rises to the upper floor. The rest of the main-floor rooms have 9-ft. ceilings.
- A big patio and a storage closet adjoin a covered walkway leading to the garage.
- The exciting upper floor has lots to offer! The spacious master suite is isolated from the secondary bedrooms and features a romantic sitting area, a private balcony and a stylish bath with a garden tub and twin sinks. A nursery, den or home office lies across the hall.
- The two secondary bedrooms share another level with a skylighted 10-ft.-high TV or study area that overlooks the family room below.

Plan NW-371

Bedrooms: 3+	Baths: 2½
Living Area:	
Upper floor	1,386 sq. ft.
Main floor	1,630 sq. ft.
Total Living Area:	**3,016 sq. ft.**
Garage	572 sq. ft.
Exterior Wall Framing:	2x6

Foundation Options:

Crawlspace

(All plans can be built with your choice of foundation and framing. A generic conversion diagram is available. See order form.)

BLUEPRINT PRICE CODE: E

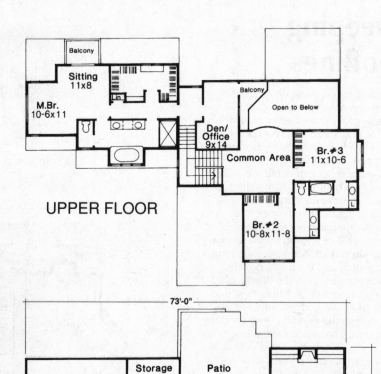

UPPER FLOOR

MAIN FLOOR

TO ORDER THIS BLUEPRINT, CALL TOLL-FREE 1-800-547-5570

Plan NW-371

PRICES AND DETAILS ON PAGES 12-15

One-Story Convenience

- High ceilings and a bright, open floor plan highlight this convenient and economical one-story home.
- The tiled foyer leads to the 10½-ft.-high vaulted Great Room, which features a cozy fireplace and access to the backyard through sliding glass doors. A sunny formal dining bay extends to one side.
- Brightened by recessed fluorescent lighting, the gourmet kitchen boasts a windowed sink, a pantry closet and an oversized island cooktop and snack bar.
- Nestled into a beautiful bay window, the breakfast nook overlooks a decorative brick planter and is perfect for quiet spring mornings!
- A skylighted hall leads to the home's sleeping wing. The master bedroom showcases an elegant coved ceiling, a walk-in closet and a private bath with a spa tub and a separate shower.
- The two remaining bedrooms are serviced by the second full bath.
- All rooms have 9-ft.-high ceilings unless otherwise specified.

Plan S-20794

Bedrooms: 3	Baths: 2
Living Area:	
Main floor	1,776 sq. ft.
Total Living Area:	**1,776 sq. ft.**
Standard basement	1,716 sq. ft.
Three-car garage	725 sq. ft.
Exterior Wall Framing:	2x6

Foundation Options:

Standard basement

Crawlspace

Slab

(All plans can be built with your choice of foundation and framing. A generic conversion diagram is available. See order form.)

BLUEPRINT PRICE CODE: **B**

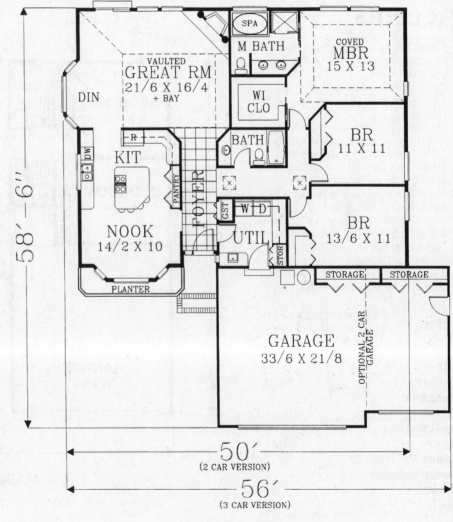

MAIN FLOOR

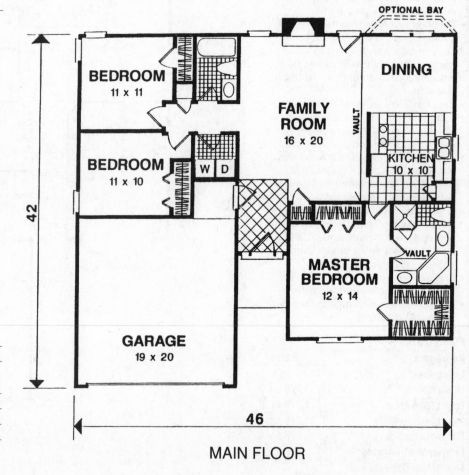

Charming Accents

- Traditional accents add warmth and charm to the facade of this affordable one-story home.
- Decorative, beveled oval glass adorns the elegant entry, which is flanked by sidelights.
- The tiled foyer introduces the spacious family room, which is enhanced by a 12-ft. vaulted ceiling and a nice fireplace. A French door provides easy access to the backyard.
- The galley-style kitchen flows into the sunny dining area, which can be extended with an optional bay window.
- The secluded master bedroom features plenty of closet space. The private master bath boasts a corner garden tub, a separate shower and two sinks. The bath may be expanded with a 13-ft. vaulted ceiling.
- Two additional bedrooms share a hall bath in the opposite wing. A nice-sized laundry room is centrally located.

Plan APS-1205

Bedrooms: 3	Baths: 2

Living Area:

Main floor	1,296 sq. ft.
Total Living Area:	**1,296 sq. ft.**
Garage	380 sq. ft.
Exterior Wall Framing:	2x4

Foundation Options:

Crawlspace

Slab

(All plans can be built with your choice of foundation and framing. A generic conversion diagram is available. See order form.)

BLUEPRINT PRICE CODE:	A

OPTIONAL BAY

BEDROOM 11 x 11

DINING

FAMILY ROOM 16 x 20

VAULT

KITCHEN 10 x 10

BEDROOM 11 x 10

W D

MASTER BEDROOM 12 x 14

VAULT

GARAGE 19 x 20

42

46

MAIN FLOOR

Plan APS-1205

PRICES AND DETAILS ON PAGES 12-15

Room to Grow

- Arched windows, cedar siding and brick veneer accents highlight the facade of this beautiful home.
- Inside, the foyer shows off an 18-ft. vaulted ceiling. All other main-floor areas have 9-ft. ceilings. The quiet den boasts double doors and functional built-in storage shelves.
- An arched opening sets off the expansive bayed living room. The adjacent formal dining room is enhanced by a tray ceiling and French-door access to a private deck.
- The gourmet kitchen includes an island cooktop and a sunny breakfast nook that extends to a second deck.
- The huge family room features a fireplace, a wet bar and a dramatic window wall with deck access. A half-bath and a utility room with a sewing counter round out this level.
- Upstairs, the master suite is entered through elegant double doors and has a private access to the fourth bedroom, ideal for a nursery. The skylighted master bath flaunts a spa tub and his-and-hers vanities and walk-in closets.
- The blueprints suggest a layout for future expansion in the basement.

Plan CDG-2054

Bedrooms: 4+	Baths: 2½
Living Area:	
Upper floor	1,584 sq. ft.
Main floor	1,876 sq. ft.
Total Living Area:	**3,460 sq. ft.**
Partial daylight basement	1,297 sq. ft.
Garage	657 sq. ft.
Exterior Wall Framing:	2x6

Foundation Options:

Partial daylight basement

(All plans can be built with your choice of foundation and framing. A generic conversion diagram is available. See order form.)

BLUEPRINT PRICE CODE: E

UPPER FLOOR

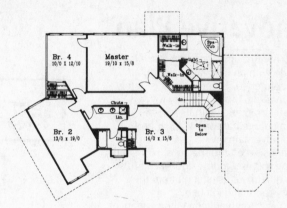

MAIN FLOOR

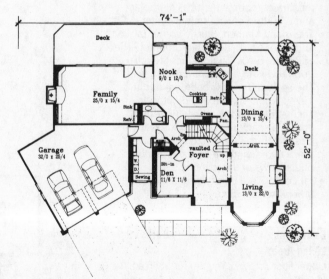

DAYLIGHT BASEMENT

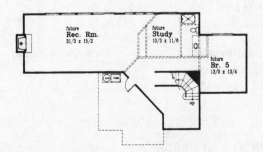

Innovative Plan

- This sharp design combines a striking facade with an innovative floor plan.
- The columned, covered entry is stately and inviting. Inside, the airy foyer is equally dramatic, with its 19½-ft. ceiling, large transom window and decorative stairway.
- Columns set off the spacious living and dining rooms. Double doors keep this area quiet by closing it off from the family room and kitchen.
- An 11-ft., 9-in. vaulted ceiling enhances the family room, which has a fireplace and a built-in entertainment center.
- The island kitchen offers a corner pantry and an open, angled snack counter. The adjoining breakfast nook has French-door access to a backyard deck.
- The secluded master bedroom flaunts a 12½-ft. vaulted ceiling and outdoor access. Beyond the private whirlpool bath is a spacious walk-in closet.
- Upstairs, three good-sized bedrooms share two skylighted baths. A balcony offers views of the foyer below.
- All ceilings are 9 ft. high unless otherwise specified.

Plan DW-2640

Bedrooms: 4	Baths: 3½
Living Area:	
Upper floor	866 sq. ft.
Main floor	1,774 sq. ft.
Total Living Area:	**2,640 sq. ft.**
Standard basement	1,774 sq. ft.
Garage	490 sq. ft.
Exterior Wall Framing:	2x4

Foundation Options:

Standard basement

Crawlspace

Slab

(All plans can be built with your choice of foundation and framing. A generic conversion diagram is available. See order form.)

BLUEPRINT PRICE CODE: D

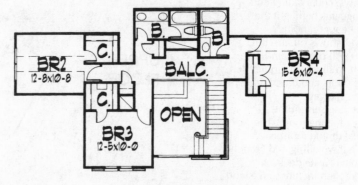

UPPER FLOOR

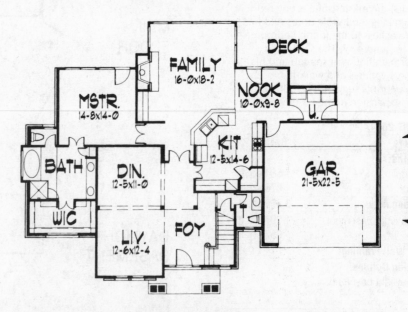

MAIN FLOOR

Bold, Creative Symmetry

- This creatively contemporary home makes a striking design statement with its vertical siding, ascending windows and symmetrical roof peaks.
- Inside, the airy foyer is open to the upper balcony and to the formal spaces on either side. This wide expanse boasts a handsome fireplace and, at nearly 35 ft. across, is great for entertaining.
- The informal spaces overlook a vast terrace at the back of the home. The family room has its own fireplace and can access the terrace through the adjacent sliding glass doors.
- A refreshing wet bar is centrally located for easy service to all main-floor areas. The kitchen's pantry and snack counter are other nice extras.
- The main-floor living spaces have 9-ft. ceilings, while all four upper-floor bedrooms are expanded by 16-ft. vaulted ceilings. The master bedroom includes a walk-in closet and a private bath with dual sinks. The secondary bedrooms share another bath, also with dual sinks.

Plan HFL-1740-JN

Bedrooms: 4	Baths: 2½
Living Area:	
Upper floor	1,146 sq. ft.
Main floor	1,301 sq. ft.
Total Living Area:	**2,447 sq. ft.**
Standard basement	1,241 sq. ft.
Garage and storage	476 sq. ft.
Exterior Wall Framing:	2x6

Foundation Options:

Standard basement
Slab
(All plans can be built with your choice of foundation and framing. A generic conversion diagram is available. See order form.)

BLUEPRINT PRICE CODE: C

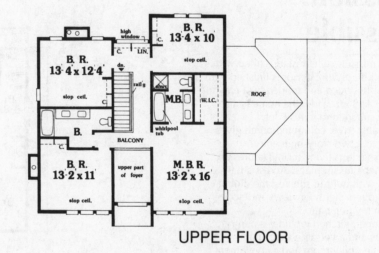

UPPER FLOOR

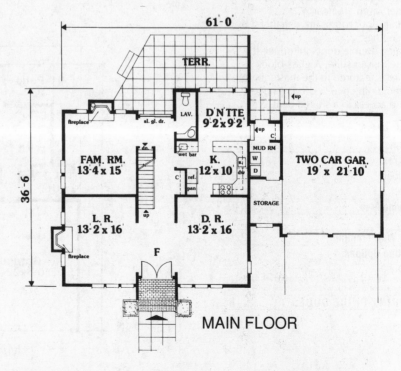

MAIN FLOOR

Mission: Possible

- This mission-style design is filled with possibilities. Its exterior is finished with durable stucco and topped by a clay tile roof. At 36 ft. wide, the home is also well suited for a narrow lot.
- The attractive, columned porch gives way to a two-story-high entry.
- The spacious living room features an efficient gas fireplace. Across a half-wall with built-in shelves, the dining area offers plenty of views and access to an inviting patio.
- The open kitchen includes a pantry closet and a versatile snack bar.
- A large utility room and a convenient powder room are nearby.
- All main-floor rooms are enhanced by 9-ft. ceilings.
- Upstairs, double doors introduce the private master suite. A glass-block shower is featured in the master bath.
- The remaining two bedrooms have private access to a shared bath.

Plan NW-421-B

Bedrooms: 3	Baths: 2½
Living Area:	
Upper floor	784 sq. ft.
Main floor	738 sq. ft.
Total Living Area:	**1,522 sq. ft.**
Garage	483 sq. ft.
Exterior Wall Framing:	2x6

Foundation Options:

Crawlspace

(All plans can be built with your choice of foundation and framing. A generic conversion diagram is available. See order form.)

BLUEPRINT PRICE CODE:	B

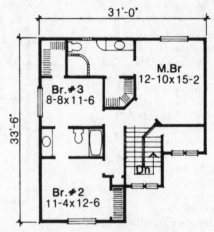

UPPER FLOOR

Br.#3
8-8x11-6

M.Br
12-10x15-2

Br.#2
11-4x12-6

31'-0"

33'-6"

Dn

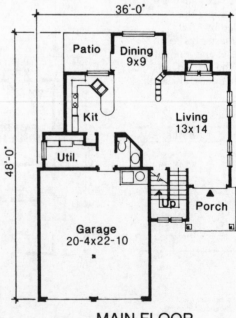

MAIN FLOOR

36'-0"

48'-0"

Patio

Dining
9x9

Kit

Living
13x14

Util.

Up

Porch

Garage
20-4x22-10

Plan NW-421-B

PRICES AND DETAILS ON PAGES 12-15

Bright Indoor/Outdoor Living

- Striking vertical siding and eye-catching rooflines create a contemporary impact for this breezy indoor/outdoor home.
- Stylish double doors open to the airy interior, which offers unlimited views of the outdoor landscape.
- The bright and spacious living and dining room area is expanded by a 13-ft., 8-in. cathedral ceiling. A functional display shelf and a warm fireplace flanked by glass are also featured. Sliding glass doors open from the dining room to one of three terraces.
- The U-shaped kitchen is flooded with light from a central skylight and adjoins a cheerful dinette and a second terrace.
- The laundry/mudroom offers a service entry from the outdoors and connects the kitchen with the two-car garage.
- Room for three bedrooms and two baths is offered in the removed sleeping wing. The master bedroom boasts a private terrace and its own bath with an optional shower extension. The third bedroom could also serve as a den.

Plan K-803-R

Bedrooms: 2+	Baths: 2
Living Area:	
Main floor	1,526 sq. ft.
Total Living Area:	**1,526 sq. ft.**
Daylight basement	1,525 sq. ft.
Garage	507 sq. ft.
Exterior Wall Framing:	2x4 or 2x6

Foundation Options:

Daylight basement
Slab

(All plans can be built with your choice of foundation and framing. A generic conversion diagram is available. See order form.)

BLUEPRINT PRICE CODE: B

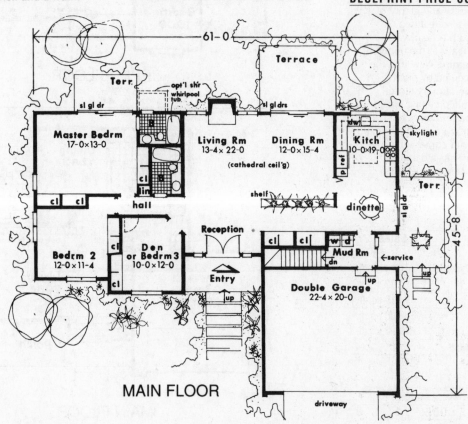

MAIN FLOOR

Open, Airy Floor Plan

- Vaulted ceilings and an open floor plan highlight this three-bedroom home.
- The main entry opens to the spacious two-story-high living room, with a dramatic see-through fireplace that is shared with the dining room. French-style sliding doors open to a nice patio.
- The modern kitchen provides an elevated serving counter for easy entertaining. A pantry and plenty of counter space are also featured. A convenient half-bath is nearby.
- A railed stairway leads to the upper floor, where a stunning view into the living room is accented by plant shelves. Ahead is a laundry closet.
- A 10½-ft.-high vaulted ceiling presides over the lovely master bedroom. The master bath features a private toilet and a whirlpool tub with corner windows.
- The front bedroom has a partially vaulted ceiling that soars to 12 ft., accenting a decorative window arrangement and a window seat.

Plan AG-1502

Bedrooms: 3	Baths: 2½
Living Area:	
Upper floor	724 sq. ft.
Main floor	792 sq. ft.
Total Living Area:	**1,516 sq. ft.**
Standard basement	780 sq. ft.
Garage	393 sq. ft.
Exterior Wall Framing:	2x4
Foundation Options:	

Standard basement
(All plans can be built with your choice of foundation and framing. A generic conversion diagram is available. See order form.)

BLUEPRINT PRICE CODE:	**B**

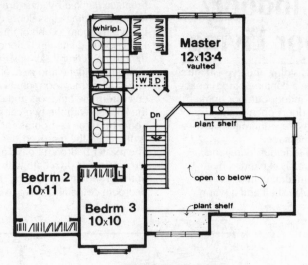

UPPER FLOOR

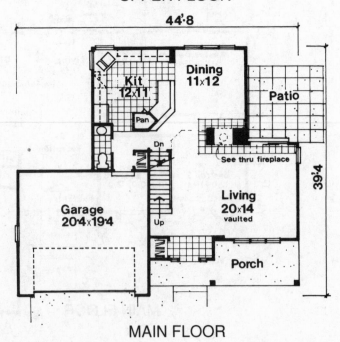

MAIN FLOOR

TO ORDER THIS BLUEPRINT, CALL TOLL-FREE 1-800-547-5570

Plan AG-1502

PRICES AND DETAILS ON PAGES 12-15

Perfect for New Families

- This compact and efficient design is perfect for the first-time home builder.
- The main floor provides an open, spacious living room for family activities or formal entertaining.
- The attached dining room opens to a lovely patio and is easily serviced by the modern U-shaped kitchen. A convenient half-bath and the garage entrance are nearby.
- Upstairs, double doors open to the handsome master bedroom, where the ceiling vaults to a flat area of 9 feet. The adjoining full bath can be entered from the master bedroom or from the hall.
- The garage may be omitted for a narrow lot, or expanded to accommodate a second car.

Plan B-92008

Bedrooms: 3	**Baths:** 1½

Living Area:	
Upper floor	676 sq. ft.
Main floor	624 sq. ft.
Total Living Area:	**1,300 sq. ft.**
Standard basement	624 sq. ft.
Garage	226 sq. ft.
Exterior Wall Framing:	2x6

Foundation Options:

Standard basement
(All plans can be built with your choice of foundation and framing. A generic conversion diagram is available. See order form.)

BLUEPRINT PRICE CODE: A

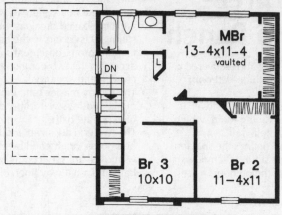

UPPER FLOOR

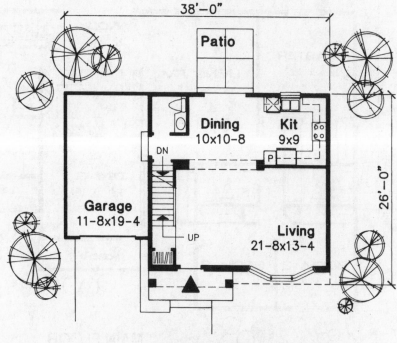

MAIN FLOOR

Rustic Three-Bedroom Ranch

- Unique angled siding and a covered front porch give this three-bedroom ranch a rustic appeal.
- Past the inviting entrance, the foyer adjoins the formal dining room, which is introduced by a half-wall.
- A second half-wall defines the spacious living room, where a trio of windows provides a view of the outdoors.

- The efficient and versatile kitchen can be laid out in a variety of ways. The adjacent bayed breakfast nook offers sliding glass doors to the backyard. A laundry room, basement stairway and access to the two-car garage are conveniently nearby.
- The roomy master suite includes a set of his-and-hers wardrobe closets and a nice private bath.
- The two equally sized additional bedrooms, brightened by front-facing windows, are serviced by a second full bath and a hallway linen closet.

Plan GL-1618

Bedrooms: 3	**Baths:** 2

Living Area:	
Main floor	1,618 sq. ft.
Total Living Area:	**1,618 sq. ft.**
Standard basement	1,618 sq. ft.
Garage	484 sq. ft.

Exterior Wall Framing: 2x6

Foundation Options:

Standard basement

(All plans can be built with your choice of foundation and framing. A generic conversion diagram is available. See order form.)

BLUEPRINT PRICE CODE: B

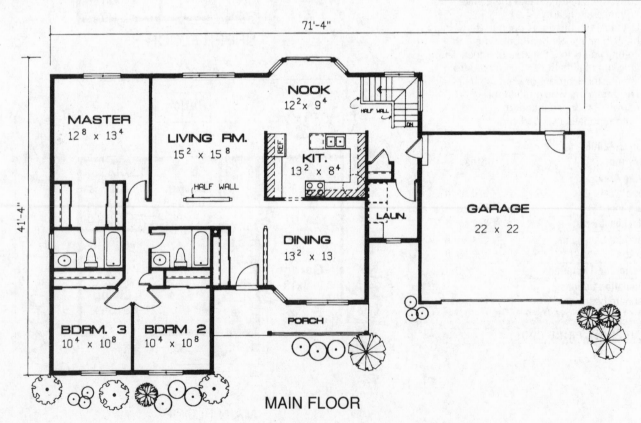

MAIN FLOOR

TO ORDER THIS BLUEPRINT, CALL TOLL-FREE 1-800-547-5570

Plan GL-1618

PRICES AND DETAILS ON PAGES 12-15

Angles Open Rear of Home to More Sunshine

PATIO

PORCH
12' x 6'

DINING
12' x 12'

MASTER SUITE
16' x 12'

BED RM.
14' x 12'

LIVING
18' x 16'

KITCHEN

BAR

DW | SINK

RANGE

REF

BATH

HALL

BATH
LIN

CLO.

WASH | DRY

UTIL
9' x 6'

PANT
BRM
STO.

STORAGE
10' x 6'

CLO.

ENTRY

CLO.

BED RM.
14' x 12'

PORCH
8' x 4'

ATTIC STAIRS

GARAGE
22' x 22'

50'

56'

AREAS

Living	1415 sq. ft.
Porches	114 sq. ft.
Garage, Storage	
Equip.	565 sq. ft.
Total	2094 sq. ft.

Exterior walls are 2x6 construction.
Specify crawlspace or slab foundation.

**TO ORDER THIS BLUEPRINT,
CALL TOLL-FREE 1-800-547-5570**

Blueprint Price Code A
Plan E-1424

*PRICES AND DETAILS
ON PAGES 12-15*   161

Open Plan Includes Circular Dining Room

- Innovative architectural features and a functional, light-filled floor plan are the hallmarks of this attractive design.
- The facade is graced by a stone chimney and a circular glass bay which houses the spectacular dining room with its domed ceiling.
- A bright, sunny kitchen is set up for efficient operation and adjoins a dinette area which echoes the circular shape of the formal dining room.
- The living room features a stone fireplace, and opens to the dining room to make a great space for entertaining.
- The bedrooms are zoned to the left, with the master suite including a private bath, large walk-in closet and access to an outdoor terrace.

Plan K-663-N

Bedrooms: 3	Baths: 2

Space:

Total living area:	1,560 sq. ft.
Basement:	1,645 sq. ft.
Garage:	453 sq. ft.
Mudroom & stairs:	122 sq. ft.

Exterior Wall Framing:	2x4/2x6

Foundation options:
Standard basement.
Slab.
(Foundation & framing conversion diagram available — see order form.)

Blueprint Price Code:	B

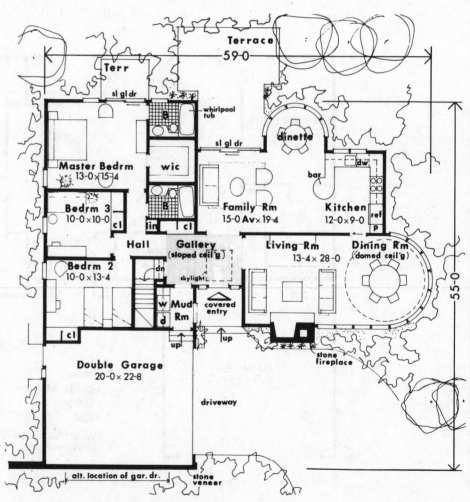

Classic Columns
Grace Wide Veranda

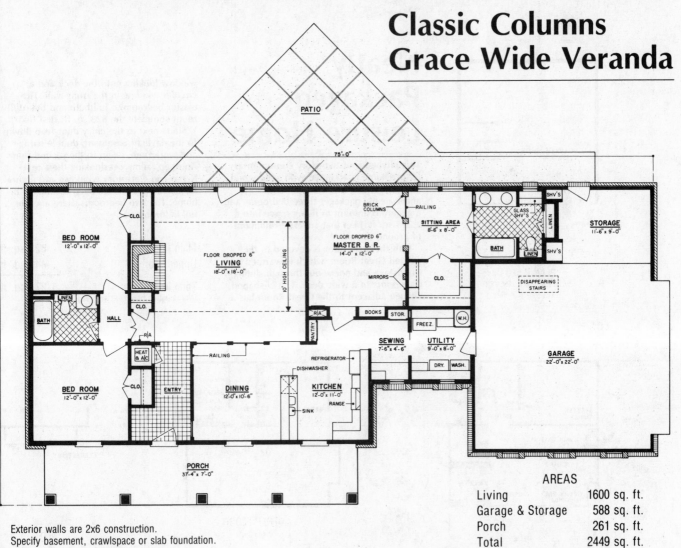

PATIO

75'-0"

BED ROOM
12'-0" x 12'-0"

CLO.

LINEN

BATH

HALL

HEAT & A/C

BED ROOM
12'-0" x 12'-0"

CLO.

CLO.

FLOOR DROPPED 6"
LIVING
18'-0" x 18'-0"

10' HIGH CEILING

ENTRY

RAILING

DINING
12'-0" x 10'-6"

R/A

BRICK COLUMNS   RAILING

SITTING AREA
8'-6" x 8'-0"

FLOOR DROPPED 6"
MASTER B. R.
14'-0" x 12'-0"

MIRRORS

CLO.

GLASS SHV'S

BATH

SHV'S

SHV'S

LINEN

LINEN

STORAGE
11'-6" x 9'-0"

DISAPPEARING STAIRS

PANTRY

BOOKS

STOR.

FREEZ.

W.H.

SEWING
7'-6" x 4'-6"

UTILITY
9'-0" x 8'-0"

DRY.   WASH.

GARAGE
22'-0" x 22'-0"

REFRIGERATOR

DISHWASHER

KITCHEN
12'-0" x 11'-0"

SINK

RANGE

PORCH
37'-4" x 7'-0"

AREAS

Living	1600 sq. ft.
Garage & Storage	588 sq. ft.
Porch	261 sq. ft.
Total	2449 sq. ft.

Exterior walls are 2x6 construction.
Specify basement, crawlspace or slab foundation.

Neatly Packaged Leisure Home

This pitched-roof two-story contemporary leisure home is accented with solid wood siding, placed vertically and diagonally, and it neatly packages three bedrooms and a generous amount of living space into a 1,271 sq. ft. plan that covers a minimum of ground space.

Half the main floor is devoted to the vaulted Great Room, which is warmed by a woodstove and opens out through sliding glass doors to a wide deck. The U-shaped kitchen adjacent to the Great Room has a window looking onto the deck and a circular window in the front wall. The master bedroom, a full bath and the utility room complete the 823 sq. ft. first floor.

Stairs next to the entry door lead down to the daylight basement, double garage and workroom, or up to the second floor. An open railing overlooking the Great Room and clerestory windows add natural light and enhance the open feeling of the home. The two bedrooms share another full bathroom.

Main floor:	823 sq. ft.
Upper floor:	448 sq. ft.
Total living area:	1,271 sq. ft.
(Not counting basement or garage)	

BASEMENT
PLAN P-520-D
WITH DAYLIGHT BASEMENT

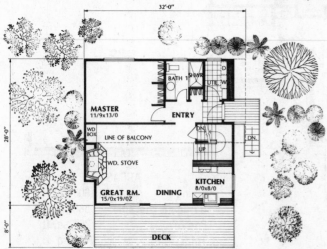

MAIN FLOOR

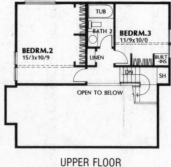

UPPER FLOOR

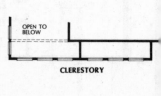

CLERESTORY

Blueprint Price Code A

Plan P-520-D

Appealing Contemporary Styling

- Contemporary wood exterior allows for economical construction.
- Spacious, open floor plan permits easy traffic flow, minimal wasted hall space.
- U-shaped kitchen includes pantry and eating bar.
- Isolated master suite features generous walk-in closet with built-in drawers and shelves and a private bath with separate sinks and large whirlpool.

Plan E-1430

Bedrooms: 3	Baths: 2

Space:

Total living area:	1,430 sq. ft.
Garage and storage:	465 sq. ft.
Porches:	128 sq. ft.

Exterior Wall Framing:	2x4

Foundation options:
Crawlspace.
Slab.
(Foundation & framing conversion diagram available — see order form.)

Blueprint Price Code:	A

Plan E-1430

Vertical Elegance

- This spacious two-story has unique features that give it a vertical elegance.
- The two-story-high foyer offers an open-railed stairway that adjoins a second stairway from the family room. The two stairways bridge together before reaching the upper floor.
- Behind high, decorative columns is the formal living room. To the rear is a spacious family room with an exciting fireplace flanked by windows. The kitchen and breakfast room overlook the outdoors, accessed through a French door.
- Three secondary bedrooms share a compartmentalized bath on the upper floor. The luxurious master bedroom features a private sitting room with a stunning two-sided fireplace, a big walk-in closet and a private vaulted bath with a separate tub and shower.

Plan FB-2600

Bedrooms: 4	Baths: 2½
Living Area:	
Upper floor	1,348 sq. ft.
Main floor	1,252 sq. ft.
Total Living Area:	**2,600 sq. ft.**
Daylight basement	1,252 sq. ft.
Garage	448 sq. ft.
Storage	36 sq. ft.
Exterior Wall Framing:	2x4

Foundation Options:
Daylight basement
Crawlspace
(Typical foundation & framing conversion diagram available—see order form.)

BLUEPRINT PRICE CODE: D

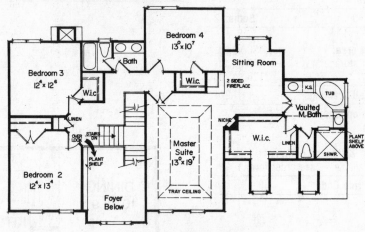

UPPER FLOOR

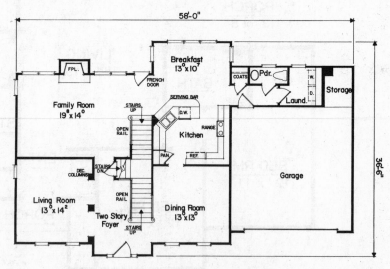

MAIN FLOOR

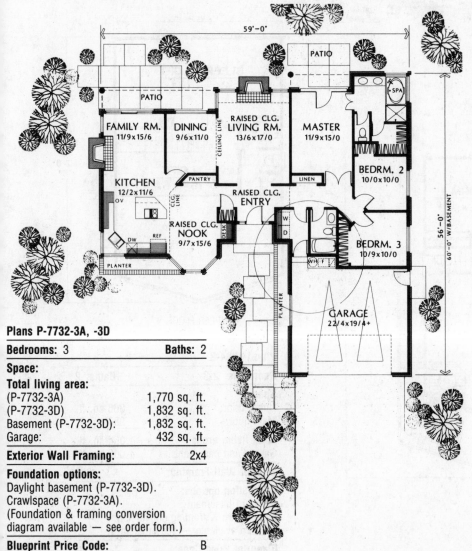

Stately Character

- Brick with kneewall planters, stylish hip rooflines and a covered entry with transom glass give a stately character to this exciting one-story design.
- A raised ceiling at the entry and on into the living room enhances the feeling of spaciousness.
- The formal dining room flows into the living room and enjoys the fireplace view.
- The island kitchen opens to both the raised ceilinged breakfast bay with built-in desk and to the family room with second fireplace and sliders to the rear patio.
- The master suite enjoys double doors, private patio access, walk-in closet and spa bath.

Plans P-7732-3A, -3D

Bedrooms: 3	Baths: 2

Space:

Total living area:

(P-7732-3A)	1,770 sq. ft.
(P-7732-3D)	1,832 sq. ft.
Basement (P-7732-3D):	1,832 sq. ft.
Garage:	432 sq. ft.

Exterior Wall Framing:	2x4

Foundation options:
Daylight basement (P-7732-3D).
Crawlspace (P-7732-3A).
(Foundation & framing conversion diagram available — see order form.)

Blueprint Price Code:	B

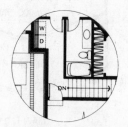

LOCATION OF STAIRS IN
BASEMENT VERSION.

TO ORDER THIS BLUEPRINT,
CALL TOLL-FREE 1-800-547-5570

Plans P-7732-3A, -3D

PRICES AND DETAILS
ON PAGES 12-15

167

Massive, Windowed Great Room

- This attractive, open design can function as a cabin, mountain retreat or permanent residence.
- The kitchen and Great Room merge to form a large family activity area; an open balcony loft above offers an elevated view of the massive front window wall.
- A third sleeping room upstairs could be split into two smaller bedrooms.
- The main level of the home is entered via a split-landing deck off the Great Room.

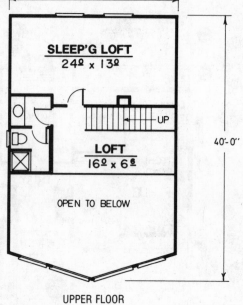

UPPER FLOOR

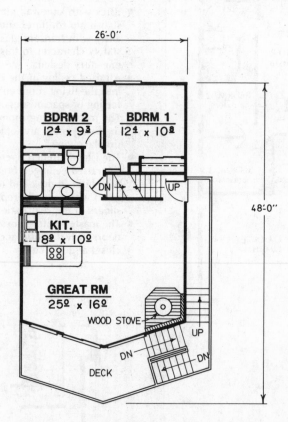

MAIN FLOOR

Plan I-1354-B

Bedrooms: 2-3	Baths: 2
Space:	
Upper floor:	366 sq. ft.
Main floor:	988 sq. ft.
Total living area:	1,354 sq. ft.
Garage and basement:	1,000 sq. ft.
Exterior Wall Framing:	2x6

Foundation options:
Standard basement.
(Foundation & framing conversion diagram available — see order form.)

Blueprint Price Code: A

Symmetry and Style

- This appealing one-story home boasts a striking facade with symmetrical rooflines, stately columns and terrific transoms.
- The formal living spaces have a classic split design, perfect for quiet times and conversation.
- The unique design of the bedroom wing gives each bedroom easy access to a full bath. The rear bedroom also enjoys pool and patio proximity.
- The huge family room, which opens up to the patio with 12-ft. pocket sliding doors, has plenty of space for a fireplace and media equipment.
- The master suite just off the kitchen and nook is private yet easily accessible. One unique feature is its bed wall with high glass above. The master bath offers a walk-in closet, a corner tub, a step down shower and a private toilet room.
- Throughout the home, volume ceilings to a height of at least ten feet increase the spacious, airy feeling.

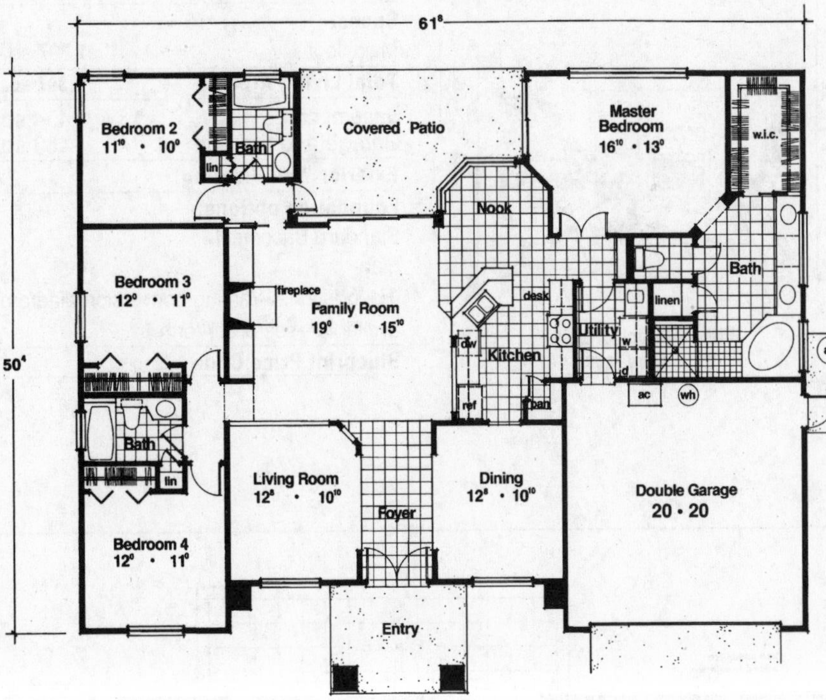

MAIN FLOOR

Floor plan labels:
- 61⁶ (width)
- 50⁴ (height)
- Bedroom 2 11¹⁰ · 10⁰
- Bath
- lin
- Covered Patio
- Master Bedroom 16¹⁰ · 13⁰
- w.l.c.
- Nook
- Bedroom 3 12⁰ · 11⁰
- fireplace
- Family Room 19⁰ · 15¹⁰
- Bath
- desk
- linen
- Kitchen
- Utility
- w
- d
- dw
- ref
- pan
- ac
- wh
- ac
- Bath
- lin
- Bedroom 4 12⁰ · 11⁰
- Living Room 12⁰ · 10¹⁰
- Foyer
- Dining 12⁰ · 10¹⁰
- Double Garage 20 · 20
- Entry

Plan HDS-99-147

Bedrooms: 4	Baths: 3
Living Area:	
Main floor	2,089 sq. ft.
Total Living Area:	**2,089 sq. ft.**
Garage	415 sq. ft.
Exterior Wall Framing:	2x4
Foundation Options:	
Slab	
(Typical foundation & framing conversion diagram available—see order form.)	
BLUEPRINT PRICE CODE:	C

Design Harmony

- This house combines several different architectural styles to achieve a design harmony all its own.
- The columns of the front porch are reminiscent of ancient Greece, while the Palladian window in the master bedroom originates from the Renaissance period. The sleek rectangular shape of the home is in keeping with more contemporary times.
- The columns are repeated inside, where they are used to visually divide the foyer from the living room and to dramatize the cathedral ceiling. Columns also frame the heat-circulating fireplace.
- Note the twin closets in the foyer. Straight ahead is the combination dining room and kitchen, which basks in an abundance of natural light from two skylights, a large bow window, plus a sliding glass door that opens to the terrace.
- Another back entrance separates the kitchen from the large mud room. The mud room has loads of closet space, with two closets and cabinets above the washer and dryer.
- The sleeping wing has three large bedrooms and two full baths. Here, as elsewhere, closet space is well accounted for.

View into living room from entry foyer.

Plan HFL-1200-FH	
Bedrooms: 3	**Baths: 2**
Space:	
Main floor	1,397 sq. ft.
Total Living Area	**1,397 sq. ft.**
Basement	1,434 sq. ft.
Garage and Storage	463 sq. ft.
Exterior Wall Framing	2x6
Foundation options:	
Standard Basement	
Slab	
(Foundation & framing conversion diagram available—see order form.)	
Blueprint Price Code	A

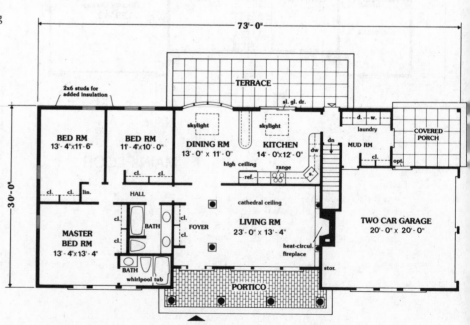

TO ORDER THIS BLUEPRINT, CALL TOLL-FREE 1-800-547-5570

Plan HFL-1200-FH

PRICES AND DETAILS ON PAGES 12-15

UPPER FLOOR

BEDROOM 12'-1"×9'-6"
STOR
STOR
Shwr
BATH
BEDROOM 12'-1"×10'-0"
STOR
STOR
DECK
26'-0"

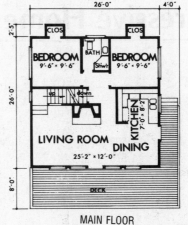

MAIN FLOOR PLAN H-720-11

26'-0" 4'-0"
CLOS
BEDROOM 10'-0"×9'-6"
BATH
Shwr
KITCHEN 9'-6"×8'-2"
DINING 12'-9"×5'-8"
down
LIVING ROOM 25'-2"×12'-0"
DECK
2'-5"
26'-0"
8'-0"

MAIN FLOOR PLAN H-720-10

26'-0" 4'-0"
CLOS   CLOS
BEDROOM 9'-6"×9'-6"   BATH Shwr   BEDROOM 9'-6"×9'-6"
up   down
KITCHEN 7'-0"×8'-2"
LIVING ROOM 25'-2"×12'-0"
DINING
DECK
2'-5"
26'-0"
8'-0"

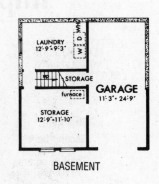

BASEMENT

LAUNDRY 12'-9"×9'-3"
D
W
STORAGE
furnace
GARAGE 11'-3"×24'-9"
STORAGE 12'-9"×11'-10"

Chalet with Variations

- Attractive chalet offers several main level variations, with second floor and basement layouts identical.
- All versions feature well-arranged kitchen, attached dining area, and large living room.
- Second-floor amenities include private decks off each bedroom and storage space in every corner!

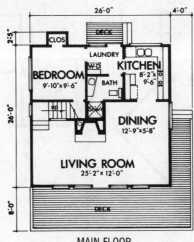

MAIN FLOOR PLAN H-720-12A WITHOUT BASEMENT

26'-0" 4'-0"
DECK
CLOS
LAUNDRY
W D
KITCHEN 8'-2"×9'-6"
BEDROOM 9'-10"×9'-6"
BATH
Shwr
up
DINING 12'-9"×5'-8"
LIVING ROOM 25'-2"×12'-0"
DECK
2'-5"
26'-0"
8'-0"

Plans H-720-10, -11 & -12A	
Bedrooms: 3-4	**Baths:** 2

Space:	
Upper floor:	328 sq. ft.
Main floor:	686 sq. ft.

Total living area:	1,014 sq. ft.
Basement:	approx. 686 sq. ft.
Garage: (incl. in basement)	278 sq. ft.

Exterior Wall Framing:	2x4

Foundation options:
Daylight basement
 (Plans H-720-10 or -11).
Crawlspace (Plan H-720-12A)
(Foundation & framing conversion
diagram available — see order form.)

Blueprint Price Code:	
Without basement:	A
With basement:	B

Impressive Home for Sloping Lot

PLAN Q-3080-1A
WITHOUT BASEMENT
(SLAB-ON-GRADE FOUNDATION)

First floor: 1,505 sq. ft.
Second floor: 1,575 sq. ft.

Total living area: 3,080 sq. ft.
(Not counting garage)

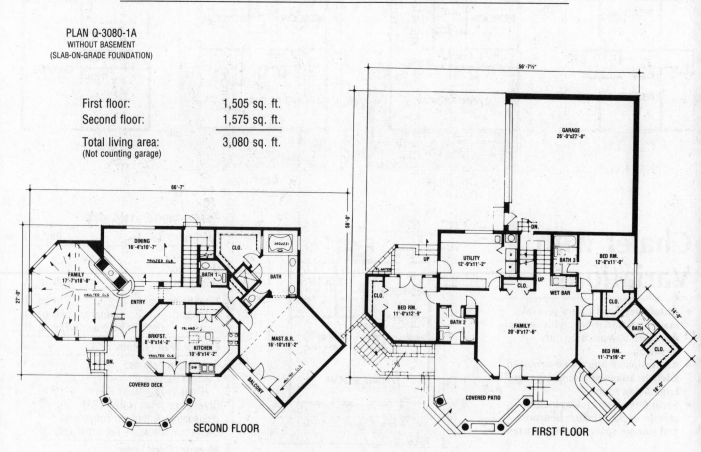

SECOND FLOOR

FIRST FLOOR

↙ NOTE: This house was designed for a lot sloping down in the direction of the arrow.

Blueprint Price Code E

Plan Q-3080-1A

Panoramic View for Scenic Site

● Large deck offers a panoramic view and plenty of space for outdoor living.

● Sunken living room features big windows and impressive fireplace.

● Living room is set off by railings, not walls, to create visual impact of big space.

● Master suite includes private bath, large closet, sitting area and access to deck.

● Lower level includes rec room with fireplace, two bedrooms, two baths and large utility area.

Plan NW-779

Bedrooms: 3	Baths: 3½
Space:	
Main floor:	1,450 sq. ft.
Lower floor:	1,242 sq. ft.
Total living area:	2,692 sq. ft.
Exterior Wall Framing:	2x6

Foundation options:
Daylight basement only.
(Foundation & framing conversion diagram available — see order form.)

Blueprint Price Code:	D

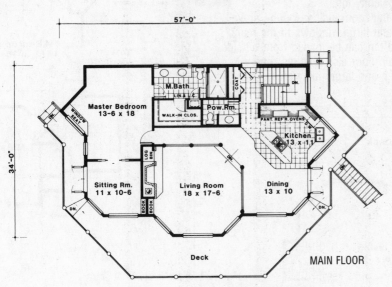

MAIN FLOOR

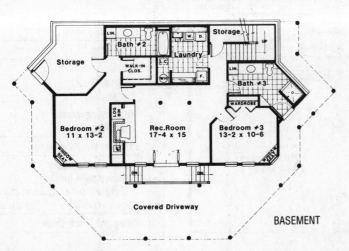

BASEMENT

Upstairs Suite Creates Adult Retreat

- This multi-level design is ideal for a gently sloping site with a view to the rear.

- Upstairs master suite is a sumptuous "adult retreat" complete with magnificent bath, vaulted ceiling, walk-in closet, private deck and balcony loft.
- Living room includes wood stove area and large windows to the rear. Wood bin can be loaded from outside.
- Main floor also features roomy kitchen and large utility area.

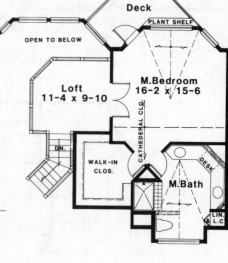

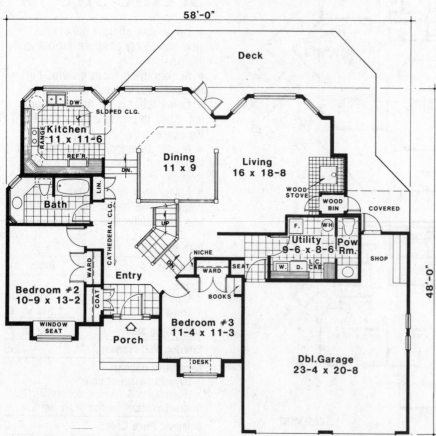

Plan NW-544-S

Bedrooms: 3	**Baths:** 2½

Space:

Upper floor:	638 sq. ft.
Main floor:	1,500 sq. ft.
Total living area:	**2,138 sq. ft.**
Garage:	545 sq. ft.

Exterior Wall Framing:	2x6

Foundation options:
Crawlspace only.
(Foundation & framing conversion diagram available — see order form.)

Blueprint Price Code:	C

Customize Your Floor Plan!

- An optional bonus room and a choice between a loft or a bedroom allow you to customize the floor plan of this striking two-story traditional.
- The vaulted foyer leads guests past a handy powder room and directly into the vaulted family room straight ahead or into the formal dining room on the right. A beautiful open-railed staircase pleasantly breaks up the spaces while giving more privacy to the kitchen and the breakfast room.
- The sunny breakfast room is open to the island kitchen. A pantry closet, loads of counter space and direct access to the laundry room and the garage add to the kitchen's efficiency.
- The main-floor master suite is a treasure, with its tray ceiling and vaulted, amenity-filled master bath.
- Upstairs, two bedrooms, a full bath and an optional loft as well as a bonus room provide plenty of opportunity for expansion and customization.

Plan FB-1874

Bedrooms: 3+	Baths: 2½
Living Area:	
Upper floor	554 sq. ft.
Main floor	1,320 sq. ft.
Bonus room	155 sq. ft.
Total Living Area:	**2,029 sq. ft.**
Daylight basement	1,320 sq. ft.
Garage	240 sq. ft.
Storage	38 sq. ft.
Exterior Wall Framing:	2x4

Foundation Options:
Daylight basement
(Typical foundation & framing conversion diagram available—see order form.)

BLUEPRINT PRICE CODE: C

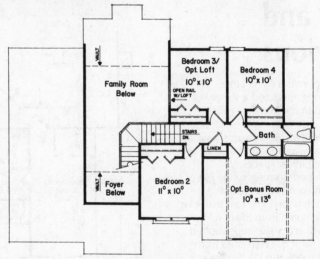

UPPER FLOOR

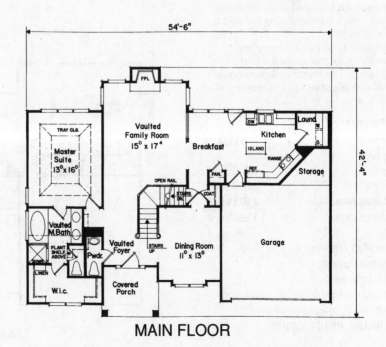

MAIN FLOOR

Large and Luxurious

- This two-story home offers large, luxurious living areas and a variety of options to tailor the home to your needs.
- The oversized, two-story foyer shows off an angled stairway and, to the right, elegant formal living spaces.
- A den or fifth bedroom sits to the left of the foyer and could be accessed through French doors. The hall bath can be privately entered from the den.
- The family will enjoy the huge vaulted family room, which is separated from the breakfast room and kitchen by an open railing. The sunken family room offers a wet bar and a warm fireplace.
- The gourmet kitchen boasts a cooktop island with a handy serving bar and a walk-in pantry.
- The upper floor has a convenient laundry room and space for four bedrooms. The fourth bedroom could serve as a playroom or a hobby room.

Plan FB-3071

Bedrooms: 3-5	Baths: 4
Living Area:	
Upper floor	1,419 sq. ft.
Main floor	1,652 sq. ft.
Total Living Area:	**3,071 sq. ft.**
Daylight basement	1,652 sq. ft.
Garage	456 sq. ft.
Exterior Wall Framing:	2x4

Foundation Options:
Daylight basement
(Typical foundation & framing conversion diagram available—see order form.)

BLUEPRINT PRICE CODE: E

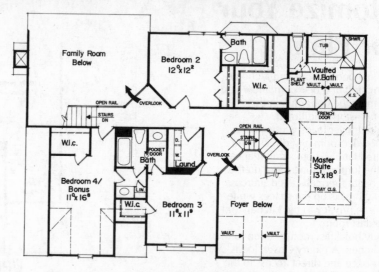

UPPER FLOOR

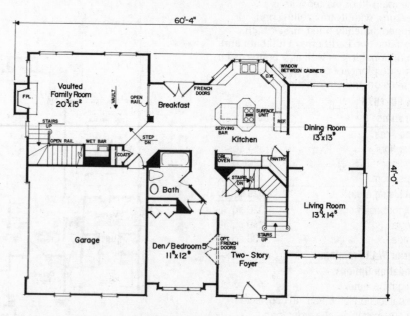

MAIN FLOOR

Plan FB-3071

PRICES AND DETAILS ON PAGES 12-15

Maximum Value and Excitement

- This well-planned 1,231 sq. ft. ranch design gives the first-time home buyer the most value and excitement for the dollar.
- The front porch, stone chimney, divided windows, and gable louvre all highlight a nostalgic charm.
- The interior spaces feature vaulted ceilings for an airy feel.
- The den could serve several functions, including guest quarters or a formal dining room.
- The master bedroom has a full-wall closet and a divided bath with private toilet.

Plan B-88021

Bedrooms: 2-3	Baths: 2
Space:	
Total living area:	1,231 sq. ft.
Basement:	1,231 sq. ft.
Garage:	400 sq. ft.
Exterior Wall Framing:	2x4

Foundation options:
Standard basement.
(Foundation & framing conversion diagram available — see order form.)

Blueprint Price Code:	A

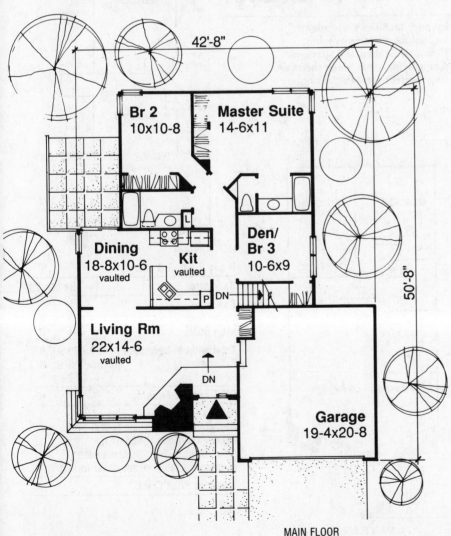

42'-8"

Br 2
10x10-8

Master Suite
14-6x11

Dining
18-8x10-6
vaulted

Kit
vaulted

Den/ Br 3
10-6x9

L

P DN

Living Rm
22x14-6
vaulted

DN

50'-8"

Garage
19-4x20-8

MAIN FLOOR

Eye-Catching Prow-Shaped Chalet

- Steep pitched roof lines and wide cornices give this chalet a distinct alpine appearance.
- Prowed shape, large windows, and 10' deck provide view and enhancement of indoor/outdoor living.
- Functional division of living and sleeping areas by hallway and first floor full bath.

- Laundry facilities conveniently located near bedroom wing.
- U-shaped kitchen and spacious dining/living areas make the main floor perfect for entertaining.

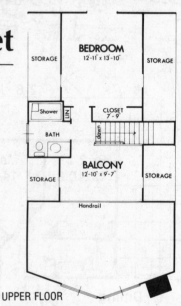

UPPER FLOOR

Plans H-886-3 & -3A

Bedrooms: 3	Baths: 2

Space:

Upper floor:	486 sq. ft.
Main floor:	994 sq. ft.

Total without basement:	1,480 sq. ft.
Basement:	approx. 715 sq. ft.
Garage:	279 sq. ft.

Exterior Wall Framing:	2x6

Foundation options:
Daylight basement (Plan H-886-3).
Crawlspace (Plan H-886-3A).
(Foundation & framing conversion diagram available — see order form.)

Blueprint Price Code:	A

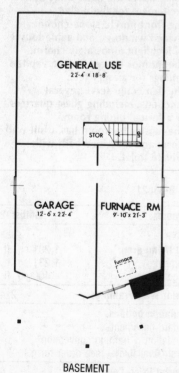

BASEMENT

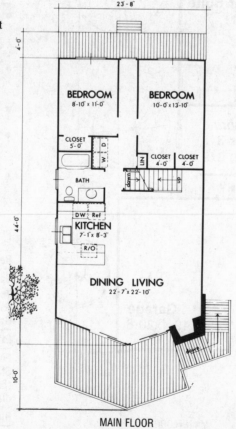

MAIN FLOOR

Plans H-886-3 & -3A

Distinctive Two-Story

- A playful and distinctive exterior invites you into a functional, contemporary interior.
- The sunken living room features a soaring cathedral ceiling open to the second floor balcony.
- The adjoining step-down family room is connected to allow for overflow and easy circulation of traffic.
- A luxurious master suite and room for three additional bedrooms are found on the second floor, with a dramatic balcony and a view of the foyer and the living room.

Plan AX-8922-A

Bedrooms: 3-4	Baths: 2½
Living Area:	
Upper floor	840 sq. ft.
Main floor	1,213 sq. ft.
Optional fourth bedroom	240 sq. ft.
Total Living Area:	**2,293 sq. ft.**
Standard basement	1,138 sq. ft.
Garage	470 sq. ft.
Exterior Wall Framing:	2x4

Foundation Options:
Standard basement
Slab
(Typical foundation & framing conversion diagram available—see order form.)

BLUEPRINT PRICE CODE: C

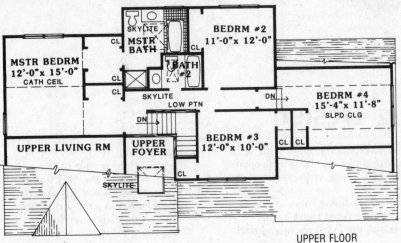

CER TILE LEDGE

SKYLITE

MSTR BATH

BEDRM #2
11'-0" x 12'-0"

BATH #2

MSTR BEDRM
12'-0" x 15'-0"
CATH CEIL

SKYLITE

LOW PTN

DN

BEDRM #4
15'-4" x 11'-8"
SLPD CLG

DN

UPPER LIVING RM

UPPER FOYER

BEDRM #3
12'-0" x 10'-0"

SKYLITE

UPPER FLOOR

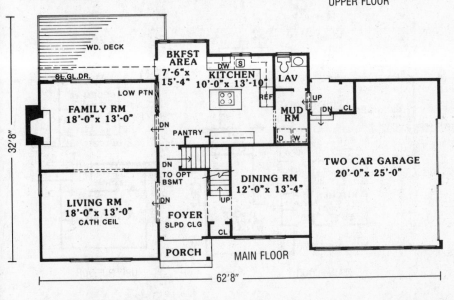

WD. DECK

BKFST AREA
7'-6" x 15'-4"

DW   S

KITCHEN
10'-0" x 13'-10"

LAV

SL. GL. DR.

LOW PTN

REF

UP

FAMILY RM
18'-0" x 13'-0"

DN

PANTRY

MUD RM

DN   CL

32'-8"

DN
TO OPT BSMT

D W

TWO CAR GARAGE
20'-0" x 25'-0"

DN

DINING RM
12'-0" x 13'-4"

UP

LIVING RM
18'-0" x 13'-0"
CATH CEIL

FOYER
SLPD CLG

CL

PORCH

MAIN FLOOR

62'8"

TO ORDER THIS BLUEPRINT,
CALL TOLL-FREE 1-800-547-5570

Plan AX-8922-A

PRICES AND DETAILS
ON PAGES 12-15

179

Spectacular Sloping Design

- For the lake or mountain-view sloping lot, this spectacular design hugs the hill and takes full advantage of the views.
- A three-sided wrap-around deck makes indoor-outdoor living a pleasure.

- The sunken living room, with cathedral ceiling, skylight, fireplace, and glass galore, is the heart of the plan.
- The formal dining room and the kitchen/breakfast room both overlook the living room and deck

views beyond.
- The main-floor master bedroom has private access to the deck and the bath.
- Two more bedrooms upstairs share a skylit bath and flank a dramatic balcony sitting area overlooking the living room below.

Plan AX-98607

Bedrooms: 3	Baths: 2

Space:	
Upper floor:	531 sq. ft.
Main floor:	1,098 sq. ft.

Total living area:	1,629 sq. ft.
Basement:	894 sq. ft.
Garage:	327 sq. ft.

Exterior Wall Framing:	2x4

Foundation options:
Standard basement.
Slab.
(Foundation & framing conversion diagram available — see order form.)

Blueprint Price Code:	B

MAIN FLOOR

UPPER FLOOR

Plan AX-98607

Appealing Arches

- Elegant arches add drama to the covered front porch of this two-story.
- Interior arches offer an attractive entrance to the formal dining room and the living room, which flank the foyer.
- The decorative niche off the foyer attractively displays your favorite conversation pieces.
- A dramatic fireplace and an array of windows frame the spacious two-story family room. An arched opening leads into the adjoining kitchen, which offers a convenient serving bar. A pantry closet and open shelving are featured in the sunny attached breakfast area.
- The upper floor includes a large master suite, three secondary bedrooms, and a compartmentalized bath. Bedroom 2 has a window seat, while Bedroom 4 has a private dressing area.
- The master bedroom flaunts a tray ceiling, a beautiful window showpiece and a private vaulted bath with a garden tub. The bedroom may be extended to include a sitting area.

Plan FB-2368

Bedrooms: 4	Baths: 2½
Living Area:	
Upper floor	1,168 sq. ft.
Main floor	1,200 sq. ft.
Total Living Area:	**2,368 sq. ft.**
Daylight basement	1,200 sq. ft.
Garage	504 sq. ft.
Exterior Wall Framing:	2x4

Foundation Options:

Daylight basement

Slab

(Typical foundation & framing conversion diagram available—see order form.)

BLUEPRINT PRICE CODE: C

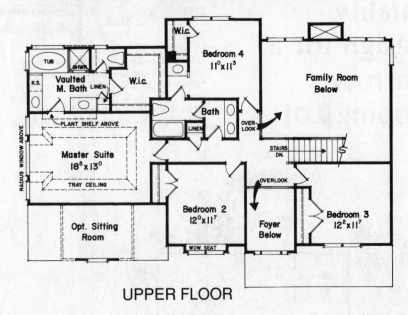

UPPER FLOOR

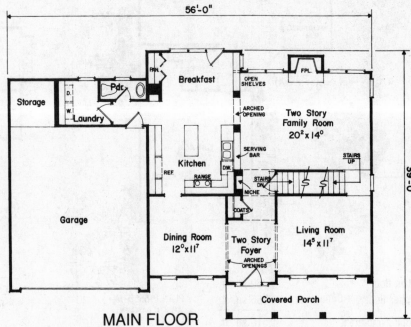

MAIN FLOOR

Quality Design for a Narrow, Sloping Lot

Multi-pitched rooflines, custom window treatments and beveled board siding add a distinctive facade to this two-level home of only 1,516 sq. ft. Its slim 34' width allows it to fit nicely on a narrow lot while offering ample indoor and outdoor living areas.

The enclosed entry courtyard is a pleasant area for al fresco breakfasts or spill-over entertaining. The wide, high-ceilinged entry hall opens directly into the sweeping Great Room and dining area. This room is warmed by a large fireplace and has a door to a large wood deck. Also off the entry hall is the morning room with a vaulted ceiling and a matching arched window overlooking the courtyard. A half-bath and utility room is on the other side of the entry.

An open-railed stairway leads from the entry to the bedrooms on the second level. The master suite has a high dormer with peaked windows, a walk-in closet and a private bathroom. The larger of the other bedrooms could be used as a den, and it also overlooks the morning room and entry hall. If additional room is required, this plan is available with a daylight basement.

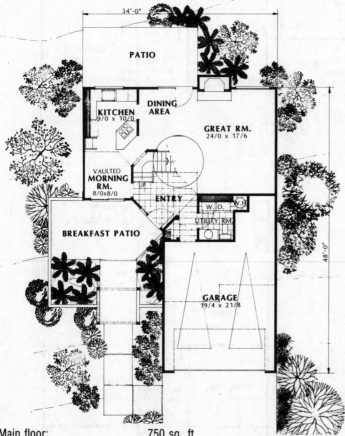

PLAN P-6563-4A
WITHOUT BASEMENT

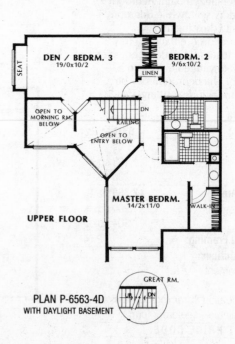

PLAN P-6563-4D
WITH DAYLIGHT BASEMENT

Main floor:	750 sq. ft.
Upper floor:	766 sq. ft.
Total living area:	1,516 sq. ft.
Basement level:	809 sq. ft.

Blueprint Price Code B

Plans P-6563-4A & -4D

TO ORDER THIS BLUEPRINT, CALL TOLL-FREE 1-800-547-5570

PRICES AND DETAILS ON PAGES 12-15

Design for Today's Lifestyle

- Compact and affordable, this home is designed for today's young families.
- The kitchen/dining room combination offers space for two people to share food preparation and clean-up chores.
- The master suite is impressive for a home of this size, and includes a cozy window seat, large walk-in closet and a private bath.
- The Great Room features an impressive fireplace and vaulted ceiling.
- The optional third bedroom could be used as a den or an expanded dining area.

Plan B-8317

Bedrooms: 2-3	**Baths:** 2
Total living area:	1,016 sq. ft.
Exterior Wall Framing:	2x4

Foundation options:
Slab only.
(Foundation & framing conversion diagram available — see order form.)

Blueprint Price Code: A

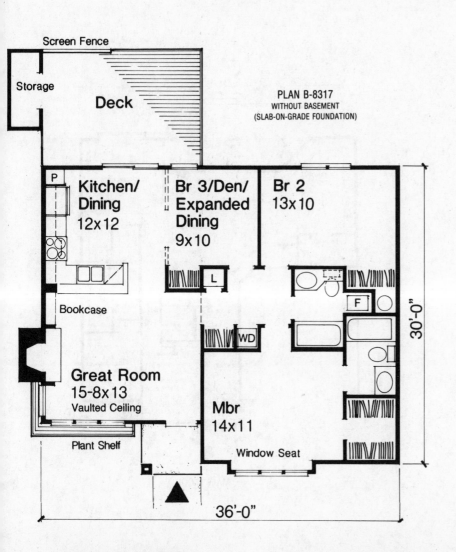

PLAN B-8317
WITHOUT BASEMENT
(SLAB-ON-GRADE FOUNDATION)

Screen Fence

Storage

Deck

Kitchen/Dining 12x12

Br 3/Den/Expanded Dining 9x10

Br 2 13x10

Bookcase

Great Room 15-8x13 Vaulted Ceiling

Plant Shelf

Mbr 14x11

Window Seat

30'-0"

36'-0"

TO ORDER THIS BLUEPRINT,
CALL TOLL-FREE 1-800-547-5570

Plan B-8317

PRICES AND DETAILS
ON PAGES 12-15

183

Sweet Master Suite

- Traditional stone veneer & New England shingle exterior.
- Arch top window at bedroom/study.
- Bedroom/study can also be used as an office.
- Great Room features vaulted ceiling, fireplace & French doors to outdoor living deck.
- Kitchen includes all amenities plus breakfast eating bar.
- Main floor laundry/mudroom.
- Master suite features coffered ceiling and Master bath with walk-in closets.
- Full basement.

Plan CPS-1155-C

Bedrooms: 3	Baths: 2

Space:	
Total living area:	1,848 sq. ft.
Basement:	1,848 sq. ft.
Garage:	513 sq. ft.

Exterior Wall Framing:	2x6

Foundation options:
Standard basement.
(Foundation & framing conversion diagram available — see order form.)

Blueprint Price Code:	B

MAIN FLOOR

Plan CPS-1155-C

PRICES AND DETAILS
ON PAGES 12-15

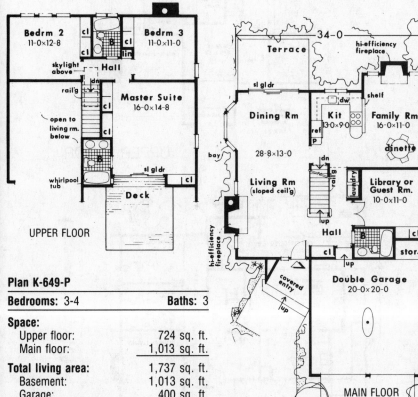

Upper Floor

Bedrm 2
11-0×12-8

Bedrm 3
11-0×11-0

skylight above

Hall

rail'g

dn

open to living rm. below

Master Suite
16-0×14-8

sl gl dr

whirlpool tub

Deck

UPPER FLOOR

Plan K-649-P

Bedrooms: 3-4	**Baths:** 3

Space:

Upper floor:	724 sq. ft.
Main floor:	1,013 sq. ft.

Total living area:	**1,737 sq. ft.**
Basement:	1,013 sq. ft.
Garage:	400 sq. ft.

Exterior Wall Framing: 2x4
(with 2x6 option included)

Foundation options:
Standard basement.
Slab.
(Foundation & framing conversion
diagram available — see order form.)

Blueprint Price Code:	B

Main Floor

34-0

Terrace

hi-efficiency fireplace

sl gl dr

Dining Rm

28-8×13-0

Kit
13-0×9-0

dw

shelf

ref

P

Family Rm
16-0×11-0

Terr.

dinette

bay

Living Rm
(sloped ceil'g)

dn

rail'g

laundry

Library or Guest Rm.
10-0×11-0

sl gl dr

up

hi-efficiency fireplace

Hall

cl

B

cl

stor.

cl

up

covered entry

up

Double Garage
20-0×20-0

52-8

MAIN FLOOR

Contemporary Features Unusual Roof Deck

- Upstairs master suite includes a private deck, sunken into a cavity in the garage roof.
- Balance of the plan is also designed to be open and airy.
- The living room has a sloped ceiling and an impressive fireplace, and flows into the dining area.
- The kitchen, family room and dinette area function well together for family dining and other activities.
- A library or guest bedroom with a full bath also offers the option of becoming a home office.

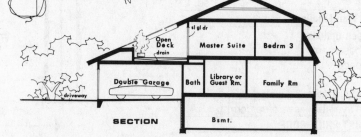

Open Deck
drain

sl gl dr

Master Suite

Bedrm 3

Double Garage

driveway

Bath

Library or Guest Rm.

Family Rm

SECTION

Bsmt.

TO ORDER THIS BLUEPRINT, CALL TOLL-FREE 1-800-547-5570

Plan K-649-P

PRICES AND DETAILS ON PAGES 12-15

185

Sunlit Elegance

- This elegant contemporary design offers just about all the amenities today's families expect in a home.
- The formal dining room is large enough for a good-sized dinner party.
- The living room is sunken and vaulted and includes a handsome fireplace.
- The spacious kitchen includes a large island and a pantry, and is open to the vaulted family room.
- Upstairs, the master bedroom is impressive, with a private master bath, large closets and easy access to a private deck. (If the greenhouse is built, stairs go from the master bath down to the hot tub.)
- The second floor also includes a roomy library and a bonus room or extra bedroom.
- The plan also offers an optional solar greenhouse, which may contain a hot tub or simply offer a great space for green plants and sunbathing.

Plan S-8217

Bedrooms: 3-4	Baths: 2
Living Area:	
Upper floor	789 sq. ft.
Main floor	1,709 sq. ft.
Bonus room	336 sq. ft.
Total Living Area:	**2,834 sq. ft.**
Partial basement	1,242 sq. ft.
Garage	441 sq. ft.
Exterior Wall Framing:	2x6

Foundation Options:

Partial basement
Crawlspace
Slab
(Typical foundation & framing conversion diagram available—see order form.)

BLUEPRINT PRICE CODE: D

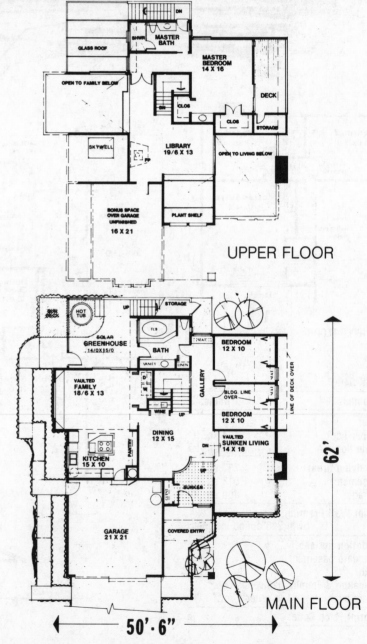

UPPER FLOOR

MAIN FLOOR

50'-6"

62'

Exciting Exterior Options

- Two exciting elevations are available with this striking stucco design. (Both are included with blueprint purchase.)
- The stately, covered front entry and elegant window treatments are just the beginning of the excitement. Inside is a huge formal living area with volume ceilings.
- The adjoining family room offers built-in shelving and provisions for an optional corner fireplace or media center. Triple sliders open to the rear covered patio.
- The eat-in country kitchen overlooks the family room and features a handy serving counter, a pantry and a laundry closet.
- Separated from the two secondary bedrooms, the master bedroom is a quiet retreat. It offers patio access and an oversized private bath with a huge walk-in closet, a big corner tub and separate vanities that flank a sitting area.

ELEVATION A

ELEVATION B

Plan HDS-99-140

Bedrooms: 3	**Baths:** 2

Living Area:

Main floor	1,550 sq. ft.
Total Living Area:	**1,550 sq. ft.**
Garage	475 sq. ft.
Exterior Wall Framing:	2x4

Foundation Options:

Slab

(Typical foundation & framing conversion diagram available—see order form.)

BLUEPRINT PRICE CODE: B

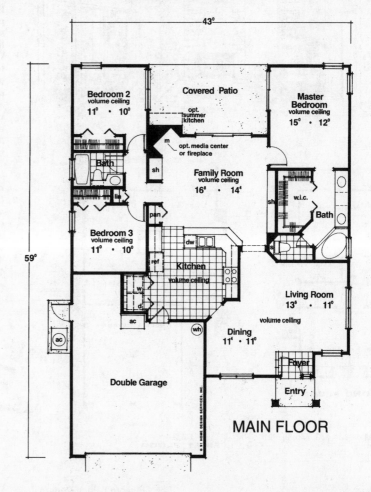

MAIN FLOOR

TO ORDER THIS BLUEPRINT,
CALL TOLL-FREE 1-800-547-5570

Plan HDS-99-140

PRICES AND DETAILS
ON PAGES 12-15

187

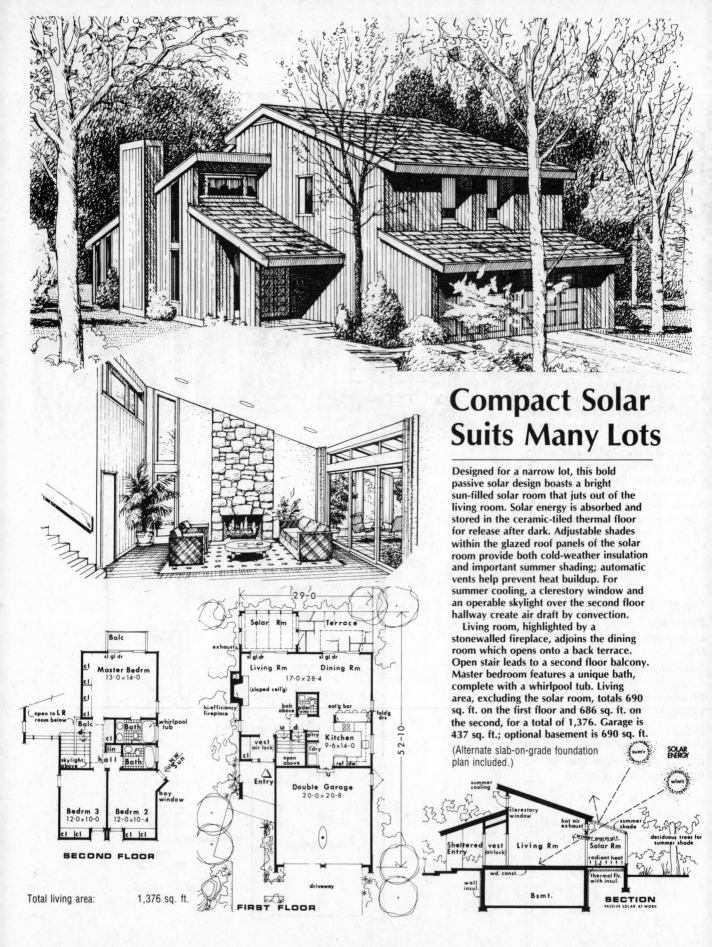

Compact Solar Suits Many Lots

Designed for a narrow lot, this bold passive solar design boasts a bright sun-filled solar room that juts out of the living room. Solar energy is absorbed and stored in the ceramic-tiled thermal floor for release after dark. Adjustable shades within the glazed roof panels of the solar room provide both cold-weather insulation and important summer shading; automatic vents help prevent heat buildup. For summer cooling, a clerestory window and an operable skylight over the second floor hallway create air draft by convection.

Living room, highlighted by a stonewalled fireplace, adjoins the dining room which opens onto a back terrace. Open stair leads to a second floor balcony. Master bedroom features a unique bath, complete with a whirlpool tub. Living area, excluding the solar room, totals 690 sq. ft. on the first floor and 686 sq. ft. on the second, for a total of 1,376. Garage is 437 sq. ft.; optional basement is 690 sq. ft.

(Alternate slab-on-grade foundation plan included.)

SECOND FLOOR

FIRST FLOOR

Total living area: 1,376 sq. ft.

SECTION
PASSIVE SOLAR AT WORK

Blueprint Price Code A
Plan K-521-C

PRICES AND DETAILS ON PAGES 12-15

A Taste of Europe

- A European exterior and modern interior enhance this beautiful one-story home.
- The huge, central Great Room has a 10' ceiling that extends into the foyer and formal dining room; a large fireplace and entrance to the rear porch are other attractions in the Great Room.
- Traffic flows smoothly into the bayed nook and kitchen for an open feeling; a pantry and counter bar are nice extras.
- The private master suite opens out to the porch; an attached luxury bath features an exciting corner garden tub, separate shower, dual vanities and generous walk-in closet.
- Two additional bedrooms, a full bath and a front study or home office complete the plan.

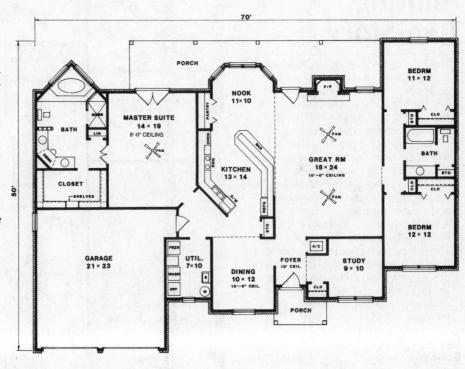

Plan VL-2162		
Bedrooms: 3		**Baths:** 2
Space:		
Main floor		2,162 sq. ft.
Total Living Area		**2,162 sq. ft.**
Garage		498 sq. ft.
Exterior Wall Framing		2x4

Foundation options:

Crawlspace

Slab

(Foundation & framing conversion diagram available—see order form.)

Blueprint Price Code   C

Alluring
Two-Story

- This dramatic contemporary is adorned with staggered rooflines that overlap and outline large expanses of glass.
- The interior features a floor plan that is both practical and functional, with individual rooms equally exciting.
- Flanking the two-story-high foyer are a formal dining room and a sunken living room. The living room boasts a cathedral ceiling and unfolds to a sunken family room with a fireplace and a patio overlook.
- A bright breakfast area and a U-shaped kitchen adjoin the family room.
- The second level features a spacious master bedroom with dual closets and a private bath. Two secondary bedrooms, another bath and an optional expansion room above the garage are also included.

Plan AX-8596-A

Bedrooms: 3+	Baths: 2½
Living Area:	
Upper floor	738 sq. ft.
Main floor	1,160 sq. ft.
Bonus room	226 sq. ft.
Total Living Area:	**2,124 sq. ft.**
Standard basement	1,160 sq. ft.
Garage	465 sq. ft.
Exterior Wall Framing:	2x4

Foundation Options:

Standard basement

(All plans can be built with your choice of foundation and framing. A generic conversion diagram is available. See order form.)

BLUEPRINT PRICE CODE: C

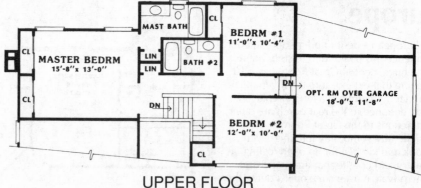

UPPER FLOOR

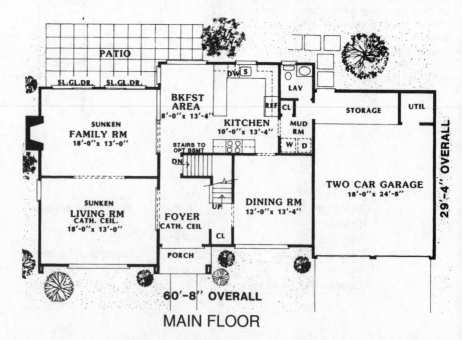

MAIN FLOOR

Smart Design for Sloping Lot

- This design is perfect for a narrow, sloping lot.
- The main entry opens to a spacious, vaulted living area. A comfortable Great Room and a sunny dining area merge with corner windows that create a dramatic boxed bay. Another attention-getter is the cozy woodstove in the corner of the beautiful Great Room.
- The dining area offers sliding glass doors that extend family activities or entertaining to the adjoining deck.
- The dining area flows into the kitchen, which features a vaulted ceiling and a windowed sink that overlooks the deck.
- Two bedrooms are located at the back of the home, each with a private, skylighted bath. The master bedroom also has a walk-in wardrobe, a lovely window seat and deck access.
- A vaulted, skylighted hall leads to the stairway to the basement, where there are a third bedroom and another full bathroom. A very large shop/storage area and a two-car garage are also included. An extra bonus is the carport/storage area below the deck.

Plan P-529-2D

Bedrooms: 3	Baths: 3
Living Area:	
Main floor	1,076 sq. ft.
Daylight basement	597 sq. ft.
Total Living Area:	**1,673 sq. ft.**
Tuck-under garage	425 sq. ft.
Exterior Wall Framing:	2x6
Foundation Options:	
Daylight basement	
BLUEPRINT PRICE CODE:	B

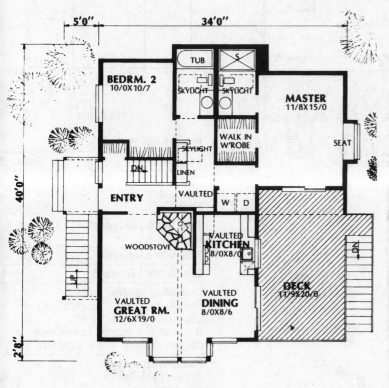

MAIN FLOOR

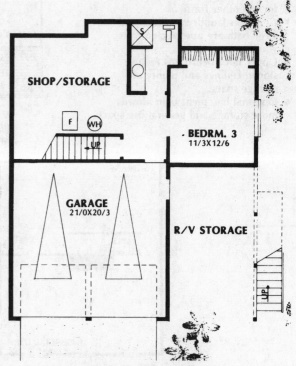

DAYLIGHT BASEMENT

Handsome Chalet Design Features View

- Roomy floor plan will make this chalet something you'll yearn for all year long.
- Massive fireplace in living room is a pleasant welcome after a day in the cold outdoors.
- Open kitchen has two entrances for smoother traffic.
- Generous laundry facilities and large bath are unexpected frills you'll appreciate.
- Upper floor bedrooms feature sloped ceilings and plenty of storage space.
- Optional basement plan affords more storage and general use space.

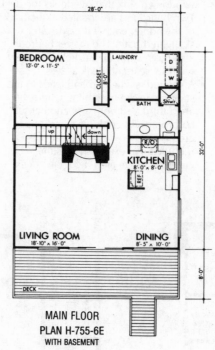

28'-0"

BEDROOM
13'-0" x 11'-5"

LAUNDRY

D / W

CLOSET 8'-0"

BATH

Shwr

up / down

K/D

KITCHEN
8'-0" x 8'-0"

REF.

32'-0"

LIVING ROOM
18'-10" x 16'-0"

DINING
8'-5" x 10'-0"

8'-0"

DECK

MAIN FLOOR
PLAN H-755-6E
WITH BASEMENT

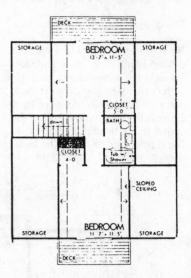

DECK

STORAGE

BEDROOM
13'-7" x 11'-5"

STORAGE

CLOSET 5'-0"

down

BATH

CLOSET 4'-0"

Tub w/ Shower

SLOPED CEILING

STORAGE

BEDROOM
11'-7" x 11'-5"

STORAGE

DECK

UPPER FLOOR

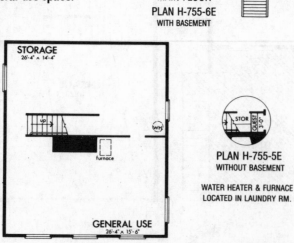

STORAGE
26'-4" x 14'-4"

up

furnace

WH

GENERAL USE
26'-4" x 15'-6"

BASEMENT

STOR

GUEST 3'-0"

PLAN H-755-5E
WITHOUT BASEMENT

WATER HEATER & FURNACE
LOCATED IN LAUNDRY RM.

Plans H-755-5E & -6E

Bedrooms: 3	Baths: 2
Space:	
Upper floor:	454 sq. ft.
Main floor:	896 sq. ft.
Total without basement:	1,350 sq. ft.
Basement:	896 sq. ft.
Total with basement:	2,246 sq. ft.
Exterior Wall Framing:	2x4

Foundation options:
Daylight basement (Plan H-755-6E).
Crawlspace (Plan H-755-5E).
(Foundation & framing conversion diagram available — see order form.)

Blueprint Price Code:
Without basement:	A
With basement:	C

Covered Wraparound Deck Featured

- A covered deck spans this home from the main entrance to the kitchen door.
- An over-sized fireplace is the focal point of the living room, which merges into an expandable dining area.
- The kitchen is tucked into one corner, but open counter space allows visual contact with living areas beyond.
- Two good-sized main-floor bedrooms are furnished with sufficient closet space.
- The basement level adds a third bedroom in an additional 673 sq. ft. of living space.

Plan H-806-2

Bedrooms: 3	Baths: 1
Living Area:	
Main floor	952 sq. ft.
Daylight basement	673 sq. ft.
Total Living Area:	**1,625 sq. ft.**
Garage	279 sq. ft.
Exterior Wall Framing:	2x6

Foundation Options:

Daylight basement
(Typical foundation & framing conversion diagram available—see order form.)

BLUEPRINT PRICE CODE: B

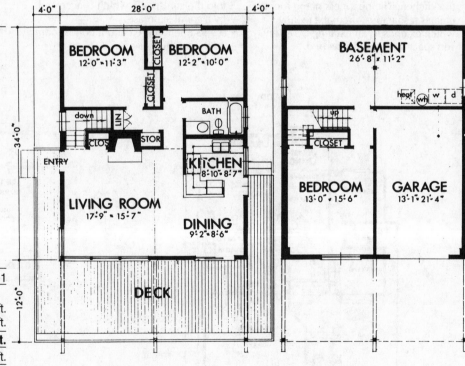

MAIN FLOOR

DAYLIGHT BASEMENT

Contemporary Elegance

- This striking contemporary design combines vertical siding with elegant traditional overtones.
- Inside, an expansive activity area is created with the joining of the vaulted living room, the family/dining room and the kitchen. The openness of the rooms creates a spacious, dramatic feeling, which extends to an exciting two-story sun space and a patio beyond.

- A convenient utility/service area near the garage includes a clothes-sorting counter, a deep sink and ironing space.
- Two main-floor bedrooms share a bright bath.
- The master suite includes a sumptuous skylighted bath with two entrances. The tub is uniquely positioned on an angled wall, while the shower and toilet are secluded behind a pocket door. An optional overlook provides views down into the sun space, which is accessed by a spiral staircase.
- A versatile loft area and a bonus room complete this design.

Plan LRD-1971	
Bedrooms: 3+	**Baths: 2**
Living Area:	
Upper floor	723 sq. ft.
Main floor	1,248 sq. ft.
Sun space	116 sq. ft.
Bonus room	225 sq. ft.
Total Living Area:	**2,312 sq. ft.**
Standard basement	1,248 sq. ft.
Garage	483 sq. ft.
Exterior Wall Framing:	2x6

Foundation Options:

Standard basement
Crawlspace
(All plans can be built with your choice of foundation and framing. A generic conversion diagram is available. See order form.)

BLUEPRINT PRICE CODE:	C

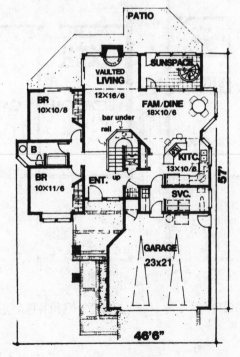

MAIN FLOOR

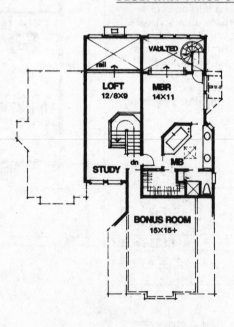

UPPER FLOOR

Plan LRD-1971

Elegant Arches

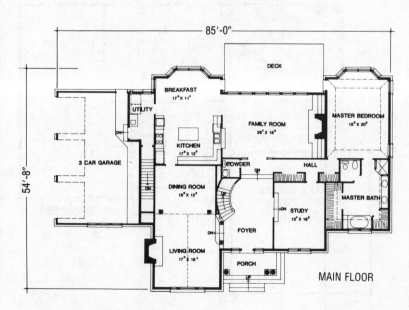

UPPER FLOOR

MAIN FLOOR

- Gracious arched windows and entry portico create a rhythm and style on this brick-clad exterior.
- An elegant curved staircase with balcony bridge overhead lend interest to the raised entry foyer.
- Two steps down to the left of the foyer lies the cathedral — vaulted living room with fireplace and formal dining room defined with column separation.
- The quiet main floor master wing features another bay window, coved ceiling, walk-in closets, and well-planned private bath.
- The island kitchen overlooks the bay-windowed breakfast wall of the adjacent family room.

Plan DD-3639

Bedrooms: 4 +	Baths: 3½

Space:	
Upper floor:	868 sq. ft.
Main floor:	2,771 sq. ft.

Total living area:	3,639 sq. ft.
Basement:	2,771 sq. ft.
Garage:	approx. 790 sq. ft.

Exterior Wall Framing:	2x4

Ceiling Heights:	
Upper floor:	8'
Main floor:	9'

Foundation options:
Standard basement
Crawlspace
Slab
(Foundation & framing conversion diagram available — see order form.)

Blueprint Price Code:	F

Affordable Country-Style

- This charming country-inspired home is economical to build and requires only a small lot.
- The powder room and the guest closet are conveniently located near the foyer and near the combination living/dining room with boxed-out window.
- A low partition visually separates the kitchen from the adjacent family room, which features an angled fireplace, a cathedral ceiling with skylight, and sliding glass doors that open to the rear yard.
- The second floor features an optional loft or fourth bedroom.

Plan AX-8923-A

Bedrooms: 3-4	Baths: 2½
Living Area:	
Upper floor	853 sq. ft.
Main floor	1,199 sq. ft.
Optional loft/bedroom	180 sq. ft.
Total Living Area:	**2,232 sq. ft.**
Standard basement	1,184 sq. ft.
Garage	420 sq. ft.
Exterior Wall Framing:	2x4

Foundation Options:

Standard basement
Slab
(Typical foundation & framing conversion diagram available—see order form.)

BLUEPRINT PRICE CODE: **C**

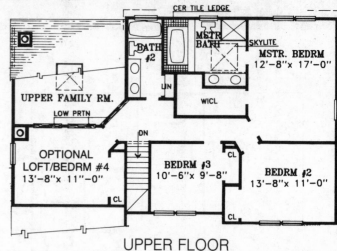

UPPER FLOOR

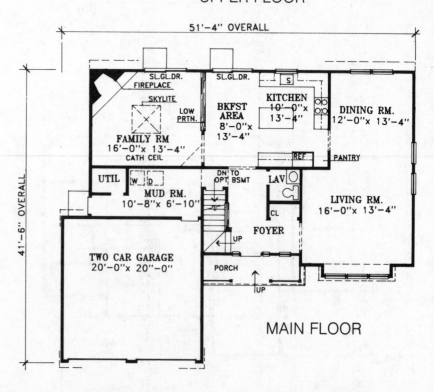

MAIN FLOOR

Plan AX-8923-A

PRICES AND DETAILS ON PAGES 12-15

Easy Living

- Large, beautiful living area with sloped ceiling and fireplace lies five steps below entry and sleeping areas.
- Attached dining room and kitchen separated by eating bar.
- Convenient main floor laundry near kitchen and side entrance.
- Secluded master suite includes personal bath and private access to sun deck.

Plans H-925-1 & -1A

Bedrooms: 3	Baths: 2

Space:

Upper floor:	288 sq. ft.
Main floor:	951 sq. ft.
Total living area:	**1,239 sq. ft.**
Basement:	approx. 951 sq. ft.
Garage:	266 sq. ft.

Exterior Wall Framing:	2x4

Foundation options:
Daylight basement (Plan H-925-1).
Crawlspace (Plan H-925-1A).
(Foundation & framing conversion diagram available — see order form.)

Blueprint Price Code:	A

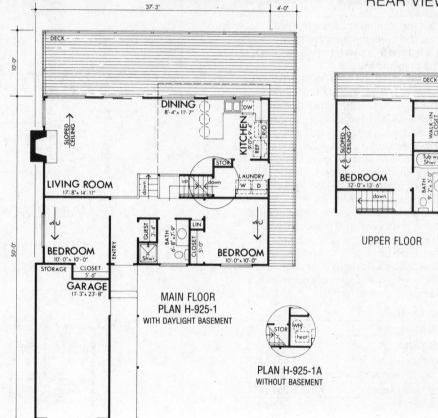

MAIN FLOOR
PLAN H-925-1
WITH DAYLIGHT BASEMENT

PLAN H-925-1A
WITHOUT BASEMENT

UPPER FLOOR

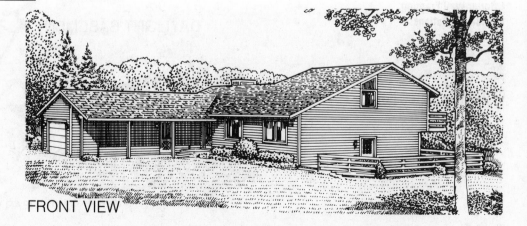

FRONT VIEW

Graceful Wings

- Past the inviting entrance to this graceful contemporary home, the skylighted foyer welcomes guests into the dramatic interior.
- Off the foyer, the tray-ceilinged dining room is graced by a wall of windows. The spacious country kitchen has a bright skylight and sliding glass doors to an enormous wraparound deck.
- The spectacular vaulted Great Room's 17-ft. ceiling soars to greet a row of large clerestory windows. Flanked by sliding glass doors, the exciting corner fireplace warms the area.
- The main-floor sleeping wing contains three bedrooms. The master bedroom has a tray ceiling, a private bath and two closets.
- The optional daylight basement includes a den, two more bedrooms, a family room and more!

Plan AX-97837

Bedrooms: 3+	Baths: 2½-3½
Living Area:	
Main floor	1,816 sq. ft.
Daylight basement (finished)	1,435 sq. ft.
Total Living Area:	**1,816/3,251 sq. ft.**
Utility and storage	381 sq. ft.
Garage	400 sq. ft.
Exterior Wall Framing:	2x4

Foundation Options:

Daylight basement

Crawlspace

Slab

(All plans can be built with your choice of foundation and framing. A generic conversion diagram is available. See order form.)

BLUEPRINT PRICE CODE: B/E

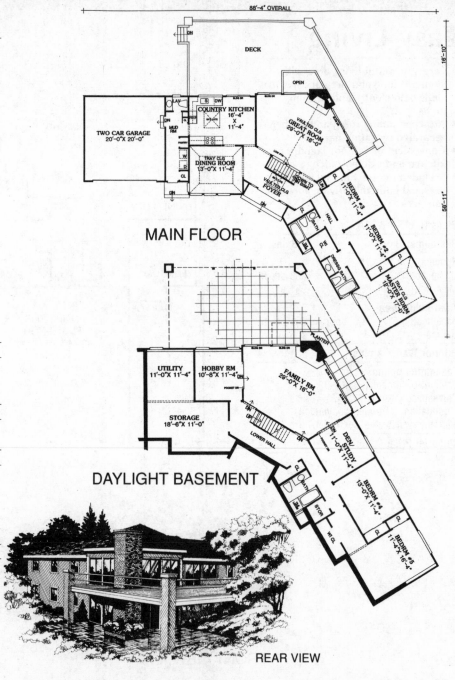

MAIN FLOOR

DAYLIGHT BASEMENT

REAR VIEW

TO ORDER THIS BLUEPRINT, CALL TOLL-FREE 1-800-547-5570

Plan AX-97837

PRICES AND DETAILS ON PAGES 12-15

Sun-Drenched Spaces

- Articulate rooflines and stone accents complement this two-story.
- Inside, radiant spaces stem from the use of glazed sun roofs and expansive windows and doors.
- The huge living room and dining room flow together for a spacious setting accentuated by a big fireplace and a cathedral ceiling. The dining room features a sunny bay and a rear sun roof and terrace.
- A second fireplace in the family room generates a warm and cozy atmosphere in the merging kitchen and bayed dinette.
- Four bedrooms and two skylighted baths share the upper level.

Plan K-651-U

Bedrooms: 4	Baths: 2 ½
Space:	
Upper floor	930 sq. ft.
Main floor	1,144 sq. ft.
Total Living Area	**2,074 sq. ft.**
Basement	1,082 sq. ft.
Garage	460 sq. ft.
Exterior Wall Framing	2x4 or 2x6

Foundation options:
Standard Basement
Slab
(Foundation & framing conversion diagram available—see order form.)

Blueprint Price Code	C

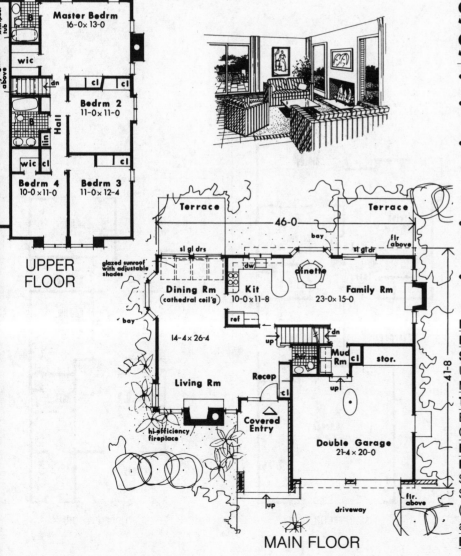

UPPER FLOOR

Master Bedrm 16-0 x 13-0
wic
Bedrm 2 11-0 x 11-0
Hall
Bedrm 4 10-0 x 11-0
Bedrm 3 11-0 x 12-4

MAIN FLOOR

Terrace
Terrace
46-0
bay
glazed sunroof with adjustable shades
Dining Rm (cathedral ceil'g) 14-4 x 26-4
Kit 10-0 x 11-8
dinette
Family Rm 23-0 x 15-0
ref
Living Rm
hi-efficiency fireplace
Recep
Covered Entry
Mud Rm
stor.
Double Garage 21-4 x 20-0
driveway
41-8

Compact Two-Story with Spanish Touch

- Living room has vaulted ceiling and wet bar.
- Large study available for home office.
- Master bedroom opens to private balcony, and includes large walk-in closet and private bath.
- Upstairs hallway looks down into living room.

Plan Q-1707-1A

Bedrooms: 3	Baths: 2½

Space:

Upper floor:	831 sq. ft.
Main floor:	876 sq. ft.
Total living area:	**1,707 sq. ft.**
Garage:	466 sq. ft.

Exterior Wall Framing:	2x4

Foundation options:
Slab only.
(Foundation & framing conversion diagram available — see order form.)

Blueprint Price Code:	B

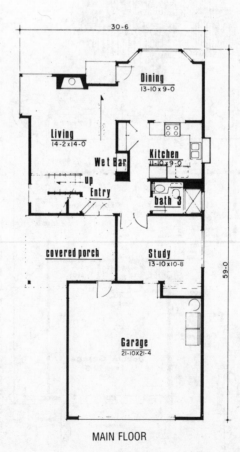

MAIN FLOOR

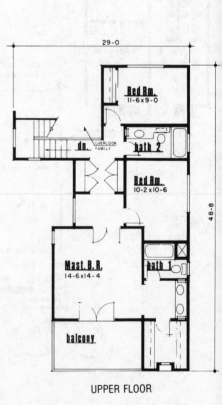

UPPER FLOOR

Plan Q-1707-1A

PRICES AND DETAILS
ON PAGES 12-15

Arresting Angles

- This arresting design, with its towering windows and vertical angles, is filled with light and luxurious spaces.
- A bridge on the upper floor visually separates the soaring reception area from the living room, which features a cathedral ceiling. The floor-to-ceiling stone-faced fireplace is framed by glass, starting with sliding glass doors and rising to triangular-shaped windows.
- The kitchen is flanked by the casual dinette and the formal dining room. The dining room is open to the living room, and both rooms view out to a partially covered backyard terrace.
- A den overlooking a side terrace and a library/guest room with a nearby bath add to the main floor's versatility.
- The upper floor is highlighted by great views and a superb master suite. The spacious sleeping area overlooks the living room below and accesses a private deck. The luxurious master bath includes a whirlpool tub, a separate dressing area and a walk-in closet.

Plan K-653-U

Bedrooms: 3+	Baths: 3
Living Area:	
Upper floor	844 sq. ft.
Main floor	1,208 sq. ft.
Total Living Area:	**2,052 sq. ft.**
Standard basement	1,208 sq. ft.
Garage	427 sq. ft.
Exterior Wall Framing:	2x4 or 2x6

Foundation Options:

Standard basement

Slab

(All plans can be built with your choice of foundation and framing. A generic conversion diagram is available. See order form.)

BLUEPRINT PRICE CODE:	C

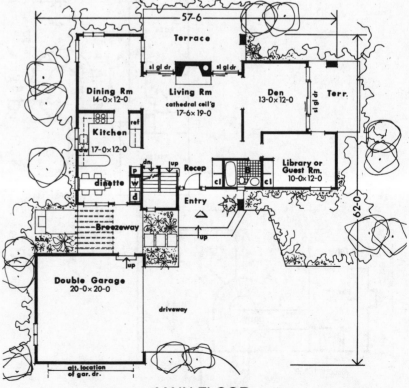

UPPER FLOOR

MAIN FLOOR

Plan Q-3811-1A

Bedrooms: 3-4	Baths: 4

Space:

Upper floor:	1,086 sq. ft.
Main floor:	2,725 sq. ft.
Total living area:	3,811 sq. ft.
Garage:	888 sq. ft.
Exterior Wall Framing:	2x4

Foundation options:
Slab only.
(Foundation & framing conversion diagram available — see order form.)

Blueprint Price Code:	E

Updated Spanish Traditional

- Here's a two-story version of the traditional Spanish hacienda, with space to spare for any family activity.
- The expansive foyer is highlighted by a beautiful semi-circular stairway.
- The spacious living room features a high, vaulted ceiling.
- A formal dining room is large enough for a good-sized dinner party.

- A huge family room also features a cathedral ceiling.
- The large kitchen includes a work island and sunny breakfast nook.
- A superb master bedroom is isolated for maximum privacy, and includes a majestic master bath and a huge closet.
- An upstairs library with a full bath could serve as a fourth bedroom if needed.

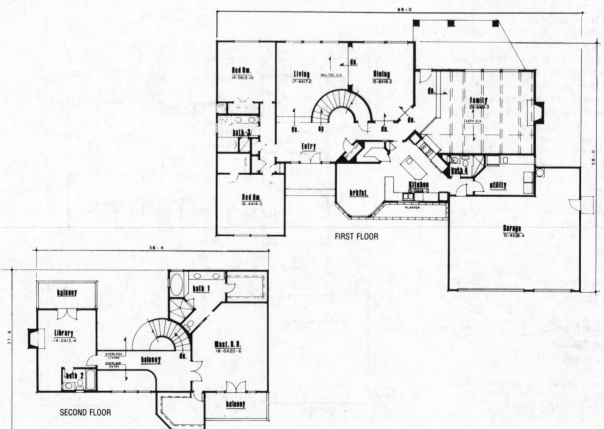

FIRST FLOOR

SECOND FLOOR

Plan Q-3811-1A

PRICES AND DETAILS
ON PAGES 12-15

Smooth Transitional

- Big, bright windows and an up-to-date floor plan give this transitional country home its modern appeal.
- Illuminated by a large clerestory window, the inviting two-story-high entry flows into the living room.
- Enhanced by a 12-ft.-high vaulted ceiling, the living room is separated from the vaulted formal dining room by a columned arch. All other main-floor rooms are expanded by 9-ft. ceilings.
- The adjacent island kitchen includes a sunny bay-windowed breakfast area, a pantry and a stylish angled counter.
- Warmed by a handsome fireplace, the spacious family room features a built-in media center and sliding glass doors to a backyard deck.
- Upstairs, the luxurious master bedroom boasts a bayed sitting area. The vaulted master bath has a spa tub, a sit-down shower and a dual-sink vanity.
- Two additional bedrooms share another full bath. The main-floor den can serve as a fourth bedroom, if needed.

Plan UDG-93004

Bedrooms: 3+	Baths: 3
Living Area:	
Upper floor	939 sq. ft.
Main floor	1,448 sq. ft.
Total Living Area:	**2,387 sq. ft.**
Standard basement	1,448 sq. ft.
Garage	420 sq. ft.
Exterior Wall Framing:	2x4

Foundation Options:

Standard basement

(All plans can be built with your choice of foundation and framing.
A generic conversion diagram is available. See order form.)

BLUEPRINT PRICE CODE:	C

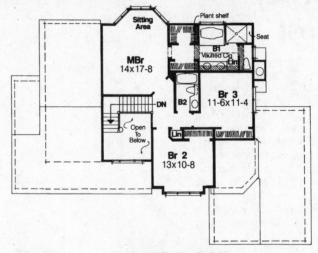

UPPER FLOOR

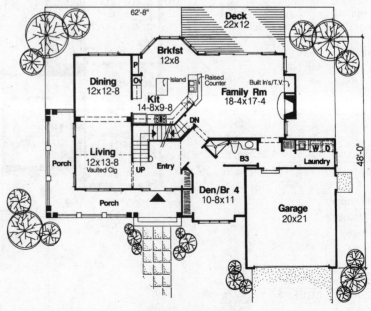

MAIN FLOOR

High Style, Low Cost

- Decorative vents, attractive window trim and shutters, and a nice blend of brick and wood create a great curb appeal for this affordable home.
- Vaulted ceilings give high style to the home's interior, starting with the Great Room and the adjoining dining room. This large living area is accentuated with a see-through gas fireplace and a ceiling that slopes to 13 feet. The work desk has a cozy location near the fireplace and is topped with a plant ledge. A French door opens to a backyard patio.
- An island with a vegetable sink sits at the center of the neatly designed kitchen. A pantry and a nice-sized laundry room are close at hand. In the basement option, the stairway would be located near the entrance from the garage, as shown above.
- The sleeping wing offers three vaulted bedrooms and two full baths.

Plan U-93-101

Bedrooms: 3	Baths: 2
Living Area:	
Main floor	1,453 sq. ft.
Total Living Area:	**1,453 sq. ft.**
Standard basement	1,430 sq. ft.
Garage	528 sq. ft.
Exterior Wall Framing:	2x6

Foundation Options:

Standard basement
Crawlspace
Slab

(All plans can be built with your choice of foundation and framing. A generic conversion diagram is available. See order form.)

BLUEPRINT PRICE CODE: **A**

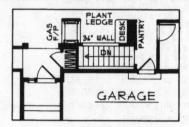

BASEMENT STAIRWAY LOCATION

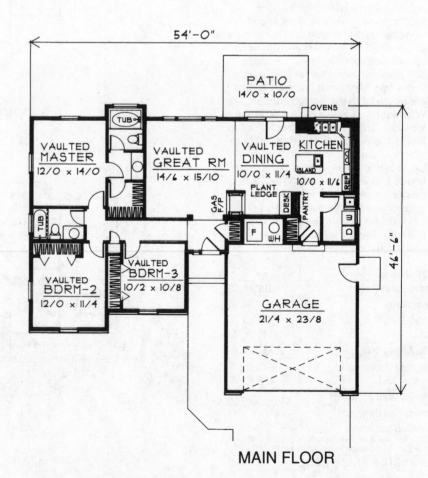

MAIN FLOOR

Spacious Single-Story

- Vaulted ceilings distinguish this bright, open single-story home.
- Designed for both formal entertaining and casual family living, this airy home features an inviting stone-hearth fireplace in the living room and a dramatic woodstove in the corner of the family room.
- The living room flows into the formal dining room, which boasts a coffered ceiling and a built-in china hutch.
- The efficiently designed kitchen is positioned to serve both the formal and the informal areas. A functional island range, a pantry, a work desk and a serving bar to the large deck are featured in the kitchen.
- A skylight brightens the hallway to the sleeping wing, which includes three bedrooms, an oversized laundry room and two bathrooms. The sumptuous master suite offers a whirlpool garden tub, a double-basin vanity and a huge walk-in closet.

Plan LMB-9576-T

Bedrooms: 3+	Baths: 2
Living Area:	
Main floor	2,185 sq. ft.
Total Living Area:	**2,185 sq. ft.**
Garage	600 sq. ft.
Exterior Wall Framing:	2x6

Foundation Options:

Crawlspace
(All plans can be built with your choice of foundation and framing. A generic conversion diagram is available. See order form.)

BLUEPRINT PRICE CODE:	C

MAIN FLOOR

TO ORDER THIS BLUEPRINT, CALL TOLL-FREE 1-800-547-5570

Plan LMB-9576-T

PRICES AND DETAILS ON PAGES 12-15

Plan AX-7622-A

Bedrooms: 3	Baths: 2

Living Area:

Upper floor	343 sq. ft.
Main floor:	924 sq. ft.

Total Living Area:	**1,267 sq. ft.**

Standard basement	924 sq. ft.

Exterior Wall Framing: 2x4

Foundation Options:
Standard basement
Slab
(Typical foundation & framing conversion diagram available—see order form.)

BLUEPRINT PRICE CODE: A

True A-Frame

- This stylish A-frame has perfect outdoor complements including two side porches, one of which is screened, a second floor deck off the attic bedroom and an optional front deck.
- Interior highlights include a 24′ living room with a corner stone fireplace, cathedral ceiling and two sets of sliding glass doors. An attractive circular stairway leads to the second level balcony which overlooks this high-activity area.
- The kitchen offers direct access to the attached porch with built-in stone barbecue for outdoor dining.

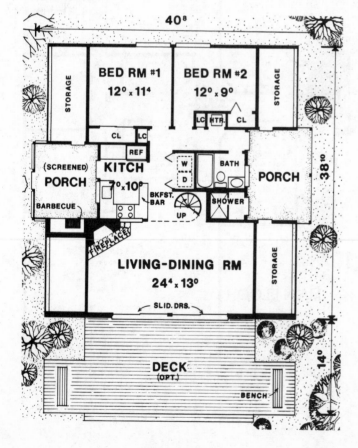

MAIN FLOOR

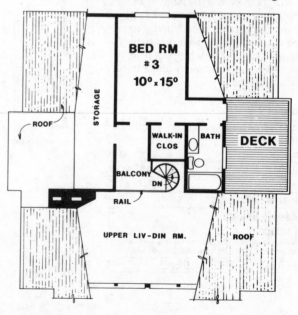

UPPER FLOOR

Modern Country Life

- Classic country features like a wrap-around porch, round louvered vents and a covered entry accent the exterior of this modern home.
- Just past the inviting entry, the spacious two-story-high living room is separated from the dining room by a see-through fireplace. All other first-floor rooms have 9-ft. ceilings.
- The dining room features a bright bay window. The adjacent kitchen, which serves the family room over a stylish counter, has a pantry and corner windows over the sink.
- The family room is brightened by sliding glass doors to a backyard patio. A convenient half-bath and a laundry room are nearby.
- Upstairs, the master bedroom boasts a 10-ft.-high vaulted ceiling. The master bath has a double-sink vanity, a walk-in closet and a linen closet.

Plan AG-1603

Bedrooms: 4	Baths: 2½
Living Area:	
Upper floor	853 sq. ft.
Main floor	789 sq. ft.
Total Living Area:	**1,642 sq. ft.**
Standard basement	760 sq. ft.
Garage	440 sq. ft.
Exterior Wall Framing:	2x4

Foundation Options:

Standard basement

(All plans can be built with your choice of foundation and framing. A generic conversion diagram is available. See order form.)

BLUEPRINT PRICE CODE: B

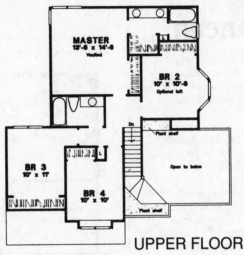

UPPER FLOOR

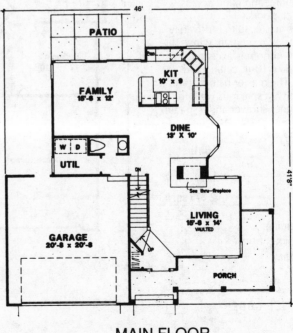

MAIN FLOOR

Creative Mediterranean

- A creative exterior composed of bright stucco with decorative corner quoins, high arched windows and a sleek roofline gives this home its modern Mediterranean look.
- Inside, the floor plan is just as creative. The bright dining area and the central living room are joined at an angle, creating a single wide-open space under a 12-ft.-high volume ceiling.
- The unique island kitchen has a walk-in pantry and a sunny breakfast area, and enjoys the warmth and atmosphere of the adjoining family room.
- The family room is warmed by a corner fireplace and boasts built-in shelves, a 10-ft.-high ceiling and patio access through French doors.
- The luxurious master suite is privately secluded in its own separate wing. The huge master bedroom is accented by large windows, a 10-ft. ceiling and patio access. The master bath features a dual-sink vanity, a spacious walk-in closet, a designer shower and a spa tub.

Plan HDS-99-159

Bedrooms: 3+	Baths: 2½

Living Area:

Main floor	2,373 sq. ft.

Total Living Area:	**2,373 sq. ft.**
Garage	400 sq. ft.

Exterior Wall Framing:

8-in. concrete block and 2x4

Foundation Options:

Slab

(All plans can be built with your choice of foundation and framing. A generic conversion diagram is available. See order form.)

BLUEPRINT PRICE CODE:	**C**

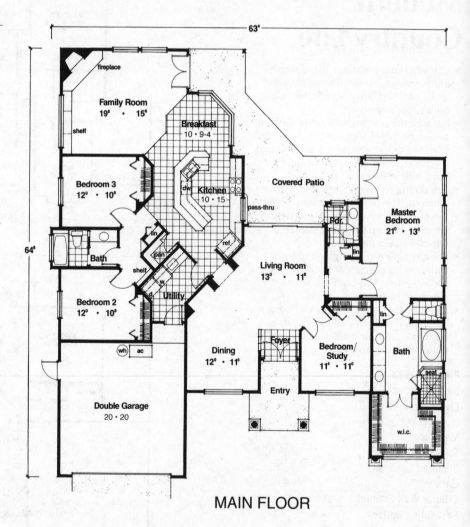

MAIN FLOOR

Plan HDS-99-159

Solar Home Soaks Up Sun

This dramatic one-story passive solar design is finished in vertical and angled wood siding, and is adaptable to many sites and conditions. Solar energy is soaked up and stored in the masonry wall and floors of the south-facing activity area and master suite. To ensure heat retention, heavy insulation is specified for ceilings and walls; sheltered entry and air-lock vestibule are planned; fireplace is the high-efficiency heat-circulating type, using outside air for combustion.

For cooling, eave overhang keeps out unwanted heat in summer. High, operable clerestory windows in the sun garden create natural ventilation. The open, interflowing plan features cathedral ceilings in the living and family rooms. Three bedrooms and two baths are ideally isolated in a private wing. Living area, excluding solarium and sun garden, is 1883 sq. ft.; garage, mud room, etc., 533 sq. ft.; optional basement, 807 sq. ft.

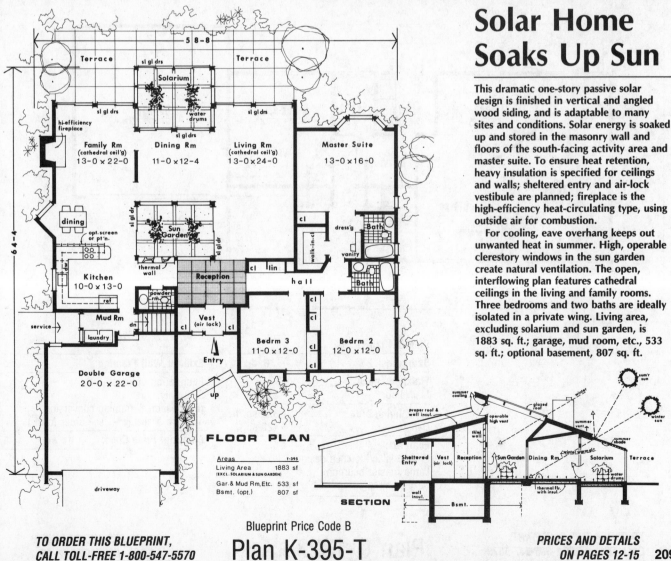

FLOOR PLAN

Areas	T-395
Living Area	1883 sf
(EXCL. SOLARIUM & SUN GARDEN)	
Gar. & Mud Rm,Etc.	533 sf
Bsmt. (opt.)	807 sf

SECTION

Blueprint Price Code B

Plan K-395-T

PRICES AND DETAILS ON PAGES 12-15

Ranch Style with Spacious Great Room

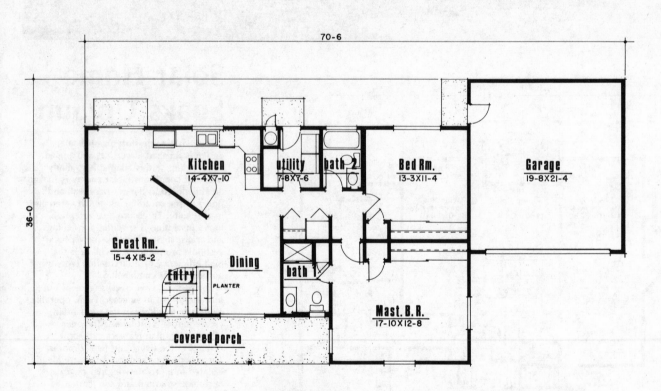

Plan Q-1323-1A

Bedrooms: 2	**Baths:** 2

Finished space:
Main floor: 1,323 sq. ft.

Total living area: 1,323 sq. ft.
Garage: 420 sq. ft.

Features:
Unique island kitchen design.
Large master bedroom.
Cozy covered porch.

Exterior Wall Framing: 2x4

Foundation options:
Slab only.
(Foundation & framing conversion
diagram available — see order form.)

Blueprint Price Code: A

Handsome Ranch Offers Symmetry

- A dramatic facade with stone chimney, vertical siding and stone veneer accents gives this ranch a distinctive custom appearance.
- Double doors at the entry open to a skylit gallery and a well-zoned floor plan.
- The formal living and dining rooms at the front of the home are highlighted by a vaulted ceiling and a stone-finished fireplace.
- The expansive informal areas at the rear are ideal for casual family living and entertaining. A vaulted ceiling hovers above a sunny, angular dinette area, an open island kitchen and a family room with built-in media center.
- Included in the sleeping wing is an isolated master bedroom with a private terrace and a personal bath with whirlpool tub.

VIEW OF DINETTE AND FAMILY ROOM FROM KITCHEN.

Plan K-673-R

Bedrooms: 3	Baths: 2
Space:	
Main floor	1,704 sq. ft.
Total Living Area	**1,704 sq. ft.**
Basement	1,600 sq. ft.
Garage	400 sq. ft.
Exterior Wall Framing	2x4 or 2x6

Foundation options:
Standard Basement
Slab
(Foundation & framing conversion diagram available—see order form.)
Blueprint Price Code   B

Multi-Level Ideal for Difficult Lot

- This compact design is well suited for a lot that slopes steeply up to the rear.
- Massive open spaces and windows create a light and airy feeling inside.
- A mid-level landing at the entry takes you to the vaulted living room, which offers a pass-through to the kitchen; completing the main level are a dining room, two bedrooms and a bath.
- The master bedroom is an upper level loft arrangement. The attached master bath is entered through double doors and features dual vanities, large tub and separate toilet.
- The basement/lower level houses the garage, utility room and fourth bedroom.

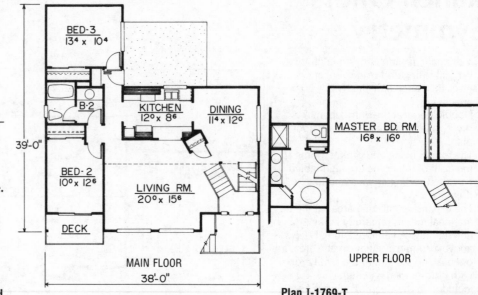

BED-3
13⁴ x 10⁴

B-2

KITCHEN
12⁰ x 8⁶

DINING
11⁴ x 12⁰

39'-0"

BED-2
10⁰ x 12⁶

LIVING RM.
20⁰ x 15⁶

DECK

MAIN FLOOR
38'-0"

MASTER BD. RM.
16⁸ x 16⁰

UPPER FLOOR

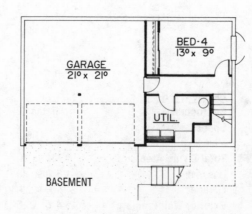

GARAGE
21⁰ x 21⁰

BED-4
13⁰ x 9⁰

UTIL.

BASEMENT

Plan I-1769-T

Bedrooms: 4	Baths: 2

Space:

Upper floor:	418 sq. ft.
Main floor:	1,021 sq. ft.
Lower floor:	330 sq. ft.
Total living area:	1,769 sq. ft.
Garage:	441 sq. ft.

Exterior Wall Framing: 2x6

Foundation options:
Daylight basement.
(Foundation & framing conversion diagram available — see order form.)

Blueprint Price Code: B

Plan I-1769-T

Fashionable Detailing

- A soaring entry portico and unusual window treatments make a bold, fashionable statement for this home.
- Inside, varied ceiling heights and special features lend a distinctive look and feel to each room.
- A 14-ft. stepped ceiling in the foyer gives way to the columned formal dining room with a 12-ft. stepped ceiling. Soffit planters outline the foyer and the living room.
- Decorative columns and a 12-ft. raised ceiling also highlight the living room, where sliding doors open to an expansive covered patio.

- A huge, angular counter with a floating soffit defines the kitchen from the sunny breakfast nook. The adjoining family room has a 10-ft. ceiling and a fireplace accented with high, fixed-glass windows and built-in shelves.
- The master suite has a French door to the patio and an arched opening to the lavish bath. The raised spa tub has louvered shutters to the sleeping area.
- A dual-access bath is across from the den. The two bedrooms at the opposite side of the home enjoy private access to another full bath.

Plan HDS-99-161

Bedrooms: 3+	**Baths:** 3½

Living Area:	
Main floor	2,691 sq. ft.
Total Living Area:	**2,691 sq. ft.**
Garage	520 sq. ft.
Exterior Wall Framing:	2x4

Foundation Options:

Slab

(All plans can be built with your choice of foundation and framing. A generic conversion diagram is available. See order form.)

BLUEPRINT PRICE CODE: D

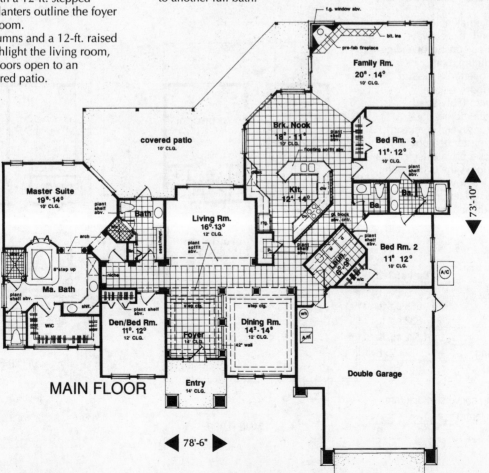

MAIN FLOOR

78'-6"

Compact Chalet

- This compact and efficient leisure home is ideal for weekends or getaways.
- The main living area consists of a large living room and dining room arrangement that overlooks the sun deck and the outdoors.
- Room for four comfortably-sized bedrooms makes the home accommodating for several weekend guests. The large master bedroom on the upper level has a private deck and a balcony that overlooks the living room, fireplace and deck below.
- A second bath and a laundry closet are located near the kitchen on the main floor.

Plan CPS-970-L

Bedrooms: 4	Baths: 1-2
Space:	
Upper floor	688 sq. ft.
Main floor	832 sq. ft.
Total Living Area	**1,520 sq. ft.**
Exterior Wall Framing	2x6

Foundation options:

Crawlspace

(Foundation & framing conversion diagram available—see order form.)

Blueprint Price Code	B

MAIN FLOOR

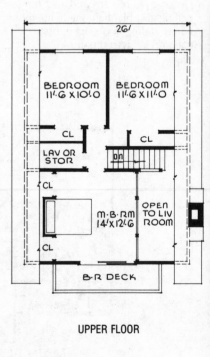

UPPER FLOOR

Quality Space in Compact Four-Bedroom Design

- This well-planned design makes good use of a small lot by putting 1,909 sq. ft. of space on a foundation less than 1,000 sq. ft. in size.
- A large family room/breakfast/kitchen area is great for family dining and other activities.
- Roomy, vaulted living room

includes an impressive fireplace, a feature not often found in homes of this modest size.
- Upstairs, you'll find four bedrooms and a balcony overlooking the living room below.
- The master bedroom includes a private bath and large walk-in closet.

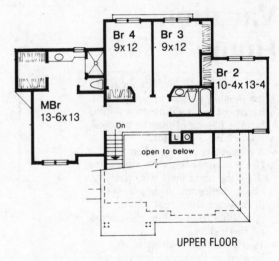

UPPER FLOOR

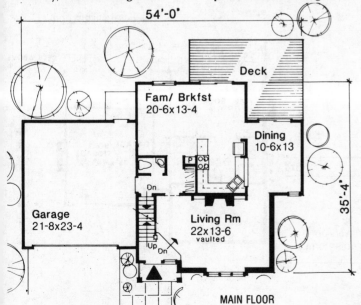

MAIN FLOOR

Plan B-117-8506

Bedrooms: 4	Baths: 2½

Space:

Upper floor:	915 sq. ft.
Main floor:	994 sq. ft.

Total living area:	1,909 sq. ft.
Basement:	994 sq. ft.
Garage:	505 sq. ft.

Exterior Wall Framing:	2x4

Foundation options:
Standard basement only.
(Foundation & framing conversion diagram available — see order form.)

Blueprint Price Code:	B

Year-Round Vacation Home

- This rustic multi-level cabin offers the flexibility of an optional basement for building on a sloping lot; the basement may be omitted if you have a level lot.
- A massive country kitchen and Great Room, each with a fireplace, share the main level with the master bedroom; an impressive deck wraps the Great Room, accessible from sliding glass doors on three sides.
- Two additional bedrooms are located on the upper level; a rec room with fireplace and sliders to an outdoor patio and a garage or boat storage area are found in the optional lower level.

Plan AX-7944-A

Bedrooms: 3	Baths: 2-3

Space:

Upper floor:	457 sq. ft.
Main floor:	1,191 sq. ft.
Total living area: (without basement)	1,648 sq. ft.
Optional basement:	809 sq. ft.
Total living area: (with basement)	2,457 sq. ft.
Garage:	382 sq. ft.

Exterior Wall Framing: 2x4

Foundation options:
Daylight basement.
Slab.
(Foundation & framing conversion diagram available — see order form.)

Blueprint Price Code:

Without basement:	B
With basement:	C

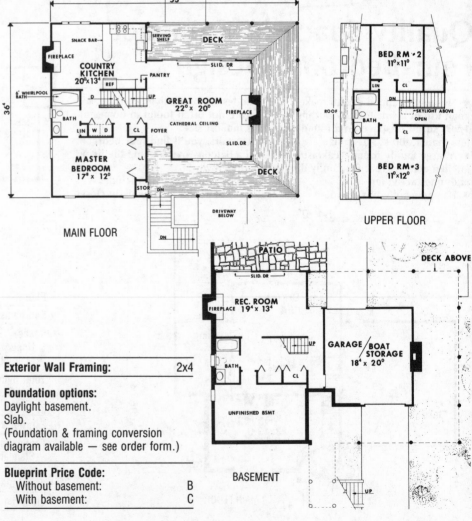

MAIN FLOOR

UPPER FLOOR

BASEMENT

Plan AX-7944-A

PRICES AND DETAILS ON PAGES 12-15

Country-Style Coziness

- Designed as a starter or retirement home, this delightful plan has a charming exterior and an open, airy interior.
- The spacious front porch gives guests a warm welcome and provides added space for relaxing or entertaining. The modified hip roof, half-round louver vent and decorative porch railings are other distinguishing features of the facade.
- Inside, the open dining and living rooms are heightened by dramatic vaulted ceilings. The streamlined kitchen has a snack counter joining it to the dining room. All three rooms reap the benefits of the fireplace.
- A laundry closet is in the hall leading to the three bedrooms. The main bath is close by.
- The master bedroom suite offers its own bath, plus a private patio sequestered behind the garage.

Plan APS-1002

Bedrooms: 3	**Baths:** 2

Space:	
Main floor	1,050 sq. ft.
Total Living Area	**1,050 sq. ft.**
Garage	288 sq. ft.
Exterior Wall Framing	2x4

Foundation options:

Slab

(Foundation & framing conversion diagram available—see order form.)

Blueprint Price Code	A

Floor Plan Labels

- 36 (top width)
- 42 (left height)
- PATIO
- MASTER BEDROOM 11 X 12
- BEDROOM 9 X 12
- W D
- KITCHEN 9 x 11
- BEDROOM 9 x 10
- GARAGE 12 x 24
- VAULT
- VAULT
- DINING 9 x 10
- LIVING 14 x 14

Open Living for Weekend or Forever

- This cozy, 1 1/2 story home is perfect for a weekend retreat, summer home, or casual permanent residence.
- A large, open living area on the first level combines the kitchen, dining area and living room for a spacious setting; sliding doors to the front offer an outdoor relaxing or dining alternative.
- Two bedrooms and a full bath are located at the rear, both with closet space.
- The upper loft would be ideal for a private master bedroom or quiet study area.

Plan CPS-1095

Bedrooms: 2-3	Baths: 1
Space:	
Upper floor	320 sq. ft.
Main floor	784 sq. ft.
Total Living Area	**1,104 sq. ft.**
Basement	784 sq. ft.
Exterior Wall Framing	**2x6**

Foundation options:

Standard Basement

(Foundation & framing conversion diagram available—see order form.)

Blueprint Price Code	**A**

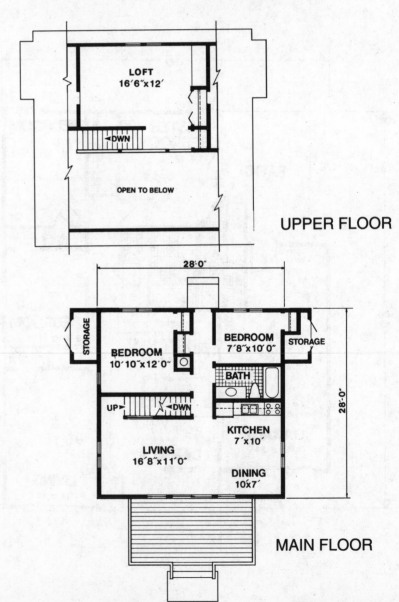

UPPER FLOOR

MAIN FLOOR

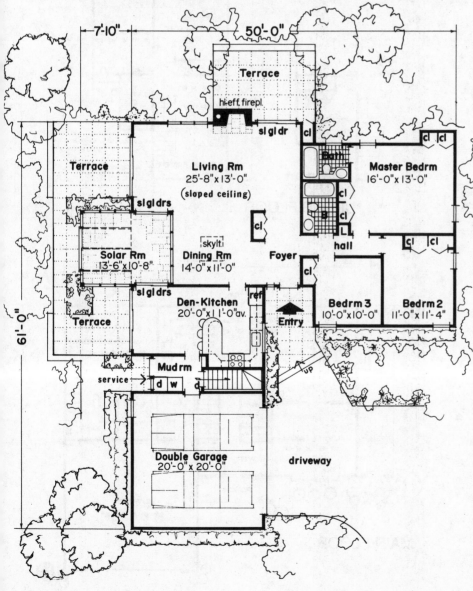

Passive Solar Plan Unites Practicality and Beauty

This handsome one-story passive solar house, characterized by minimal maintenance and smart flexibility, incorporates many energy-saving features. Of main interest is the south-facing solar room that helps provide heat. The interior layout is open and airy with a feeling of expansiveness, allowing plenty of sunlight.

From the foyer, dramatic views begin to unfold. A sloped ceiling in the living room rises overhead as the fireplace provides cozy warmth.

The efficient U-shaped kitchen features a breakfast bar and a bright den that flows into a side terrace. Isolated in a quiet wing are three bedrooms. The master bedroom is highlighted by ample closets and a private bathroom that includes a whirlpool tub. Living area, excluding the solar room, is 1,464 sq. ft.; optional basement, 1,414 sq. ft.; garage, mud room, etc., come to 502 sq. ft.

Total living area:	1,464 sq. ft.
Garage, etc.:	502 sq. ft.
Basement (Optional):	1,414 sq. ft.

Blueprint Price Code A

Plan K-528-C

TO ORDER THIS BLUEPRINT,
CALL TOLL-FREE 1-800-547-5570

PRICES AND DETAILS
ON PAGES 12-15   **219**

Single-Level Conveniences

- This modern-day Cape Cod offers the convenience of single-level living with secondary bedrooms and a separate bath located on the upper level.
- The open floor plan allows a view of the family room fireplace from the kitchen and the bayed dining area.
- Pocket doors between the family room and the living room provide the modest-sized home flexibility. They may be closed for a cozy, private sitting area or opened for frequent traffic flow or entertaining.
- The generous-sized master bedroom is convenient to the kitchen and the laundry room. It features a large walk-in closet and a private bath.
- Joining the two bedrooms on the upper level is a skylighted library loft that overlooks the foyer below. A larger alternate bath may replace the smaller bath, adding 48 sq. ft.

Plan GL-1654-P

Bedrooms: 3	Baths: 2½
Space:	
Upper floor	462 sq. ft.
Main floor	1,192 sq. ft.
Total Living Area	**1,654 sq. ft.**
Exterior Wall Framing	2x4

Foundation options:
Standard Basement
(Foundation & framing conversion diagram available—see order form.)

Blueprint Price Code	B

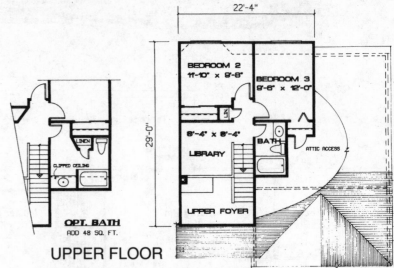

UPPER FLOOR

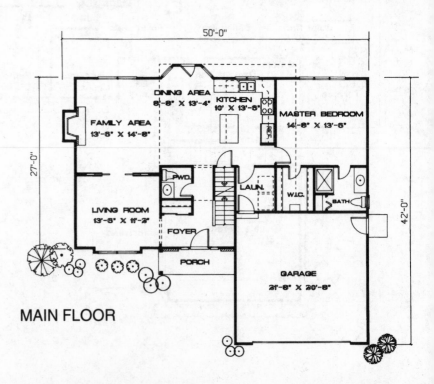

MAIN FLOOR

Plan GL-1654-P

Tri-Level Living

- Upper level provides spectacular private master retreat with deluxe bath, private deck, raised bed area, large walk-in closet and large windows to the rear.
- Main floor includes spacious living room, library and formal dining room.
- Large kitchen adjoins sunny nook. Utility area also on main floor.
- Lower level features large family room, game room, wine cellar, two bedrooms and bath.

Plan NW-855

Bedrooms: 3	Baths: 2½

Space:	
Upper floor:	549 sq. ft.
Main floor:	1,388 sq. ft.
Lower floor:	1,371 sq. ft.
Total living area:	**3,308 sq. ft.**
Garage:	573 sq. ft.

Exterior Wall Framing:	2x6

Foundation options:
Daylight basement only.
(Foundation & framing conversion diagram available — see order form.)

Blueprint Price Code:	E

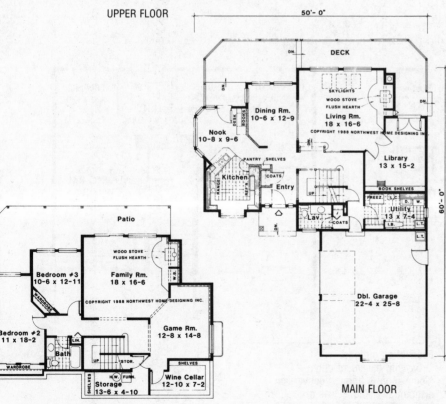

UPPER FLOOR

MAIN FLOOR

LOWER FLOOR

TO ORDER THIS BLUEPRINT,
CALL TOLL-FREE 1-800-547-5570

Plan NW-855

PRICES AND DETAILS
ON PAGES 12-15

221

Three Bedrooms in Daylight Basement

- Front porch offers warm welcome to vaulted entry area.
- Main floor offers plenty of space for family living and entertaining.
- Lower level provides three bedrooms, with the master suite including a private bath and walk-in closet.

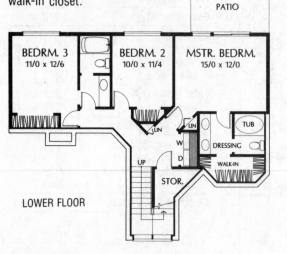

LOWER FLOOR

BEDRM. 3
11/0 x 12/6

BEDRM. 2
10/0 x 11/4

MSTR. BEDRM.
15/0 x 12/0

PATIO

LIN
TUB
DRESSING
WALK-IN
W
D
UP
STOR.

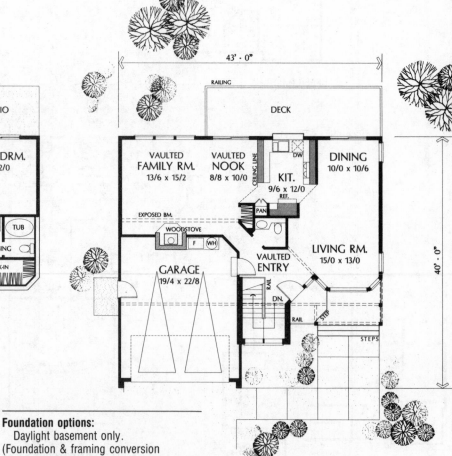

MAIN FLOOR

43' - 0"
40' - 0"

RAILING
DECK

VAULTED FAMILY RM.
13/6 x 15/2

VAULTED NOOK
8/8 x 10/0

KIT.
9/6 x 12/0
REF.

DINING
10/0 x 10/6

DW

CEILING LINE

EXPOSED BM.

WOODSTOVE
F
WH
PAN

GARAGE
19/4 x 22/8

VAULTED ENTRY

LIVING RM.
15/0 x 13/0

RAIL
DN.
RAIL
STEP
STEPS

Plan P-7725-2D

Bedrooms: 3	Baths: 2½

Space:	
Main floor:	921 sq. ft.
Lower floor:	921 sq. ft.
Total living area:	**1,842 sq. ft.**
Garage:	438 sq. ft.
Exterior Wall Framing:	**2x6**

Foundation options:
Daylight basement only.
(Foundation & framing conversion diagram available — see order form.)

Blueprint Price Code: B

Room for Work and Play

- Stately columns, an arched porch and dramatic rooflines add attractive and distinguishing touches to this four-bedroom home.
- Amenities inside include a two-story foyer with a curved staircase, a two-story library with a full-length arched window, and a spacious central living room with a fireplace and adjoining patio.
- A modern island kitchen and bayed breakfast area merge with the living room for an open feel.
- The large main-floor master suite boasts a bay area with private patio access and a generous-sized personal bath with twin vanities, dual walk-in closets and a separate tub and shower.
- A large workshop off the garage is an added feature that will be appreciated by hobbyists.
- On the second floor, a versatile media room and a computer work room provide plenty of space for work and play. The upper level also has three nice-sized bedrooms and two full baths.

Plan DD-3583

Bedrooms: 4	Baths: 3½
Space:	
Upper floor	1,436 sq. ft.
Main floor	2,147 sq. ft.
Total Living Area	**3,583 sq. ft.**
Basement	2,147 sq. ft.
Garage	454 sq. ft.
Exterior Wall Framing	2x4

Foundation options:

Standard Basement

Crawlspace

Slab

(Foundation & framing conversion diagram available—see order form.)

Blueprint Price Code	F

UPPER FLOOR

- COMPUTER 11⁸ x 7⁴
- STOR. 8⁸ x 7⁴
- MEDIA 20⁸ x 14⁸
- BEDROOM 3 13⁸ x 13⁴
- LIVING. BELOW
- BATH 3
- BALCONY
- BEDROOM 2 15⁰ x 12⁰
- BATH 2
- BEDROOM 4 12⁸ x 11⁰
- FOYER BELOW
- LIBRARY BELOW

75⁰ / 42⁸

MAIN FLOOR

- WORKSHOP 15⁰ x 9⁴
- UTIL.
- BRKFST. 13⁸ x 11⁴
- PATIO
- LIVING 16⁰ x 21⁴
- MASTER BEDROOM 16⁰ x 17⁰
- KITCHEN 14⁸ x 10⁴
- GARAGE 20⁸ x 22⁴
- LOGGIA
- ½ BATH
- M/BATH 14⁸ x 18⁰
- FOYER 10⁸ x 16⁴
- DINING 12⁸ x 14⁴
- LIBRARY 12⁸ x 17¹⁰
- PORCH

77⁰ / 46¹⁰

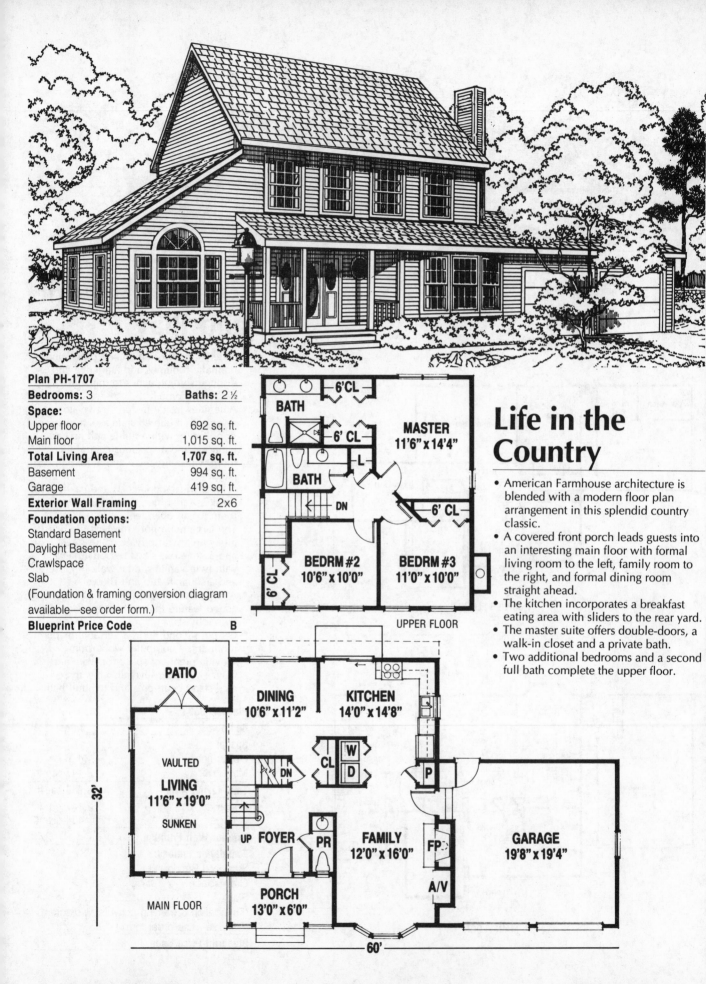

Plan PH-1707

Bedrooms: 3	Baths: 2 ½

Space:

Upper floor	692 sq. ft.
Main floor	1,015 sq. ft.
Total Living Area	**1,707 sq. ft.**
Basement	994 sq. ft.
Garage	419 sq. ft.
Exterior Wall Framing	**2x6**

Foundation options:

Standard Basement
Daylight Basement
Crawlspace
Slab

(Foundation & framing conversion diagram available—see order form.)

Blueprint Price Code	**B**

UPPER FLOOR

6'CL

BATH

6' CL

MASTER
11'6" x 14'4"

BATH

L

DN

6' CL

BEDRM #2
10'6" x 10'0"

BEDRM #3
11'0" x 10'0"

6' CL

Life in the Country

- American Farmhouse architecture is blended with a modern floor plan arrangement in this splendid country classic.
- A covered front porch leads guests into an interesting main floor with formal living room to the left, family room to the right, and formal dining room straight ahead.
- The kitchen incorporates a breakfast eating area with sliders to the rear yard.
- The master suite offers double-doors, a walk-in closet and a private bath.
- Two additional bedrooms and a second full bath complete the upper floor.

PATIO

DINING
10'6" x 11'2"

KITCHEN
14'0" x 14'8"

32'

VAULTED

LIVING
11'6" x 19'0"

SUNKEN

CL

W
D

DN

UP FOYER

PR

FAMILY
12'0" x 16'0"

FP

P

A/V

GARAGE
19'8" x 19'4"

MAIN FLOOR

PORCH
13'0" x 6'0"

60'

**TO ORDER THIS BLUEPRINT,
CALL TOLL-FREE 1-800-547-5570**

Plan PH-1707

**PRICES AND DETAILS
ON PAGES 12-15**

Every Room with a View

- Unique, octagonal design allows an outdoor view from each room.
- Three bordering decks extend first-level living areas.
- Generous living room features dramatic stone fireplace and central skylight open to second floor.
- Second level features circular balcony connecting all bedrooms.
- Alternate second-floor plan replaces one bedroom with a viewing deck.

Plan H-27: 4-Bedroom Version

Bedrooms: 4	Baths: 2½
Space:	
Upper floor:	1,167 sq. ft.
Main floor:	697 sq. ft.
Total living area:	1,864 sq. ft.
Exterior Wall Framing:	2x4

Foundation options:
Crawlspace only.
(Foundation & framing conversion diagram available — see order form.)

Blueprint Price Code:	B

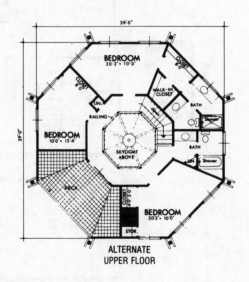

ALTERNATE
UPPER FLOOR

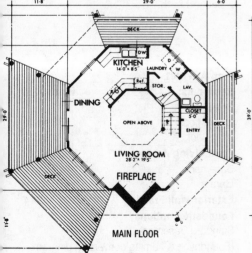

MAIN FLOOR

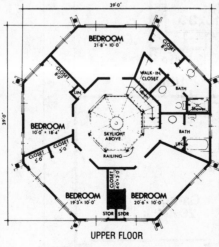

UPPER FLOOR

Plan H-27: 3-Bedroom Version

Bedrooms: 3	Baths: 2½
Space:	
Upper floor:	960 sq. ft.
Main floor:	697 sq. ft.
Total living area:	1,657 sq. ft.
Exterior Wall Framing:	2x4

Foundation options:
Crawlspace only.
(Foundation & framing conversion diagram available — see order form.)

Blueprint Price Code:	B

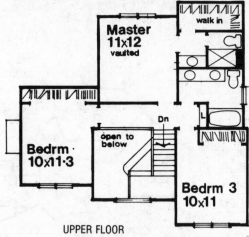

Master
11x12
vaulted

walk in

Bedrm
10x11·3

open to below

Dn

Bedrm 3
10x11

UPPER FLOOR

Delightful, Open Spaces

- A lot of room is offered in this compact but open three-bedroom home.
- The volume entry opens to a spacious living room with a fireplace, an open stairway to the upper level and windows that overlook the front porch and the rear patio.
- Between the living room and kitchen is a dining area with sliders that access the patio.
- Near the kitchen and garage entrance are handy laundry facilities and a powder room.
- The upper-level hallway connects the three bedrooms and overlooks the foyer below. At the center is a vaulted master bedroom with a private bath and a walk-in closet.
- Two secondary bedrooms share a second bath.

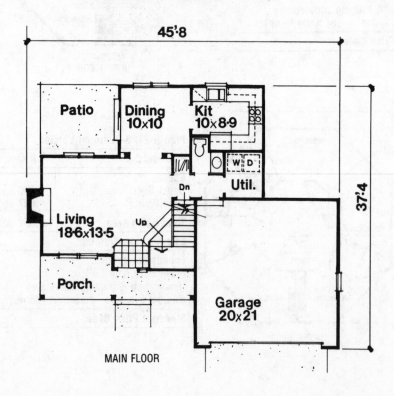

45'·8

Patio

Dining
10x10

Kit
10x8·9

W D

Util.

Dn

Living
18·6x13·5

Up

37'·4

Porch

Garage
20x21

MAIN FLOOR

Plan AG-1201	
Bedrooms: 3	Baths: 2 ½
Space:	
Upper floor	668 sq. ft.
Main floor	620 sq. ft.
Total Living Area	**1,288 sq. ft.**
Basement	620 sq. ft.
Garage	420 sq. ft.
Exterior Wall Framing	2x4
Foundation options:	
Standard Basement	
(Foundation & framing conversion diagram available—see order form.)	
Blueprint Price Code	**A**

Cottage Design Offers Comfort and Style

- Upper balcony bedroom overlooks living room below.
- Combined living/dining area makes great space for entertaining.
- Unique kitchen arrangement includes laundry area.
- Master suite features bay window sitting area.

Plan E-1002

Bedrooms: 1-2	Baths: 2

Space:

Upper floor	267 sq. ft.
Main floor	814 sq. ft.
Total Living Area	**1,081 sq. ft.**
Basement	814 sq. ft.
Unheated area	59 sq. ft.
Exterior Wall Framing	**2x4**

Foundation options:

Standard Basement
Crawlspace
Slab
(Foundation & framing conversion diagram available—see order form.)

Blueprint Price Code	**A**

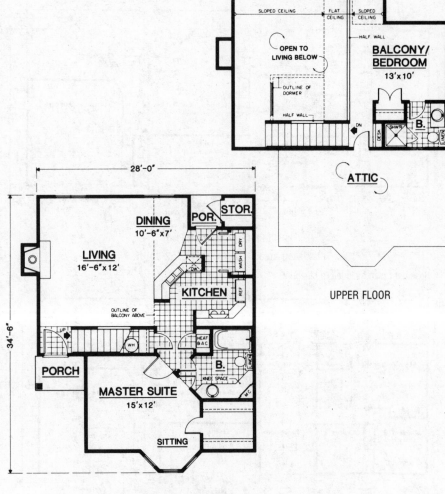

UPPER FLOOR

MAIN FLOOR

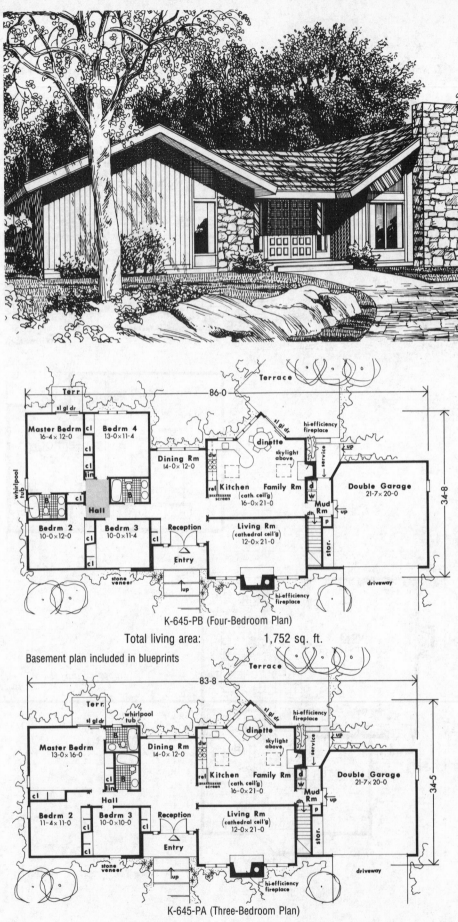

K-645-PB (Four-Bedroom Plan)

Total living area: 1,752 sq. ft.

Basement plan included in blueprints

K-645-PA (Three-Bedroom Plan)

Total living area: 1,548 sq. ft.

Blueprint Price Code B

Flexible Design

This distinctive contemporary ranch offers a three-bedroom or a four-bedroom version of a nearly identical basic plan. Natural stone and wood finish generates an exterior appeal and requires little maintenance. Double doors at the entry open onto a wide reception hall and a stunning view of the rear garden.

A dramatic cathedral ceiling crowns the living room and the family room/kitchen area. The living room features a woodburning fireplace amid a glass wall. Overlooking the backyard is the informal area; the family room is graced with operable skylights and a second fireplace. An efficient kitchen serves both the cheerful dinette and the formal dining room.

The privately zoned sleeping wing comes with either three bedrooms or four bedrooms. The master bedroom suite boasts a private terrace, ample closet space and a full bath. Living area is 1,548 sq. ft. for the three-bedroom and 1,752 sq. ft. for the four. Garage, mud room, etc., total 563 sq. ft.

The home features 2x6 exterior walls for energy efficiency.

CONTEMPORARY EXTERIOR

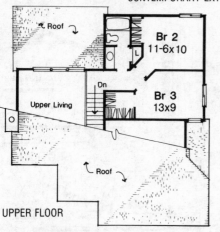

UPPER FLOOR

Br 2
11-6x10

Dn

Br 3
13x9

Roof

Upper Living

Roof

Two-Story with Alternate Exteriors

- This moderate-sized plan gives you a choice of exteriors (both included in blueprints).
- An open planning concept allows efficient use of downstairs space, providing a large living/dining area for both family living and entertaining.
- The living room offers both a fireplace and a vaulted ceiling.

- A roomy kitchen offers good cabinet and counter space as well as a breakfast bar.
- The downstairs master bedroom includes a large walk-in closet and easy access to a compartmentalized bathroom.
- Two bedrooms upstairs share a second full bath.

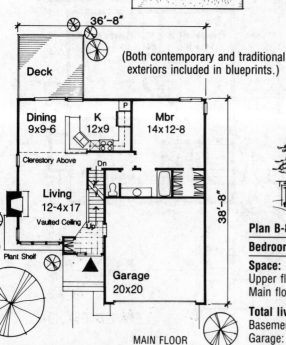

36'-8"

(Both contemporary and traditional exteriors included in blueprints.)

Deck

Dining
9x9-6

K
12x9

P

Mbr
14x12-8

Clerestory Above

Dn

38'-8"

Living
12-4x17
Vaulted Ceiling

Up

Plant Shelf

Garage
20x20

MAIN FLOOR

TRADITIONAL EXTERIOR

Plan B-8323

Bedrooms: 3		**Baths:** 2

Space:
Upper floor: 400 sq. ft.
Main floor: 846 sq. ft.

Total living area: 1,246 sq. ft.
Basement: 846 sq. ft.
Garage: 400 sq. ft.

Exterior Wall Framing: 2x4

Foundation options:
Standard basement only.
(Foundation & framing conversion diagram available — see order form.)

Blueprint Price Code: A

Sunny Chalet

- This captivating home is designed to maximize indoor and outdoor living. It features expansive windows, an open main floor and a large deck.
- A lower-level entry leads up a staircase to the spacious living room, which features a high cathedral ceiling with a balcony overhead, an energy-efficient fireplace and sliding glass doors to a sizable deck.
- The adjacent dining room boasts a bay window and easy access to the kitchen, which offers ample counter space and a sunny skylight. A half-bath is nearby.
- The lower floor features two spacious bedrooms that share a full bath, complete with a whirlpool tub.
- A quiet den could serve as a third bedroom or a guest room.

Plan K-532-L

Bedrooms: 2+	Baths: 1½
Living Area:	
Main floor	492 sq. ft.
Lower floor	488 sq. ft.
Total Living Area:	**980 sq. ft.**
Exterior Wall Framing:	2x4 or 2x6
Foundation Options:	
Crawlspace	
BLUEPRINT PRICE CODE:	**A**

VIEW INTO LIVING ROOM
AND DINING ROOM

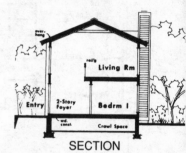

SECTION

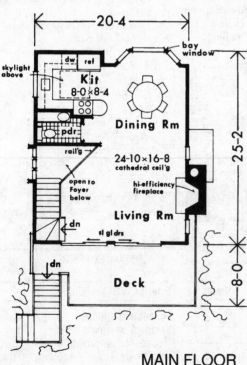

MAIN FLOOR

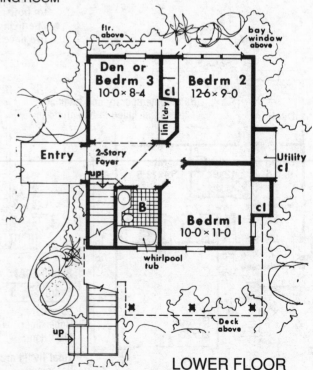

LOWER FLOOR

TO ORDER THIS BLUEPRINT, CALL TOLL-FREE 1-800-547-5570　　　Plan K-532-L　　　*PRICES AND DETAILS ON PAGES 12-15*

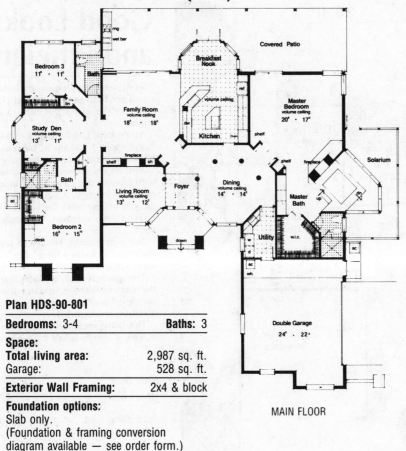

◄ 82'-4" ►

80'-4"

Bedroom 3
11' · 11'

Bath

Study Den
volume ceiling
13' · 11'

Bath

Bedroom 2
16' · 15'⁸

desk

mg
wet bar

Family Room
volume ceiling
18' · 18'⁰

Breakfast Nook

volume ceiling

Kitchen

dw

ref

Covered Patio

Master Bedroom
volume ceiling
20' · 17'⁰

shelf

fireplace   shelf   sh

Living Room
volume ceiling
13' · 12'²

Foyer

Dining
volume ceiling
14' · 14'⁰

shelf

fireplace

Solarium

up

Master Bath

Utility

w.i.c.

ac

down

w
d

ac
wh

Double Garage
24'⁰ · 22'⁰

MAIN FLOOR

Plan HDS-90-801

Bedrooms: 3-4	Baths: 3

Space:

Total living area:	2,987 sq. ft.
Garage:	528 sq. ft.

Exterior Wall Framing:	2x4 & block

Foundation options:
Slab only.
(Foundation & framing conversion
diagram available — see order form.)

Blueprint Price Code:	D

Gracious Mediterranean Style

- This design speaks of elegance and luxury both inside and out.
- A cloud shade and arched windows add elegance to the entrance.
- The foyer opens up to the breathtaking openness of high vaulted ceilings and a gorgeous octagonal dining room.
- The generously sized family room expands visually as the eye follows the high interior vaults.
- The kitchen also features a vaulted ceiling, and adjoins a nook which lends an open-air appearance to the area.
- The spectacular suite boasts a raised-hearth fireplace that's open to both the bath and bedroom sides.
- Bedroom 2 is spacious, and shares a connecting bath with the den, which could serve as a guest bedroom.
- Bedroom 3 adjoins another bath, and includes a large closet.
- A large covered patio across the back of the home includes a built-in wet bar and outdoor grill.

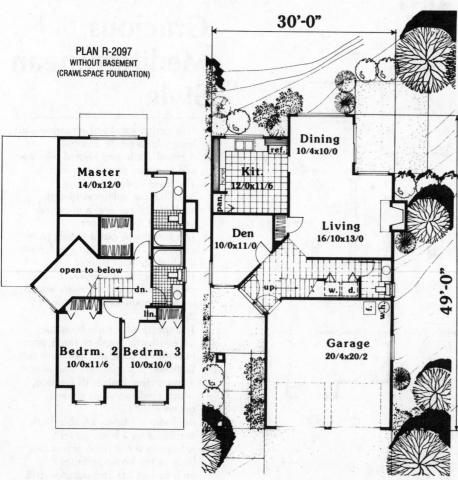

PLAN R-2097
WITHOUT BASEMENT
(CRAWLSPACE FOUNDATION)

30'-0"

49'-0"

Master
14/0x12/0

open to below

dn.

lin.

Bedrm. 2
10/0x11/6

Bedrm. 3
10/0x10/0

Dining
10/4x10/0

ref.

Kit.
12/0x11/6

pan.

Den
10/0x11/0

Living
16/10x13/0

up

w. d.

f.

w.h.

Garage
20/4x20/2

Good Looks and Efficiency

This two-story contemporary home combines both good looks and efficiency. Together they make this home a sure winner.

You'd have to look long and hard for a home under 1,500 sq. ft., such as this, that has more pizzazz or amenities.

Visitors are greeted by a dramatic entry with illuminating clerestory window and overhead balcony. A vaulted den is located directly off the entry for easy access and boasts corner windows for plenty of natural light.

The cozy country kitchen to the rear of the house includes a large pantry and extra room for a breakfast table.

The spacious walk-in closet featured in the master bedroom, upstairs, frees up additional wall space in the room itself for furniture arrangement.

This home measures only 30' in width, making it ideally suited for a narrow lot.

Main floor:	768 sq. ft.
Upper floor:	698 sq. ft.
Total living area: (Not counting garage)	1,466 sq. ft.

Blueprint Price Code A

Plan R-2097

Four-Bedroom Contemporary Style

Steeply pitched, multi-level gable rooflines accented by diagonal board siding and tall windows add imposing height to this contemporary, 2,289 sq. ft. home. With most of the 1,389 sq. ft. main floor devoted to the living, dining and family rooms, and a long patio or wood deck accessible off the nook, the home lends itself ideally to family activities and gracious entertaining.

Directly off the spacious foyer is the vaulted-ceiling living room and dining area, brightened with high windows and warmed by a log-sized fireplace. The wide U-shaped kitchen, nook and family room, with wood stove, join and extend across the back half of the main floor. With doors off the nook and utility room leading to a large patio, this area combines for large, informal activities. Also off the front entry hall is a full bathroom, a den or fourth bedroom, and the open stairway, brightened by a skylight, leading to the upper floor.

The master bedroom suite, occupying about half of the upper floor, has a wide picture window, walk-in dressing room/wardrobe, and a skylighted bathroom with sunken tub and separate shower. The other two bedrooms share the hall bathroom. A daylight basement version of the plan further expands the family living and recreation areas of this home.

Main floor:	1,389 sq. ft.
Upper floor:	900 sq. ft.
Total living area:	2,289 sq. ft.
(Not counting basement or garage)	
Basement level:	1,389 sq. ft.

MAIN FLOOR

PLAN P-7627-4A
WITHOUT BASEMENT

PLAN P-7627-4D
WITH DAYLIGHT BASEMENT

UPPER FLOOR

Blueprint Price Code C

Plans P-7627-4A & -4D

Cathedral Ceiling Featured

The open floor plan of this modified A-Frame design virtually eliminates wasted hall space. The centrally located Great Room features a 15'4" cathedral ceiling with exposed wood beams and large areas of fixed glass on both front and rear. Living and dining areas are visually separated by a massive stone fireplace.

The isolated master suite features a walk-in closet and sliding glass doors opening onto the front deck.

A walk-thru utility room provides easy access from the carport and outside storage area to the compact kitchen. On the opposite side of the Great Room are two additional bedrooms and a second full

bath. All this takes up only 1,454 square feet of heated living area. A full length deck and vertical wood siding with stone accents on the corners provide a rustic yet contemporary exterior.

Total living area: 1,454 sq. ft.
(Not counting basement or garage)

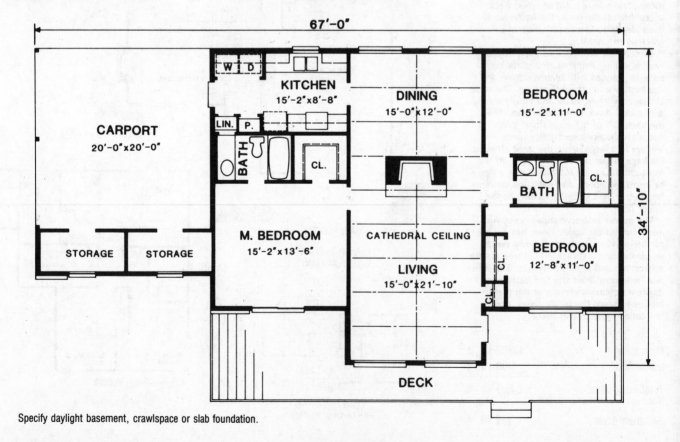

Specify daylight basement, crawlspace or slab foundation.

Blueprint Price Code A

Plan C-7360

Rear of Home As Attractive As Front

The rear of this rustic/contemporary home features a massive stone fireplace and a full-length deck which make it ideal for mountain, golf course, lake or other locations where both the front and rear offer scenic views.

Sliding glass doors in the family room and breakfast nook open onto the deck. The modified A-Frame design combines a 20'6" cathedral ceiling over the sunken family room with a large studio over the two front bedrooms. An isolated master suite features a walk-in closet and compartmentalized bath with double vanity and linen closet. The front bedrooms include ample closet space and share a unique bath-and-a-half arrangement.

On one side of the U-shaped kitchen and breakfast nook is the formal dining room which opens onto the foyer. On the other side is a utility room which can be entered from either the kitchen or garage.

The exterior features a massive stone fireplace, large glass areas and a combination of vertical wood siding and stone.

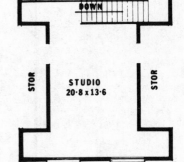

SECOND FLOOR

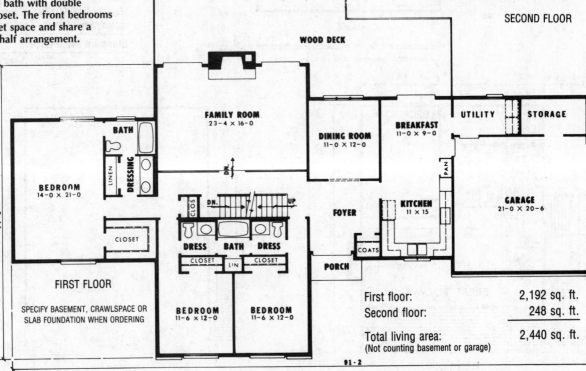

First floor: 2,192 sq. ft.
Second floor: 248 sq. ft.

Total living area: 2,440 sq. ft.
(Not counting basement or garage)

The Simple & Economical Housing Solution

- This compact plan could serve as a second home or a primary residence for a small family.
- Spacious Great Room features woodstove and a large adjoining deck.
- Efficent kitchen is close to storage and laundry area.
- Large, overlooking loft offers infinite possibilities, such as extra sleeping quarters, a home office, art studio, or recreation room.
- Clerestory window arrangement and sloped-ceilings top the loft for added light.

Plan H-963-2A

Bedrooms: 1	Baths: 1
Space:	
Loft:	432 sq. ft.
Main floor:	728 sq. ft.
Total living area:	1,160 sq. ft.
Lower level/garage:	728 sq. ft.
Exterior Wall Framing:	2x4

Foundation options:
Slab.
(Foundation & framing conversion diagram available — see order form.)

Blueprint Price Code:	A

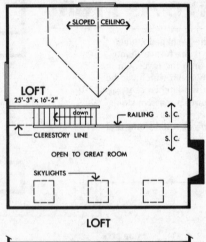

LOFT
25'-3" x 16'-2"

CLERESTORY WINDOWS OVER LOFT AND STAIRS

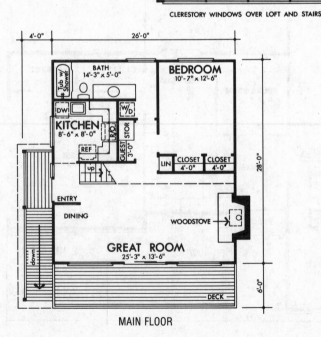

MAIN FLOOR

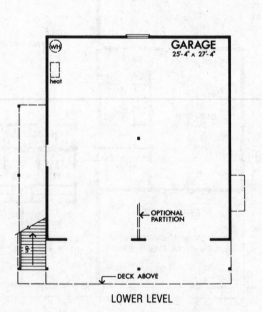

LOWER LEVEL

TO ORDER THIS BLUEPRINT, CALL TOLL-FREE 1-800-547-5570

Plan H-963-2A

PRICES AND DETAILS ON PAGES 12-15

Exciting, Economical Design

Exciting but economical, this 1,895 sq. ft., three-bedroom house is arranged carefully for maximum use and enjoyment on two floors, and is only 42 feet wide to minimize lot size requirements. The multi-paned bay windows of the living room and an upstairs bedroom add contrast to the hip rooflines and lead you to the sheltered front entry porch.

The open, vaulted foyer is brightened by a skylight as it sorts traffic to the downstairs living areas or to the upper bedroom level. A few steps to the right puts you in the vaulted living room and the adjoining dining area. Sliding doors in the dining area and the nook, and a pass-through window in the U-shaped kitchen, make the patio a perfect place for outdoor activities and meals.

A large fireplace warms the spacious family room, which has a corner wet bar for efficient entertaining. A utility room leading to the garage and a powder room complete the 1,020 sq. ft. main floor.

An open stairway in the foyer leads to the 875 sq. ft. upper level. The master bedroom has a large walk-in wardrobe, twin vanity, shower and bathroom. The front bedroom has a seat in the bay window and the third bedroom has a built-in seat overlooking the vaulted living room. A full bath with twin vanity serves these bedrooms.

The daylight basement version of the plan adds 925 sq. ft. of living space.

Main floor:	1,020 sq. ft.
Upper floor:	875 sq. ft.
Total living area:	**1,895 sq. ft.**
(Not counting basement or garage)	

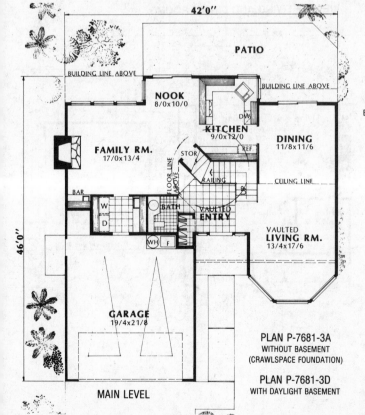

PLAN P-7681-3A
WITHOUT BASEMENT
(CRAWLSPACE FOUNDATION)

PLAN P-7681-3D
WITH DAYLIGHT BASEMENT

MAIN LEVEL

PLAN P-7681-3D
BASEMENT LEVEL: 925 sq. ft.

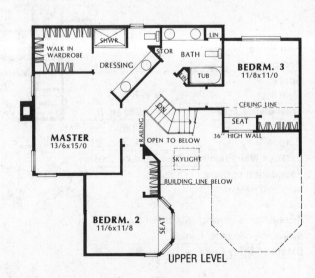

UPPER LEVEL

Blueprint Price Code B

Plans P-7681-3A & 3D

PRICES AND DETAILS
ON PAGES 12-15

Panoramic Rear View

- This rustic but elegant country home offers an open, airy interior.
- At the center of the floor plan is a spacious living room with a sloped ceiling, fireplace and an all-glass circular wall giving a panoramic view of the backyard.
- The adjoining dining room shares the sloped ceiling and offers sliders to the rear terrace.
- The bright kitchen has a large window, an optional skylight and a counter bar that separates it from the bayed dinette.
- The bedroom wing includes two secondary bedrooms and a large, bayed master bedroom with dual walk-in closets and a private bath with a sloped ceiling and a garden whirlpool tub.

VIEW OF LIVING AND DINING ROOMS.

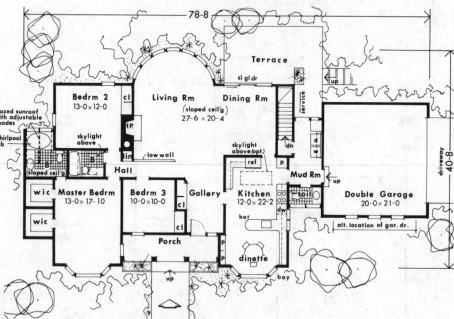

Plan K-685-DA

Bedrooms: 3	Baths: 2 ½
Space:	
Main floor	1,760 sq. ft.
Total Living Area	**1,760 sq. ft.**
Basement	1,700 sq. ft.
Garage	482 sq. ft.
Exterior Wall Framing	2x4 or 2x6

Foundation options:

Standard Basement

Slab

(Foundation & framing conversion diagram available—see order form.)

Blueprint Price Code	**B**

TO ORDER THIS BLUEPRINT, CALL TOLL-FREE 1-800-547-5570

Plan K-685-DA

PRICES AND DETAILS ON PAGES 12-15

Classy Touches in Compact Home

- **Charming window treatments, a quality front door, covered porch and detailed railings add class to this smaller home.**
- **The beautiful kitchen is brightened and enlarged by a sunny bay window.**
- **The spacious family room enjoys easy access to a patio in the back yard.**
- **The roomy living room features an impressive corner fireplace and a large bay window in the front.**
- **The master bedroom boasts a large bathroom, dressing area and closet in addition to the sleeping area.**
- **Both secondary bedrooms feature cozy window seats.**

UPPER FLOOR

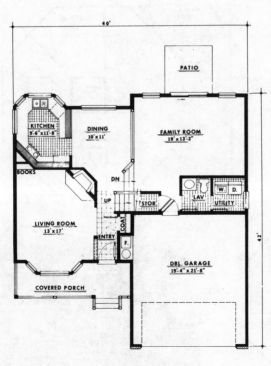

MAIN FLOOR

Plan NW-836

Bedrooms: 3	Baths: 2½

Space:

Upper floor:	684 sq. ft.
Main floor:	934 sq. ft.
Total living area:	**1,618 sq. ft.**
Garage:	419 sq. ft.

Exterior Wall Framing:	2x6

Foundation options:
   Crawlspace only.
(Foundation & framing conversion diagram available — see order form.)

Blueprint Price Code:	B

FRONT VIEW

Octagonal Sunshine Special

- Octagon homes offer the ultimate for taking advantage of a view, and are fascinating designs even for more ordinary settings.
- This plan offers a huge, house-spanning living/dining area with loads of glass and a masonry collector wall to store solar heat.
- The 700-square-foot upper level is devoted entirely to an enormous master suite, with a balcony overlooking the living room below, a roomy private bath and a large closet/dressing area.
- Scissor-trusses allow vaulted ceilings over the two-story-high living room and the master suite.
- A second roomy bedroom and full bath are offered downstairs, along with an efficient kitchen, a laundry area and inviting foyer.
- A daylight basement option offers the potential for more bedrooms, hobbies, work rooms or recreational space.

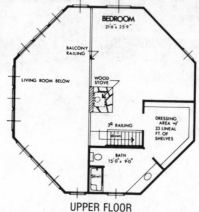

UPPER FLOOR

Plans H-948-1A & -1B	
Bedrooms: 2-4	**Baths:** 2
Space:	
Upper floor:	700 sq. ft.
Main floor:	1,236 sq. ft.
Total without basement:	1,936 sq. ft.
Daylight basement:	1,236 sq. ft.
Total with basement:	3,172 sq. ft.
Garage:	550 sq. ft.
Exterior Wall Framing:	2x6

Foundation options:
Daylight basement (H-948-1B).
Crawlspace (H-948-1A).
(Foundation & framing conversion diagram available — see order form.)

Blueprint Price Code:
Without basement:	B
With basement:	E

MAIN FLOOR

WITHOUT BASEMENT (CRAWLSPACE FOUNDATION)

SCALE
0 1 2 3 4 5 6 7 8 9 10

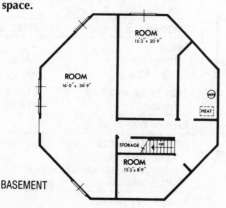

BASEMENT

REAR VIEW

Plans H-948-1A & -1B

PRICES AND DETAILS ON PAGES 12-15

Vaulted Ceilings, Open Planning, Compact Luxury

- A protected entryway opens into a foyer which immediately shows off the impressive fireplace and vaulted ceiling in the living room.
- The dining room, breakfast nook and kitchen flow logically together as an efficient unit, with a pass-through from the kitchen to the breakfast area.
- The master suite is spectacular for a home of this size, with a vaulted ceiling, sunny sitting area, large closet and sumptuous master bath with separate tub and shower.
- The front bedroom, with its beautiful palladian window and vaulted ceiling, would serve equally well as a den or impressive home office.
- Note the convenient placement of the laundry area, garage entrance and basement stairs.

Plan B-89020

Bedrooms: 2-3	Baths: 2

Space:

Total living area:	1,642 sq. ft.
Basement:	approx. 1,642 sq. ft.
Garage:	455 sq. ft.
Exterior Wall Framing:	2x4

Foundation options:
Standard basement only.
(Foundation & framing conversion diagram available — see order form.)

Blueprint Price Code: B

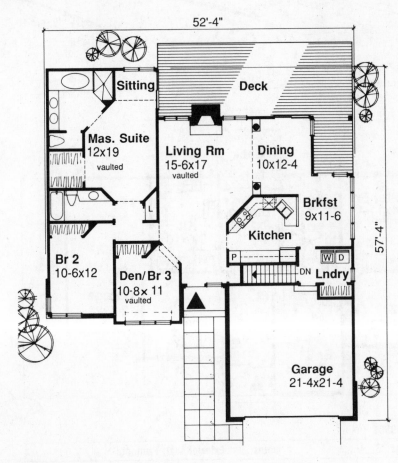

MAIN FLOOR

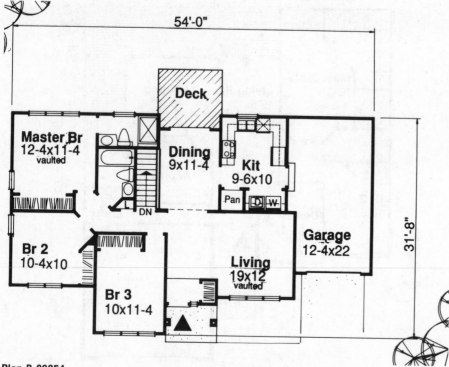

Deck

Master Br
12-4x11-4
vaulted

Dining
9x11-4

Kit
9-6x10

Pan | D | W.

Br 2
10-4x10

DN

Br 3
10-11-4

Living
19x12
vaulted

Garage
12-4x22

54'-0"

31'-8"

Affordable Style & Excitement

- Style and excitement is not reserved exclusively for large homes. This modest-sized home offers plenty of style and excitement, both outside and in.
- Multiple gables and rooflines, with transom windows and important-looking entry columns create exterior style.
- A vaulted ceiling in the living room and a long view through the dining room to the deck offer entry impact.
- The master suite has a vaulted ceiling and private bath while the other two bedrooms share a second full bath.

Plan B-89054

Bedrooms: 3	Baths: 2

Space:	
Total living area:	1,135 sq. ft.
Basement:	1,135 sq. ft.
Garage:	271 sq. ft.

Exterior Wall Framing: 2x4

Foundation options:
Standard basement.
(Foundation & framing conversion diagram available — see order form.)

Blueprint Price Code: A

TO ORDER THIS BLUEPRINT,
CALL TOLL-FREE 1-800-547-5570

Plan B-89054

PRICES AND DETAILS
ON PAGES 12-15

Southwest Design
Fits Long, Narrow Lot

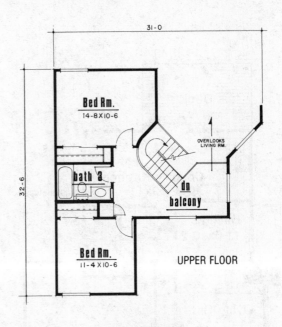

MAIN FLOOR

- 31-0
- 70-0
- covered patio
- Family 12-8 x 17-0
- Kitchen 10-8 x 9-0
- CATH CLG
- CATH CLG
- Dining 10-8 x 7-8
- Mast. B.R. 15-0 x 14-8
- Living 15-4 x 12-4
- VAULTED CLG.
- Up
- Entry
- bath 1
- bath 2
- CLOSET
- Study/opt. b.r. 10-8 x 10-6
- utility
- Garage 19-4 x 20-2

UPPER FLOOR

- 31-0
- 32-6
- Bed Rm. 14-8 X 10-6
- bath a
- OVERLOOKS LIVING RM.
- dn
- balcony
- Bed Rm. 11-4 X 10-6

PLAN Q-1915-1A
WITHOUT BASEMENT
(SLAB-ON-GRADE FOUNDATION)

First floor:	1,400 sq. ft.
Second floor:	515 sq. ft.
Total living area: (Not counting garage)	1,915 sq. ft.

Blueprint Price Code B

Plan Q-1915-1A

Spacious Country Kitchen

Main floor:	834 sq. ft.
Upper floor:	722 sq. ft.
Total living area:	1,556 sq. ft.
(Not counting basement or garage)	

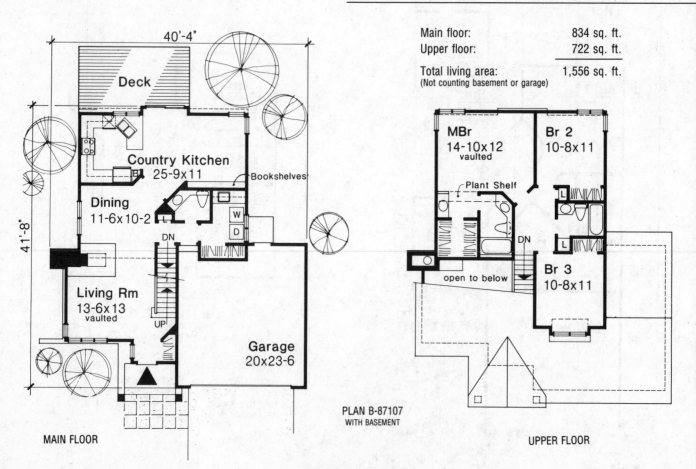

MAIN FLOOR

40'-4"

41'-8"

Deck

Country Kitchen
25-9x11

Bookshelves

Dining
11-6x10-2

W
D

DN

Living Rm
13-6x13
vaulted

UP

Garage
20x23-6

UPPER FLOOR

MBr
14-10x12
vaulted

Plant Shelf

Br 2
10-8x11

DN

open to below

Br 3
10-8x11

PLAN B-87107
WITH BASEMENT

Blueprint Price Code B

Plan B-87107

Weekend Retreat

For those whose goal is a small, affordable retreat at the shore or in the mountains, this plan may be the answer. Although it measures less than 400 sq. ft. of living space on the main floor, it lacks nothing in comfort and convenience. A sizeable living room boasts a masonry hearth on which to mount your choice of a wood stove or a pre-fab fireplace. There is plenty of room for furniture, including a dining table.

The galley-type kitchen is a small marvel of compact convenience and utility, even boasting a dishwasher and space for a stackable washer and dryer. The wide open nature of the first floor guarantees that even the person working in the kitchen area will still be included in the party. On the floor plan, a dashed line across the living room indicates the limits of the balcony bedroom above. In front of this line, the A-frame shape of the living room soars from the floor boards to the ridge beam high above. Clerestory windows lend a further note of spaciousness and unity with nature's outdoors. A huge planked deck adds to the indoor-outdoor relationship.

A modest-sized bedroom on the second floor is approached by a standard stairway, not an awkward ladder or heavy pull-down stairway as is often the case in small A-frames. The view over the balcony rail to the living room below adds a note of distinction. The unique framing pattern allows a window at either end of the bedroom, improving both outlook and ventilation.

A compact bathroom serves both levels and enjoys natural daylight through a skylight window.

First floor:	391 sq. ft.
Upper level:	144 sq. ft.
Total living area:	535 sq. ft.

FRONT VIEW

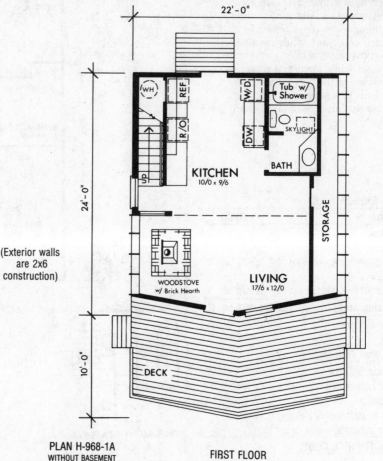

(Exterior walls are 2x6 construction)

UPPER LEVEL
144 SQUARE FEET

PLAN H-968-1A
WITHOUT BASEMENT
(CRAWLSPACE FOUNDATION)

FIRST FLOOR
391 SQUARE FEET

Blueprint Price Code A
Plan H-968-1A

**PRICES AND DETAILS
ON PAGES 12-15**

Vaulted Design for Narrow Lot

- Vaulted living spaces add to the spacious feel of this narrow-lot home.
- The focal point is a large fireplace flanked by windows that give views of a lovely patio and the yard beyond.
- The dining room offers access to a secluded courtyard, while the bayed kitchen overlooks a front garden.
- The master suite features a sitting room with sliders to the patio. The master bath leads to a large walk-in closet.
- The two remaining bedrooms share the hall bath.

Plans P-6588-2A & -2D

Bedrooms: 3	Baths: 2

Living Area:

Main floor (non-basement version)	1,362 sq. ft.
Main floor (basement version)	1,403 sq. ft.
Total Living Area:	**1,362/1,403 sq. ft.**
Daylight basement	1,303 sq. ft.
Garage	427 sq. ft.
Exterior Wall Framing:	2x6

Foundation Options:	Plan #
Daylight basement	P-6588-2D
Crawlspace	P-6588-2A

(Typical foundation & framing conversion diagram available—see order form.)

BLUEPRINT PRICE CODE:	**A**

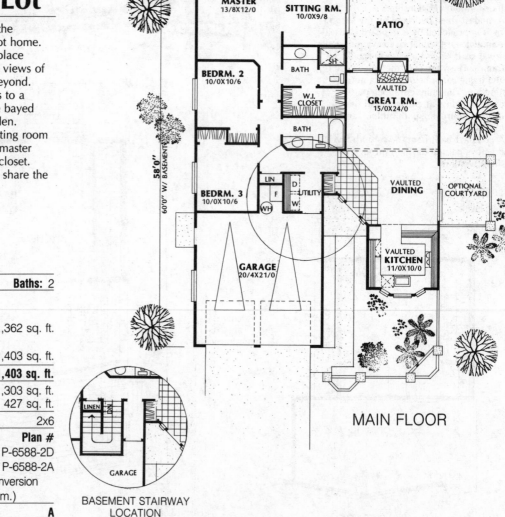

MAIN FLOOR

BASEMENT STAIRWAY LOCATION

TO ORDER THIS BLUEPRINT, CALL TOLL-FREE 1-800-547-5570

Plans P-6588-2A & -2D

PRICES AND DETAILS ON PAGES 12-15

A-Frame Chalet with Popular Features

Ski chalets bring to mind Alpine comforts and evenings by the hearth. Schussing down nearby slopes is much more enjoyable when you don't have to worry about long drives home. Also, being on hand means you won't miss the fresh snowfall. In addition, summer time finds the mountain setting ideal for refreshing weekends away from the crowds and heat.

This class A-Frame is designed for optimum comfort and minimum cost, yet allows for variety and individual taste in setting and decor. Your home away from home can vary from plush to rustic, depending on personal preferences.

A special feature of this plan is the natural stone fireplace located where it can be enjoyed from indoors and outdoors. It serves the dual function of being a standard fireplace indoors and a handy barbecue outdoors. Two sleeping rooms on the main floor are a further advantage. Upstairs, there is a third bedroom plus a half bath. A balcony room provides space for overflow guests or a playroom for the kids. All the rooms in the house have "knee walls" so the space is usable right to the wall. These walls provide handy storage places as well as space for insulation.

First floor:	845 sq. ft.
Second floor:	375 sq. ft.
Total living area:	1,220 sq. ft.

PLAN H-6
WITHOUT BASEMENT
(CRAWLSPACE FOUNDATION)

SECOND FLOOR
375 SQUARE FEET

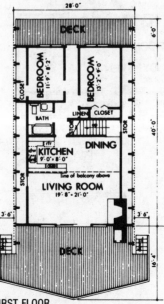

FIRST FLOOR
845 SQUARE FEET

TO ORDER THIS BLUEPRINT,
CALL TOLL-FREE 1-800-547-5570

Blueprint Price Code A
Plan H-6

PRICES AND DETAILS
ON PAGES 12-15   **247**

Bayed Morning Room Has Patio View

- This modern-looking ranch is stylishly decorated with a pair of arched-window dormers, handsome brick trim and a covered front porch.
- Inside, the main living areas are oriented to the rear, with an array of boxed and angled window walls.
- Volume 10-ft. ceilings are found throughout the home, with the exception of the three smaller bedrooms.
- The huge family room at the center of the home offers a patio view and a fireplace that can also be seen from the adjoining kitchen and eating area.
- The walk-through kitchen features an eating bar and a pantry, as well as easy service to both the bayed morning room and the formal dining room across the hall.
- A window seat and a private garden bath highlight the master suite, which is separated from the other bedrooms. The fourth bedroom may double as a study.

Plan DD-1962

Bedrooms: 3-4	Baths: 2
Space:	
Main floor	1,962 sq. ft.
Total Living Area	**1,962 sq. ft.**
Basement	1,962 sq. ft.
Garage	386 sq. ft.
Exterior Wall Framing	2x4

Foundation options:
Standard Basement
Crawlspace
Slab
(Foundation & framing conversion diagram available—see order form.)

Blueprint Price Code	**B**

MAIN FLOOR

PATIO

63⁷

MORNING
11⁴ X 10⁸

PANTRY

BEDROOM 3
11⁴ X 14⁴

FAMILY ROOM
16⁰ X 19⁸

KITCHEN
10⁴ X 12⁰

MASTER BEDROOM
13⁴ X 16⁴

M. BATH

LINEN

LINEN

BATH 2

UTILITY

48¹⁰

BEDROOM 2
13⁸ X 12

BEDROOM 4/ STUDY
12⁰ X 10⁶

ENTRY

DINING
12⁰ X 12⁸

GARAGE
19⁰ X 20⁴

PORCH

Great Room for Entertaining

- The focal point of this stylish contemporary home is its central sunken Great Room with luxurious features. Guests are easily served at a handy wet bar or at an angled counter by the kitchen and breakfast area. Open beams above and a woodstove to the left add a rustic ambience. A rear window wall gives sweeping views of the outdoors.
- A wraparound deck or patio expands the entertaining area.
- The main-floor master suite boasts a raised tub, a separate shower, a walk-in closet and outdoor access. A sunspace may be added if desired.
- Two bedrooms and a bath are located upstairs.

Plan LRD-22884

Bedrooms: 3	Baths: 2½
Living Area:	
Upper floor	674 sq. ft.
Main floor	1,686 sq. ft.
Total Living Area:	**2,360 sq. ft.**
Standard basement	1,686 sq. ft.
Garage	450 sq. ft.
Exterior Wall Framing:	2x6

Foundation Options:

Standard basement

Crawlspace

Slab

(Typical foundation & framing conversion diagram available—see order form.)

BLUEPRINT PRICE CODE: C

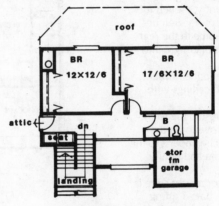

UPPER FLOOR

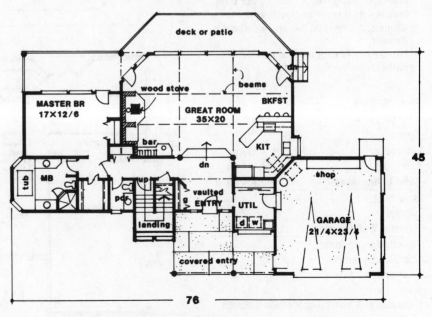

MAIN FLOOR

Sprawling French Country

- A hip roof and gable accents give this sprawling home a country, French look.
- The spectacular living room stretches from the entry of the home to the rear. Windows at both ends offer light and a nice breeze.
- Both the living room and the formal dining room have high ceilings with transom lights.
- Angled walls add interest to the roomy island kitchen, which overlooks the covered lanai. The kitchen opens to the adjoining morning room and family room.
- The spacious main-floor master suite is highlighted by a large, bayed sitting area, set apart from the bedroom with columns and dividers. The master bath features dual walk-in closets and vanities, a large spa tub and a separate shower.
- Three extra bedrooms and two more baths share the upper level.

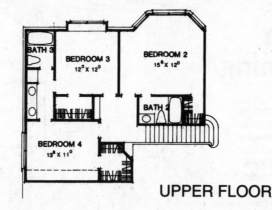

UPPER FLOOR

Plan DD-2889

Bedrooms: 4	Baths: 3 ½
Space:	
Upper floor	819 sq. ft.
Main floor	2,111 sq. ft.
Total Living Area	**2,930 sq. ft.**
Basement	2,111 sq. ft.
Garage	622 sq. ft.
Exterior Wall Framing	**2x4**

Foundation options:

Standard Basement

Crawlspace

Slab

(Foundation & framing conversion diagram available—see order form.)

Blueprint Price Code	D

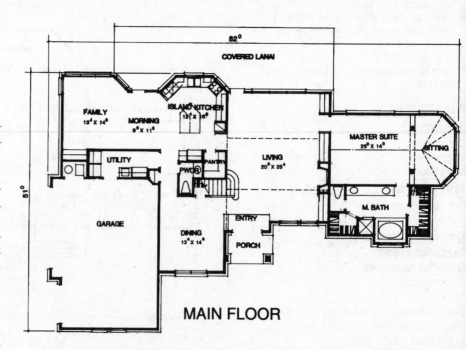

MAIN FLOOR

TO ORDER THIS BLUEPRINT, CALL TOLL-FREE 1-800-547-5570

Plan DD-2889

PRICES AND DETAILS ON PAGES 12-15

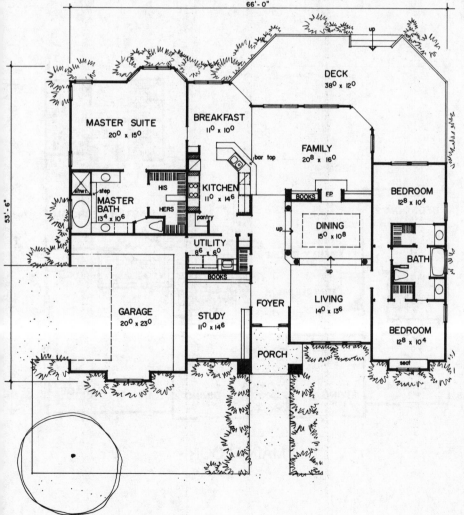

66' - 0"

53' - 6"

DECK
38⁰ x 12⁰

MASTER SUITE
20⁰ x 15⁰

BREAKFAST
11⁰ x 10⁰

FAMILY
20⁸ x 16⁰

MASTER BATH
13⁴ x 10⁶

HIS

HERS

KITCHEN
11⁰ x 14⁶

pantry

BOOKS

F.P.

BEDROOM
12⁸ x 10⁴

DINING
15⁰ x 10⁸

UTILITY
8⁶ x 6⁰

BATH

BOOKS

GARAGE
20⁰ x 23⁰

STUDY
11⁰ x 14⁶

FOYER

LIVING
14⁰ x 13⁶

PORCH

BEDROOM
12⁸ x 10⁴

seat

Brilliant Columns

- Brilliant entry columns and a stucco exterior give this one-story a distinguished look.
- Inside, the foyer offers views to a personal study or home office, a formal living room and a raised dining area with wood columns.
- The equally spectacular family room has a 14' ceiling, a fireplace, built-in book storage, and arched windows at the rear that overlook the attached deck.
- A counter bar separates the open kitchen from the family room; the kitchen also offers a pantry and an adjoining breakfast area.
- The large master suite is secluded to the rear of the home; it has a bayed sitting area and a roomy, private bath.

Plan DW-2342

Bedrooms: 3-4	**Baths: 2**

Space:

Main floor	2,342 sq. ft.
Total Living Area	**2,342 sq. ft.**
Basement	2,342 sq. ft.
Garage	460 sq. ft.
Exterior Wall Framing	2x4

Foundation options:

Standard Basement
Crawlspace
Slab

(Foundation & framing conversion diagram available—see order form.)

Blueprint Price Code	C

TO ORDER THIS BLUEPRINT,
CALL TOLL-FREE 1-800-547-5570

Plan DW-2342

PRICES AND DETAILS
ON PAGES 12-15

251

European Charm

- This distinguished European home offers all of today's most luxurious features.
- Vaulted ceilings enhance and expand the formal living and dining areas as well as the master bedroom suite.
- The informal areas are oriented to the rear of the home, entered through French doors in the foyer. The large family room features a tray ceiling, a fireplace with an adjoining entertainment center and a view of the backyard deck. The open kitchen and breakfast area is bright and cheerful, with a window wall and access to the deck.
- French doors lead into the luxurious master suite, which showcases a spectacular see-through fireplace that is shared with the vaulted spa bath. The splashy bath also includes a dual-sink vanity, a separate shower and a huge wardrobe closet and dressing area.
- Two more bedrooms and a full bath are on the opposite side of the home.

Plan APS-2006

Bedrooms: 3	Baths: 2
Living Area:	
Main floor	2,006 sq. ft.
Total Living Area:	**2,006 sq. ft.**
Standard basement	2,006 sq. ft.
Garage	448 sq. ft.
Exterior Wall Framing:	2x4

Foundation Options:

Standard basement
Slab

(All plans can be built with your choice of foundation and framing. A generic conversion diagram is available. See order form.)

BLUEPRINT PRICE CODE:	C

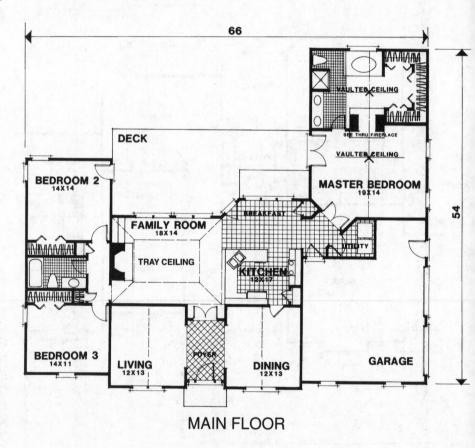

MAIN FLOOR

Plan APS-2006

UPPER FLOOR

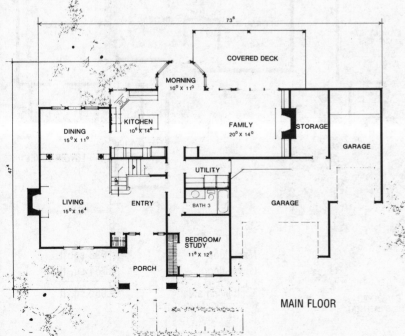

MAIN FLOOR

Executive Excellence

- This executive home with stucco exterior has an open, lighted effect with large expanses of glass and flowing spaces.
- The entry and stairwell are a two-story space opening to the formal living and dining rooms.
- Family gathering spaces are at the rear with plenty of glass opening to a large covered deck.
- A guest bedroom/study with full bath complete the lower level.
- Upstairs is the enormous master suite with a closet big enough for large wardrobes and a lavish master bath. Two more bedrooms and the hall bath are also upstairs.

Plan DD-2725

Bedrooms: 3-4	Baths: 3

Space:	
Upper floor:	1,152 sq. ft.
Main floor:	1,631 sq. ft.

Total living area:	2,783 sq. ft.
Garage:	approx. 600 sq. ft.
Storage:	approx. 100 sq. ft.

Exterior Wall Framing:	2x4

Ceiling Heights:	
Upper floor:	8'
Main floor:	9'

Foundation options:
Basement.
Crawlspace.
Slab.
(Foundation & framing conversion diagram available — see order form.)

Blueprint Price Code:	D

Bedrooms on Walkout Level

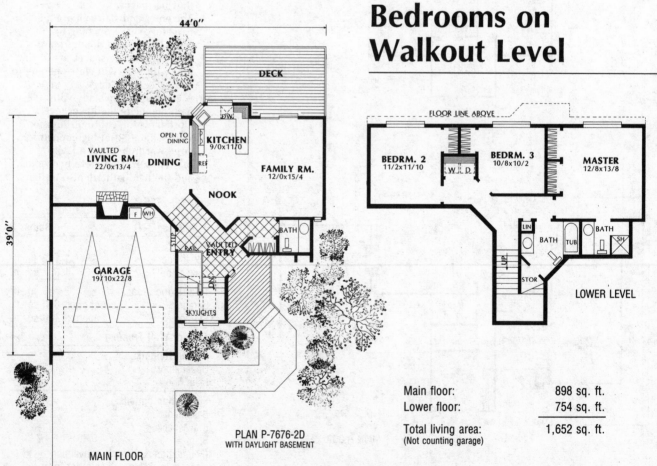

44'0"

39'0"

DECK

VAULTED
LIVING RM.
22/0x13/4

DINING

OPEN TO
DINING

DW

KITCHEN
9/0x11/0

REF

FAMILY RM.
12/0x15/4

NOOK

F | WH

GARAGE
19/10x22/8

STEP
RAIL

VAULTED
ENTRY

BATH

DN

SKYLIGHTS

PLAN P-7676-2D
WITH DAYLIGHT BASEMENT

MAIN FLOOR

FLOOR LINE ABOVE

BEDRM. 2
11/2x11/10

W | D

BEDRM. 3
10/8x10/2

MASTER
12/8x13/8

LIN

BATH

TUB

BATH

SH

UP

STOR

LOWER LEVEL

Main floor: 898 sq. ft.
Lower floor: 754 sq. ft.

Total living area: 1,652 sq. ft.
(Not counting garage)

Blueprint Price Code B

Plan P-7676-2D

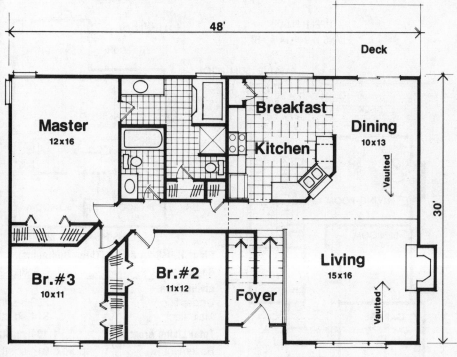

Split-Foyer Has Room for Expansion

- This popular split-foyer design provides space for expansion with the inclusion of an unfinished family room in the lower level. The garage and laundry room also share the lower level.
- A vaulted ceiling highlights both the living room and the dining room; the living room also offers a warming fireplace and a view to the backyard deck, which is accessible through the dining room.
- The roomy kitchen features an angled countertop, a pantry and an eat-in kitchen.
- Secluded to the rear, the spacious master suite features two closets, a corner window and a generous bath with a step-up tub and separate shower.
- The two additional bedrooms share a second full bath.

Plan APS-1410

Bedrooms: 3	**Baths:** 2

Living Area:

Main floor	1,428 sq. ft.
Total Living Area:	**1,428 sq. ft.**
Daylight basement	458 sq. ft.
Garage	480 sq. ft.

Exterior Wall Framing: 2x4

Foundation Options:

Daylight basement

(Typical foundation & framing conversion diagram available—see order form.)

BLUEPRINT PRICE CODE: A

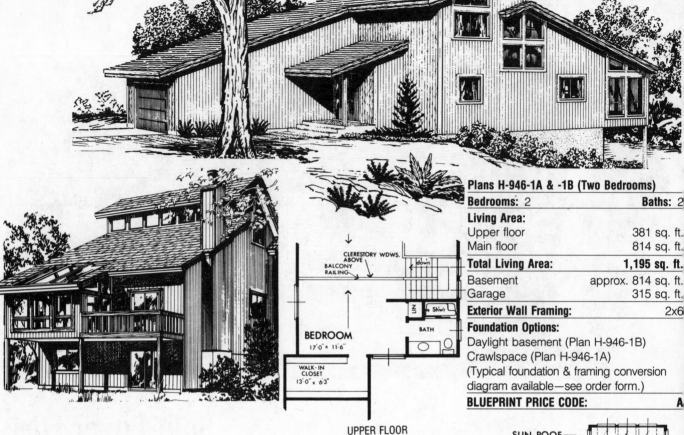

Plans H-946-1A & -1B (Two Bedrooms)

Bedrooms: 2		**Baths:** 2
Living Area:		
Upper floor		381 sq. ft.
Main floor		814 sq. ft.
Total Living Area:		**1,195 sq. ft.**
Basement		approx. 814 sq. ft.
Garage		315 sq. ft.
Exterior Wall Framing:		2x6

Foundation Options:
Daylight basement (Plan H-946-1B)
Crawlspace (Plan H-946-1A)
(Typical foundation & framing conversion diagram available—see order form.)

BLUEPRINT PRICE CODE: A

UPPER FLOOR
PLANS H-946-1A & -1B

CLERESTORY WDWS. ABOVE
BALCONY RAILING
down
LIN
Sh'wr
BATH
BEDROOM
17'-0" x 11'-6"
WALK-IN CLOSET
13'-0" x 6'-3"

Narrow-Lot Solar Design

- This design offers your choice of foundation and number of bedrooms, and it can be built on a narrow, sloping lot.
- The passive-solar dining room has windows on three sides and a slate floor for heat storage. A French door leads to a rear deck.
- The living room features a sloped ceiling, a woodstove in ceiling-high masonry, and sliding glass doors to the adjoining deck.
- The kitchen is open to the dining room but separated from the living room by a 7½-ft.-high wall.
- The upper-level variations include a choice of one or two bedrooms. Clerestory windows above the balcony railing add drama to both versions.

PASSIVE SUN ROOF
DECK
DINING
12'-3" x 10'-0"
WOOD STOVE
SLOPED CEILING
7'-6" HIGH WALL
KITCHEN
8'-0" x 8'-0"
RG
DW
REF
LIVING ROOM
16'-9" x 13'-0"
up
BEDROOM
11'-0" x 11'-9"
CLOSET 5'-6"
down
LIN
BATH
W
GARAGE
13'-3" x 23'-9"
ENTRY
CLOSET 3'-6"
58'-0"
28'-0"
MAIN FLOOR

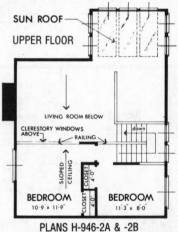

SUN ROOF
UPPER FLOOR
LIVING ROOM BELOW
CLERESTORY WINDOWS ABOVE
RAILING
down
SLOPED CEILING
CLOSET 4'-0"
CLOSET 4'-0"
BEDROOM
10'-9" x 11'-9"
BEDROOM
11'-3" x 8'-0"
PLANS H-946-2A & -2B

Plans H-946-2A & -2B (Three Bedrooms)

Bedrooms: 3		**Baths:** 2
Living Area:		
Upper floor		290 sq. ft.
Main floor		814 sq. ft.
Total Living Area:		**1,104 sq. ft.**
Basement		approx. 814 sq. ft.
Garage		315 sq. ft.
Exterior Wall Framing:		2x6

Foundation Options:
Daylight basement (Plan H-946-2B)
Crawlspace (Plan H-946-2A)
(Typical foundation & framing conversion diagram available—see order form.)

BLUEPRINT PRICE CODE: A

Attractive European Look

- Arched windows with keystones, the stucco finish with corner quoins and many other fine flourishes give this European-style home its good looks.
- The two-story foyer flaunts a handsome open stairway to the upper floor. A second stairway is offered in the family room.
- Columns act as dividers between the formal living spaces to the left of the foyer. Double doors in the dining room close off the kitchen, which features a center island, a walk-in pantry and a handy freezer room.
- A bright, bayed breakfast area is nestled between the kitchen and the family room and offers access to the deck.
- The vaulted family room also opens to the deck and has a fireplace and two built-in bookcases.
- A bonus room or fourth bedroom shares the upper floor with three other bedrooms, three full baths and a convenient laundry room.

Plan APS-3302

Bedrooms: 4+	Baths: 4
Living Area:	
Upper floor	1,276 sq. ft.
Main floor	1,716 sq. ft.
Bonus room	382 sq. ft.
Total Living Area:	**3,374 sq. ft.**
Standard basement	1,716 sq. ft.
Garage	693 sq. ft.
Exterior Wall Framing:	2x4

Foundation Options:

Standard basement
(Typical foundation & framing conversion diagram available—see order form.)

BLUEPRINT PRICE CODE:	E

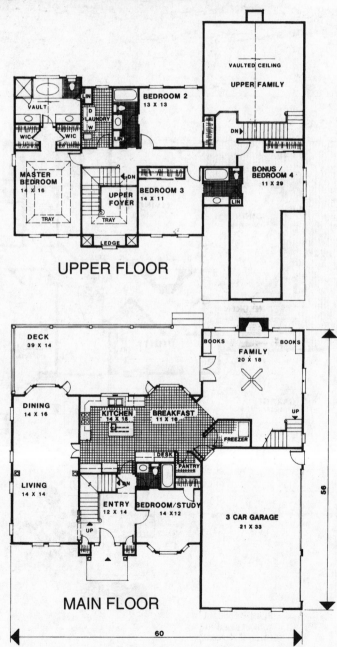

UPPER FLOOR

MAIN FLOOR

TO ORDER THIS BLUEPRINT,
CALL TOLL-FREE 1-800-547-5570

Plan APS-3302

PRICES AND DETAILS
ON PAGES 12-15

257

81'0"

RAILING

DINING
12/0x13/10

SUNKEN
LIVING RM.
23/2x19/10

DECK

STEP

WOOD

STEP

SPA TUB

SH

STEP

LINEN

DRESSING

RAILING

DECK

TUB

BATH

WALK IN
W'ROBE

MASTER SUITE
13/6x15/0

ENTRY

SKYLIGHT

KITCHEN
13/6x11/0

SK YLIGHTS

DW

REF

UTILITY

W
D

PANTRY

WH F

FRZR.

BEDRM. 3
10/3x13/4

BEDRM. 2
10/3x10/10

SEAT

SEAT

58'0"

GARAGE
31/4x25/4

Deluxe Master Bath

DW S

REF

LIN

DN

FRZR.

GARAGE

PLAN P-6600-4D
WITH DAYLIGHT BASEMENT

Main floor:	2,110 sq. ft.
Basement level:	2,080 sq. ft.

PLAN P-6600-4A
WITHOUT BASEMENT
(CRAWLSPACE FOUNDATION)

Total living area: 2,050 sq. ft.
(Not counting garage)

Blueprint Price Code C

Plans P-6600-4A & -4D

PRICES AND DETAILS
ON PAGES 12-15

A-Frame Offers Options

In this versatile A-frame, the main floor is the same in all versions, and includes one bedroom. The upper floor gives you a choice of one large bedroom or two smaller ones.

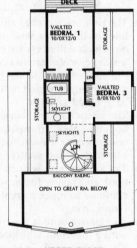

UPPER FLOOR
PLAN P-530-5A
WITH CRAWLSPACE

PLAN P-530-5D
WITH BASEMENT

UPPER FLOOR
PLAN P-530-2A
WITH CRAWLSPACE

PLAN P-530-2D
WITH BASEMENT

Upper floor:	400 sq. ft.
Main floor:	761 sq. ft.
Total living area: (Not counting basement or garage)	1,161 sq. ft.
Basement:	938 sq. ft.
Total living area with daylight basement:	2,099 sq. ft.

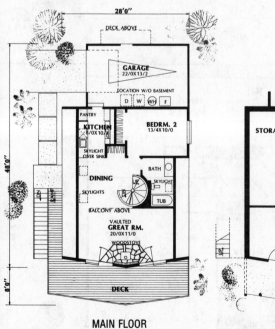

MAIN FLOOR

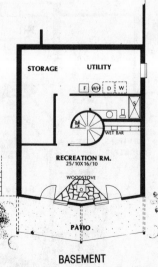

BASEMENT

Blueprint Price Code C With Basement
Blueprint Price Code A Without Basement

TO ORDER THIS BLUEPRINT,
CALL TOLL-FREE 1-800-547-5570

Plans P-530-2A/2D & -5A/5D

PRICES AND DETAILS
ON PAGES 12-15

259

Classic Lines, Elegant Flair

- The rich brick arches and classic lines of this home lend an elegant air which will never be outdated.
- Inside, graceful archways lead from the vaulted entry to the living and dining rooms, which both feature heightened ceilings.
- The kitchen offers abundant counter space, an expansive window over the kitchen sink, large island, desk and pantry.
- The kitchen also is open to the nook and family room, which combine to make a great space for family living.
- The master suite is a pure delight, with a luxurious whirlpool tub and his-and-hers walk-in closets.
- The room marked for storage could also be an exercise or hobby room.

Plan R-2083

Bedrooms: 3	Baths: 2½
Living Area:	
Upper floor	926 sq. ft.
Main floor	1,447 sq. ft.
Total Living Area:	**2,373 sq. ft.**
Garage	609 sq. ft.
Storage	138 sq. ft.
Exterior Wall Framing:	2x6

Foundation Options:

Crawlspace
(Typical foundation & framing conversion diagram available—see order form.)

BLUEPRINT PRICE CODE:	C

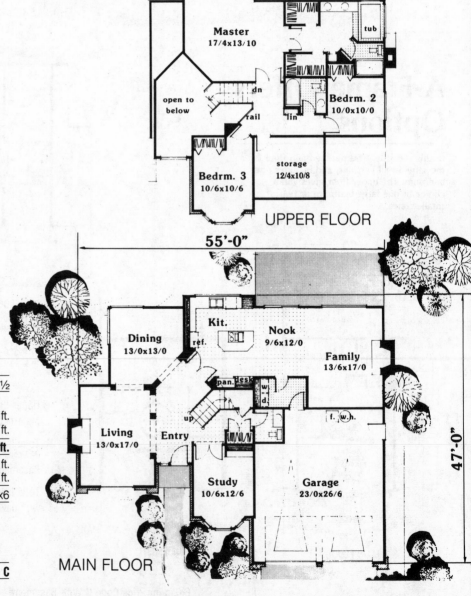

UPPER FLOOR

MAIN FLOOR

Plan R-2083

Ground-Hugging Design

- A clean-lined roof with wide overhangs blends this home into the landscape, and a low-walled entrance court adds to the effect.
- Inside, you'll find many sunny surprises, including bow windows in the living and dining rooms, a beautiful kitchen and a bright semi-circular dinette area.
- The large family room features a fireplace and cathedral ceiling.

- The master suite includes a private bath, large walk-in closet and a skylit dressing area.

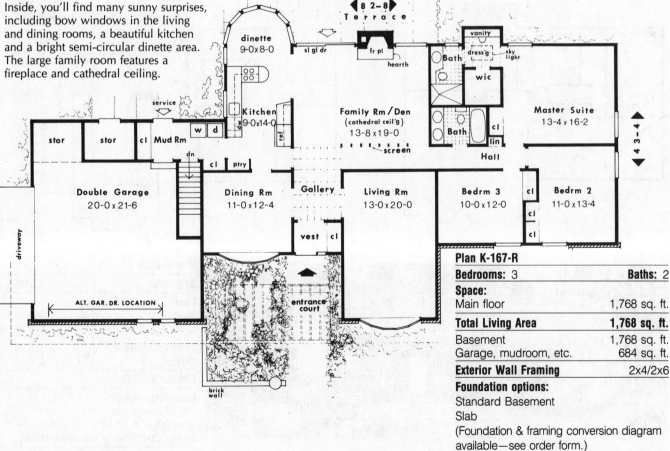

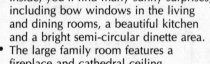

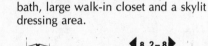

Plan K-167-R	
Bedrooms: 3	**Baths:** 2
Space:	
Main floor	1,768 sq. ft.
Total Living Area	**1,768 sq. ft.**
Basement	1,768 sq. ft.
Garage, mudroom, etc.	684 sq. ft.
Exterior Wall Framing	2x4/2x6

Foundation options:
Standard Basement
Slab
(Foundation & framing conversion diagram available—see order form.)

Blueprint Price Code   B

TO ORDER THIS BLUEPRINT,
CALL TOLL-FREE 1-800-547-5570

Plan K-167-R

PRICES AND DETAILS
ON PAGES 12-15

261

Dramatic Contemporary Takes Advantage of Slope

- Popular plan puts problem building site to work by taking advantage of the slope to create a dramatic and pleasant home.
- Spacious vaulted living/dining area is bathed in natural light from cathedral windows facing the front and clerestory windows at the peak.
- Big kitchen includes pantry and abundant counter space.
- Three main-level bedrooms are isolated for more peace and quiet.
- Lower level includes large recreation room, a fourth bedroom, third bath, laundry area and extra space for a multitude of other uses.

Photo by Kevin Robinson

NOTE:
The above photographed home may have been modified by the homeowner. Please refer to floor plan and/or drawn elevation shown for actual blueprint details.

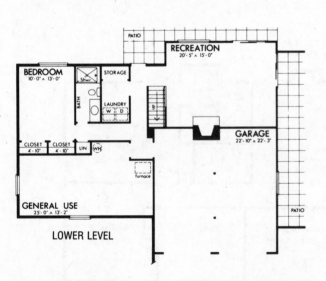

LOWER LEVEL

MAIN FLOOR

Plan H-2045-5	
Bedrooms: 4	**Baths:** 3
Space:	
Main floor:	1,602 sq. ft.
Lower floor:	1,133 sq. ft.
Total living area:	2,735 sq. ft.
Garage:	508 sq. ft.
Exterior Wall Framing:	2x4
Foundation options: Daylight basement only. (Foundation & framing conversion diagram available — see order form.)	
Blueprint Price Code:	D

Clean-Lined Design for Narrow Lot

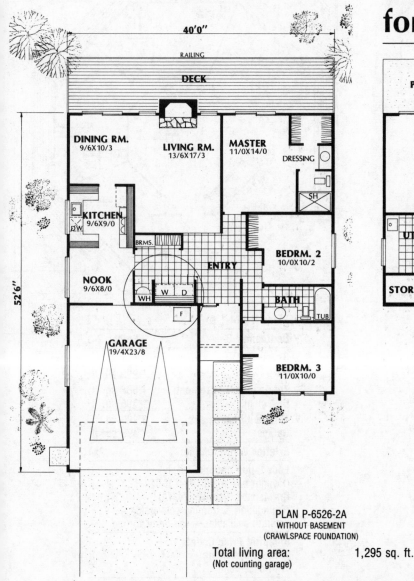

40'0"

RAILING

DECK

DINING RM.
9/6X10/3

LIVING RM.
13/6X17/3

MASTER
11/0X14/0

DRESSING

SH

KITCHEN
9/6X9/0

DW

BRMS.

52'6"

NOOK
9/6X8/0

WH W D

ENTRY

BEDRM. 2
10/0X10/2

F

BATH

TUB

GARAGE
19/4X23/8

BEDRM. 3
11/0X10/0

PLAN P-6526-2A
WITHOUT BASEMENT
(CRAWLSPACE FOUNDATION)

Total living area: 1,295 sq. ft.
(Not counting garage)

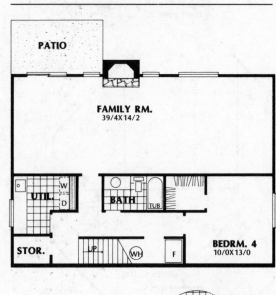

PATIO

FAMILY RM.
39/4X14/2

UTIL. W D

BATH TUB

STOR. UP WH F

BEDRM. 4
10/0X13/0

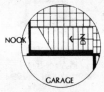

NOOK

N
D

GARAGE

PLAN P-6526-2D
WITH DAYLIGHT BASEMENT

Main floor: (Not counting garage)	1,295 sq. ft.
Basement level:	1,120 sq. ft.
Total living area with daylight basement:	2,415 sq. ft.

Blueprint Price Code A Without Basement
Blueprint Price Code C With Daylight Basement

Spacious Octagon

- Highly functional main floor plan makes traffic easy and minimizes wasted hall space.
- Double-sized entry opens to spacious octagonal living room with central fireplace and access to all rooms.
- U-shaped kitchen and attached dining area allow for both informal and formal occasions.
- Contiguous bedrooms each have independent deck entrances.
- Exciting deck borders entire home.

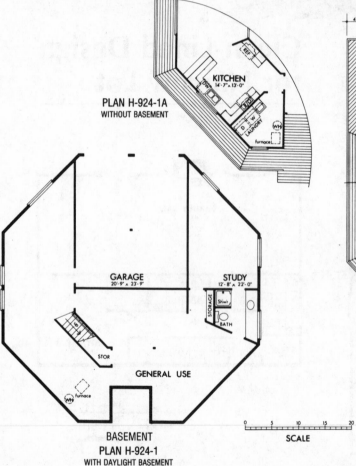

PLAN H-924-1A
WITHOUT BASEMENT

KITCHEN
14'-7" x 13'-0"

D W LAUNDRY

furnace WH

GARAGE
20'-9" x 23'-9"

STUDY
12'-8" x 22'-0"

STORAGE

Sh'wr

BATH

STOR

GENERAL USE

WH furnace

BASEMENT
PLAN H-924-1
WITH DAYLIGHT BASEMENT

SCALE
0 5 10 15 20

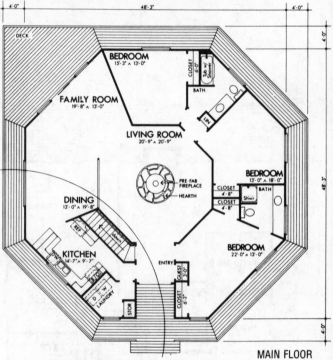

DECK

BEDROOM
15'-3" x 13'-0"

CLOSET
6'-0"

Tub w/ Shower

BATH

FAMILY ROOM
19'-8" x 13'-0"

LIVING ROOM
20'-9" x 20'-9"

BEDROOM
13'-0" x 18'-0"

CLOSET
4'-8"

BATH

PRE-FAB FIREPLACE

HEARTH

CLOSET
4'-8"

Sh'wr

DINING
13'-0" x 19'-8"

REF

KITCHEN
14'-7" x 9'-7"

D W LAUNDRY

STOR

ENTRY

BEDROOM
22'-0" x 13'-0"

CLOSET
6'-2"

GUEST
3'-0"

MAIN FLOOR

Plans H-924-1 & -1A

Bedrooms: 3-4	Baths: 2-3

Space:

Main floor:	1,888 sq. ft.
Total without basement:	1,888 sq. ft.
Basement:	1,395 sq. ft.
Total with basement:	3,283 sq. ft.
Garage:	493 sq. ft.
Exterior Wall Framing:	2x4

Foundation options:
Daylight basement (Plan H-924-1).
Crawlspace (Plan H-924-1A).
(Foundation & framing conversion diagram available — see order form.)

Blueprint Price Code:

Without basement:	B
With basement:	E

Plans H-924-1 & -1A

PRICES AND DETAILS ON PAGES 12-15

Bordered in Brick

- Decorative brick borders, front columns and arched windows give a classy look to this two-story palace.
- The entry is flanked by formal dining and living rooms, both with dramatic front windows.
- A fireplace warms the massive family room that stretches to the morning room and the kitchen at the rear of the home. The bayed morning room offers access to an attached deck; the kitchen has an island worktop.
- A unique sun room also overlooks the deck.
- Windows also surround the master bedroom, which has a large bath.
- Three nice-sized bedrooms share a second full bath on the upper level.

Plan DD-2689

Bedrooms: 4	Baths: 2 ½
Space:	
Upper floor	755 sq. ft.
Main floor	1,934 sq. ft.
Total Living Area	**2,689 sq. ft.**
Basement	1,934 sq. ft.
Garage	436 sq. ft.
Exterior Wall Framing	2×4

Foundation options:
Standard Basement
Crawlspace
Slab
(Foundation & framing conversion diagram available—see order form.)

Blueprint Price Code	D

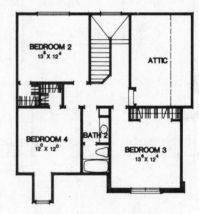

UPPER FLOOR

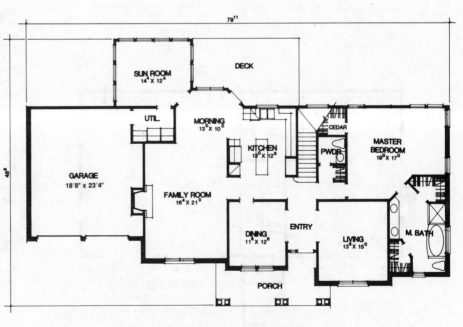

MAIN FLOOR

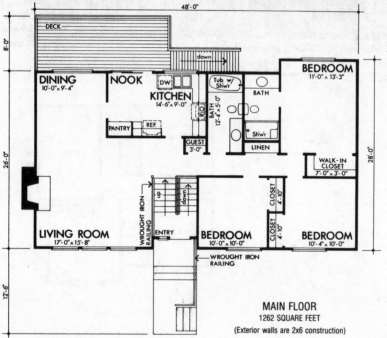

MAIN FLOOR
1262 SQUARE FEET
(Exterior walls are 2x6 construction)

DECK

DINING 10'-0" x 9'-4"

NOOK

KITCHEN 14'-6" x 9'-0"

DW

PANTRY

REF.

GUEST 3'-0"

BATH 12'-4.5-0"

Tub w/ Shwr

BATH

Sh'wr

LINEN

BEDROOM 11'-0" x 13'-3"

WALK-IN CLOSET 7'-0" x 3'-0"

LIVING ROOM 17'-0" x 15'-8"

WROUGHT IRON RAILING

ENTRY

up down

stairs

BEDROOM 10'-0" x 10'-0"

CLOSET 4'-10"

CLOSET 4'-10"

CLOSET 4'-10"

BEDROOM 10'-4" x 10'-0"

WROUGHT IRON RAILING

48'-0"
8'-0"
26'-0"
12'-6"
28'-0"

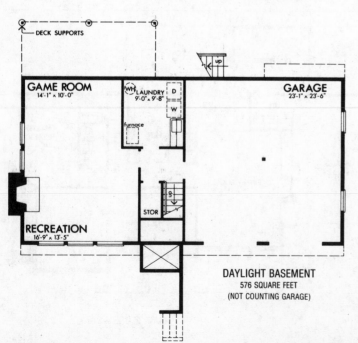

DAYLIGHT BASEMENT
576 SQUARE FEET
(NOT COUNTING GARAGE)

DECK SUPPORTS

GAME ROOM 14'-1" x 10'-0"

WH

LAUNDRY 9'-0" x 9'-8"

D

W

furnace

up

GARAGE 23'-1" x 23'-6"

STOR

RECREATION 16'-9" x 13'-5"

Economical Hillside Design

The solid, expansive, well-to-do appearance of this home plan belies the fact that it contains only 1,262 sq. ft. on the main floor and 1,152 sq. ft. on the lower level, including garage space.

This plan has a simple framing pattern, rectangular shape and straight roof line, and it lacks complicated embellishments. Even the excavation, only half as deep as usual, helps make this an affordable and relatively quick and easy house to build.

A split-level entry opens onto a landing between floors, providing access up to the main living room or down to the recreation and work areas.

The living space is large and open. The dining and living rooms combine with the stairwell to form a large visual space. A large 8'x20' deck, visible through the picture window in the dining room, adds visual expansiveness to this multi-purpose space.

The L-shaped kitchen and adjoining nook are perfect for daily food preparation and family meals, and the deck is also accessible from this area through sliding glass doors. The kitchen features a 48 cubic foot pantry closet.

The master bedroom has a complete private bathroom and oversized closet. The remaining bedrooms each have a large closet and access to a full-size bathroom.

A huge rec and game room is easily accessible from the entry, making it ideal for a home office or business.

Main floor:	1,262 sq. ft.
Lower level:	576 sq. ft.
Total living area: (Not counting garage)	1,838 sq. ft.

Blueprint Price Code B

Plan H-1332-5

PRICES AND DETAILS
ON PAGES 12-15

Loaded with Livability Features

- Inside an attractive exterior, you will find in this home a marvelous floor plan designed to provide the utmost in livability.
- The living and dining areas flow together to create a wonderful space for large gatherings.
- The family room/nook/kitchen combination provides ample space for a wide variety of activities for the busy family.
- Upstairs, the sumptuous master suite includes a deluxe bath and a large wardrobe closet.
- Two secondary bedrooms share a compartmentalized corner bath, and a large bonus room above the garage offers potential for many uses.

Plan R-2111

Bedrooms: 3	Baths: 2½
Living Area:	
Upper floor	945 sq. ft.
Main floor	1,115 sq. ft.
Bonus room	285 sq. ft.
Total Living Area:	**2,345 sq. ft.**
Garage	851 sq. ft.
Exterior Wall Framing:	2x6

Foundation Options:
Crawlspace
(Typical foundation & framing conversion diagram available—see order form.)

BLUEPRINT PRICE CODE: C

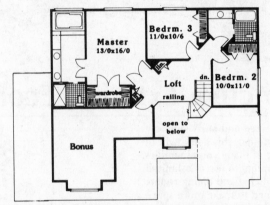

UPPER FLOOR

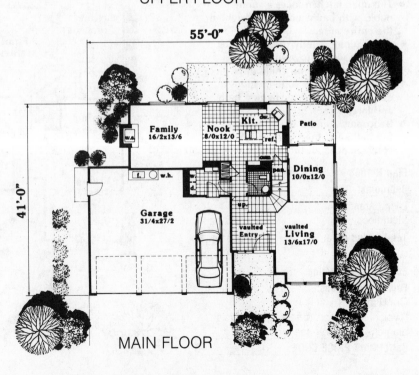

MAIN FLOOR

Distinctive Exterior, Economical Construction

- A modest-sized and fairly simple one-story design, this home will fit the budget of many young families.
- To make optimum use of a limited space, the living and dining rooms are combined to make more space for entertaining large groups.
- The open kitchen faces a sunny nook, with bay windows to brighten the entire area.
- An adjoining family room includes a corner wood stove for heat and a cozy atmosphere on chilly days.
- A pleasant master suite includes a double-door entry, skylighted bath and large closet.
- Bedrooms 2 and 3 share another full bath, and the utility area is convenient to all three bedrooms.

Plan R-1063

Bedrooms: 3	Baths: 2
Living Area:	
Main floor	1,585 sq. ft.
Total Living Area:	**1,585 sq. ft.**
Garage	408 sq. ft.
Exterior Wall Framing:	2x6

Foundation Options:

Crawlspace
(Typical foundation & framing conversion diagram available—see order form.)

BLUEPRINT PRICE CODE:	B

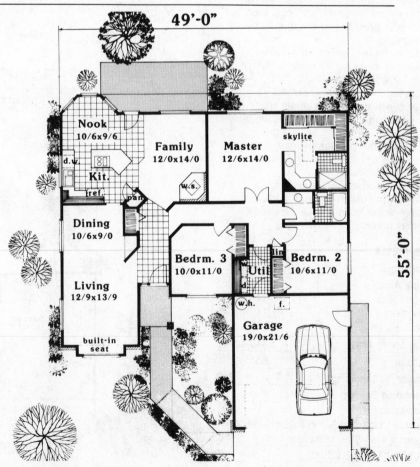

TO ORDER THIS BLUEPRINT, CALL TOLL-FREE 1-800-547-5570   Plan R-1063   **PRICES AND DETAILS ON PAGES 12-15**

Compact, Easy to Build

This compact vacation or retirement home is economical and easy to construct. Only 24' x 46' for the daylight basement version, it nonetheless contains all the necessities and some of the luxuries one desires in a three-bedroom home. The non-basement version measures 24' x 44'.

Overall width for both versions including deck and carport is 50'.

One luxury is the separate, private bath adjoining the master bedroom; another is the double "His & Hers" wardrobe closets for the same room. The other two bedrooms are equipped with good-sized closets and share a second bathroom. Even if you choose the basement version, the convenience of first floor laundry facilities is yours.

The open stairway to the basement adds 3' to the visual size of the living room. A

pre-fab fireplace is located to allow enjoyment of a cozy hearth and a beautiful view from the same chair.

The plans are so completely detailed that a handyman amateur might frame this building (with the help of a few friends). Why not try it? (Be sure to order a materials list, too!)

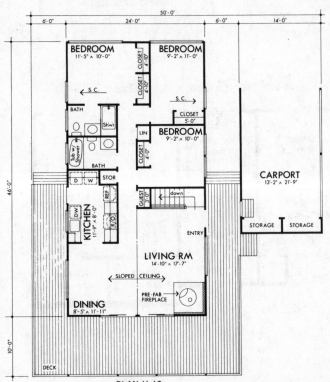

PLAN H-18
WITH DAYLIGHT BASEMENT
1104 SQUARE FEET

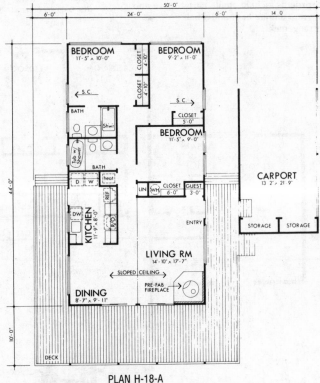

PLAN H-18-A
WITH CRAWLSPACE
1056 SQUARE FEET

Total living area: 1,104 sq. ft.
(Not counting basement or carport)

Blueprint Price Code A

Plans H-18 & H-18-A

Cathedral Ceiling With Studio

This rustic/contemporary modified A-Frame design combines a 20' high cathedral ceiling over a sunken living room with a large studio over the two rear bedrooms. The isolated master suite features a walk-in closet and compartmentalized bath with double vanity and linen closet. The two rear bedrooms include ample closet space and share a unique bath-and-a-half arrangement.

On one side of the U-shaped kitchen and breakfast nook is the formal dining room which is separated from the entry by a planter. On the other side is a utility room which can be entered from either the kitchen or garage.

All or part of the basement can be used to supplement the 2,213 sq. ft. of heated living area on the main floor. The exterior features a massive stone fireplace, large glass areas and a combination of vertical wood siding and stone.

First floor:	2,213 sq. ft.
Second floor:	260 sq. ft.
Total living area:	2,473 sq. ft.
(Not counting basement or garage)	

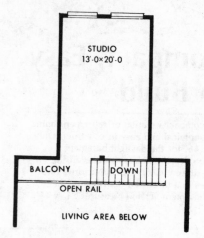

STUDIO 13'-0×20'-0

BALCONY   DOWN

OPEN RAIL

LIVING AREA BELOW

Specify basement, crawlspace or slab foundation.

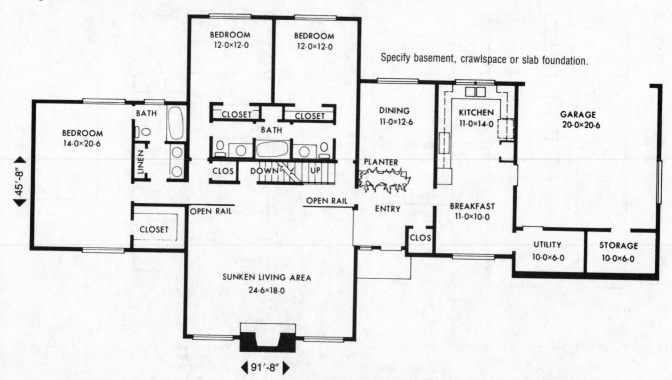

BEDROOM 12-0×12-0
BEDROOM 12-0×12-0
BATH
CLOSET
CLOSET
BATH
BEDROOM 14-0×20-6
LINEN
CLOS
DOWN
UP
DINING 11-0×12-6
KITCHEN 11-0×14-0
GARAGE 20-0×20-6
PLANTER
CLOSET
OPEN RAIL
OPEN RAIL
ENTRY
BREAKFAST 11-0×10-0
CLOS
SUNKEN LIVING AREA 24-6×18-0
UTILITY 10-0×6-0
STORAGE 10-0×6-0
45'-8"
91'-8"

Blueprint Price Code C

Plan C-7113

PRICES AND DETAILS ON PAGES 12-15

Anyone for Fun?

- A spectacular sunken game room with a corner window, vaulted ceilings, wet bar and half-wall that separates it from the family room is ideal for the active family or for those who like to entertain.
- The exciting atmosphere continues to the family room, also at a level lower than the rest of the home; here you'll find a fireplace, a rear window wall and a railing that allows a view of the adjoining vaulted nook.
- The spacious kitchen offers an island cooktop, pantry and pass-through to the game room hallway; formal, vaulted living areas are found opposite the entry.
- An upper-level bridge overlooks the game room and joins the two secondary bedrooms with the master suite and luxury, skylit master bath.

71'0"

PATIO

VAULTED NOOK 9/8x8/6

FAMILY RM. 18/4x13/6

VAULTED DINING 12/0x14/4

KITCHEN 17/0x14/0

42" HIGH WALL

SUNKEN VAULTED GAME RM. 24/6x16/0

PANTRY

UTILITY 12/0x6/2

BAR

VAULTED LIVING RM. 14/4x16/6

ENTRY

BATH

TUB   LINEN

F WH

GARAGE 32/0x22/6

DEN/ BEDRM. 4 11/0x12/0

SEAT

59'0"

MAIN FLOOR

SEAT

CEILING LINE

MASTER SUITE 18/4x13/6

SHELF   LINEN

VANITY   SKYLIGHT

SUNKEN TUB   STEP

SKYLIGHT

WALK IN WARDROBE

SKYLIGHT   RAILING

OPEN TO GAME ROOM BELOW

RAILING

OPEN TO ENTRY BELOW

BATH

TUB   LIN

BEDRM. 2 14/8x11/0

SEAT

UPPER FLOOR

BEDRM. 3

SEAT

WITH DAYLIGHT BASEMENT

ENTRY   BATH

Plans P-7665-3A & -3D

Bedrooms: 3-4	Baths: 3
Space:	
Upper floor	1,160 sq. ft.
Main floor	2,124 sq. ft.
Total Living Area	**3,284 sq. ft.**
Basement	2,104 sq. ft.
Garage	720 sq. ft.
Exterior Wall Framing	2x4
Foundation options:	Plan #
Daylight Basement	P-7665-3D
Crawlspace	P-7665-3A
(Foundation & framing conversion diagram available—see order form.)	
Blueprint Price Code	E

Private Decks Abound

- With two bedrooms opening to their own private deck, and another deck extending the full length of the living room, the scenic views can be fully enjoyed, both inside and out.

- The sunken living room features a fireplace, a dramatic 19-foot ceiling with skylights, and three sliding glass doors opening to the deck.

- The efficient kitchen overlooks the front yard and the rear view over the breakfast bar and dining room with opening to the living room.

Plan CAR-81007

Bedrooms: 3	Baths: 1½

Space:

Upper floor:	560 sq. ft.
Main floor:	911 sq. ft.
Total living area:	**1,471 sq. ft.**
Basement:	911 sq. ft.
Exterior Wall Framing:	**2x6**

Foundation options:
Standard basement.
(Foundation & framing conversion diagram available — see order form.)

Blueprint Price Code:	A

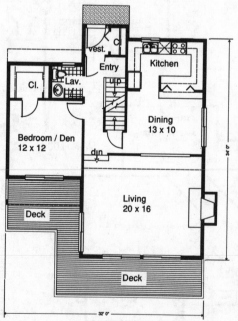

MAIN FLOOR

UPPER FLOOR

TO ORDER THIS BLUEPRINT, CALL TOLL-FREE 1-800-547-5570   Plan CAR-81007   **PRICES AND DETAILS ON PAGES 12-15**

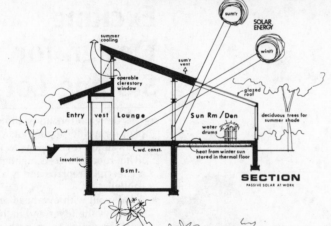

SOLAR ENERGY

summer cooling

operable clerestory window

glazed roof

Entry | vest | Lounge | Sun Rm / Den | deciduous trees for summer shade

water drums

wd. const.

insulation

heat from winter sun stored in thermal floor

Bsmt.

SECTION

PASSIVE SOLAR AT WORK

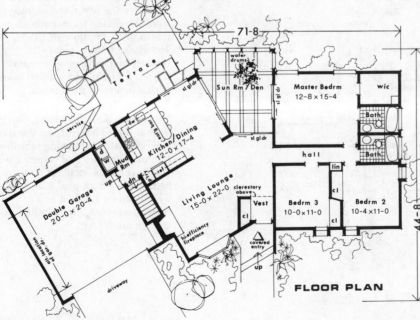

FLOOR PLAN

71-8

44-8

Terrace

service

Double Garage 20-0 x 20-4

driveway

Mud Rm

Kitchen/Dining 12-0 x 17-4

up

dn

Living Lounge 15-0 x 22-0

hi-efficiency fireplace

covered entry

up

Vest

clerestory above

Sun Rm / Den

Master Bedrm 12-8 x 15-4

wic

Bath

hall

Bath

lin

cl

Bedrm 3 10-0 x 11-0

cl

Bedrm 2 10-4 x 11-0

cl

Dramatic Angles

Dramatically angled to maximize the benefits of passive solar technology, this compact one-story home can be adapted to many sites and orientations. South-facing rooms, including sun room/den, absorb and store heat energy in thermal floors for night time radiation. Heavy insulation in exterior walls and ceilings, plus double glazing in windows, keep heat loss to a minimum. During the summer, heat is expelled through an operable clerestory window and through an automatic vent in the sun room.

Inside, entrance vestibule overlooks a breathtaking view of the sun room and the outdoors beyond; kitchen/dining area opens to a large rear terrace. Three bedrooms are isolated for total privacy. Living area, excluding sun room, is 1,223 sq. ft.; garage, mud room, etc. 504 sq. ft.; partial basement, 1,030 sq. ft.

Living Area:	1,223 sq. ft.
Garage and Mud Room:	504 sq. ft.
Basement (Opt.):	1,030 sq. ft.

(Alternate slab-on-grade foundation plan included.)

Blueprint Price Code A

Plan K-505-R

PRICES AND DETAILS ON PAGES 12-15

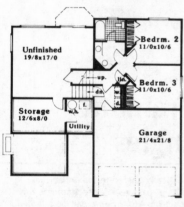

UPPER FLOOR

Plan R-4033

Bedrooms: 3	Baths: 2

Space:

Upper two levels:	1,185 sq. ft.
Lower level:	480 sq. ft.

Total living area:	**1,665 sq. ft.**
Bonus area:	334 sq. ft.
Garage:	462 sq. ft.
Storage:	100 sq. ft.

Exterior Wall Framing:	2x6

Foundation options:
Daylight basement only.
(Foundation & framing conversion
diagram available — see order form.)

Blueprint Price Code:	B

MAIN FLOOR

Exciting Design for Sloping Lot

- This design offers an exciting floor plan for a side-sloping lot.
- The vaulted foyer opens to the living room which is highlighted by a cheerful fireplace and is also vaulted.
- A half-wall with overhead arch separates the foyer and hallway from the dining room without interrupting the flow of space.
- The kitchen offers plenty of counter and cabinet space, and adjoins a brightly lit vaulted nook with a pantry in the corner.
- Separated from the rest of the household, the upper level master suite is a true haven from the day's worries, with its relaxing whirlpool tub, dual vanities and roomy closet.
- The lower level includes two bedrooms, a bath plus a large area which can be finished as a recreation room, plus a utility and storage area.

Plan R-4033

PRICES AND DETAILS
ON PAGES 12-15

Comfort and Economy on a Narrow Lot

- Since the width of this home is only 24 ft., it can be built on a 40-ft. lot — even less in some jurisdictions, and it also lends itself to zero-lot-line developments and duplex construction.
- But small doesn't mean inadequate, and this plan is proof of that.
- A covered entry leads into an efficient foyer that takes traffic into the living room or the family room.
- Also note the convenient powder room off the entry.
- The living room contains an impressive fireplace, and flows together with the family room to provide plenty of space for entertaining.
- The kitchen is efficient and fairly open, and includes a laundry area.
- Upstairs, the master bedroom includes a large walk-in closet and a private bath with an oversized shower.
- Two secondary bedrooms share a second full bath.

Plan H-1427-1A

Bedrooms: 3	Baths: 2½
Living Area:	
Upper floor	755 sq. ft.
Main floor	655 sq. ft.
Total Living Area:	**1,410 sq. ft.**
Garage	404 sq. ft.
Exterior Wall Framing:	2x4

Foundation Options:

Crawlspace
(Typical foundation & framing conversion diagram available—see order form.)

BLUEPRINT PRICE CODE: A

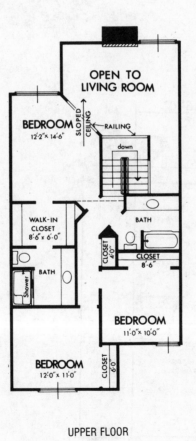

MAIN FLOOR

UPPER FLOOR

Bright, Flowing Spaces Inside

- Bright, flowing spaces are the hallmark of this handsome one-story design.
- A dramatic bay window highlights the living room, which flows into the formal dining room with a large picture window. The centrally located fireplace can be enjoyed from both rooms.
- The kitchen is strategically positioned between the dining room and the sunny, bay-windowed breakfast nook.
- A TV room or den is a great extension of the family living space but can be closed off to create a third bedroom.
- A full bath, a laundry room and two more bedrooms, including a large master suite with a private bath, complete this smart-looking, cost-efficient home.

Plan R-1028

Bedrooms: 2-3	Baths: 2
Living Area:	
Main floor	1,305 sq. ft.
Total Living Area:	**1,305 sq. ft.**
Garage	429 sq. ft.
Exterior Wall Framing:	2x6

Foundation Options:
Crawlspace
(Typical foundation & framing conversion diagram available—see order form.)

BLUEPRINT PRICE CODE: A

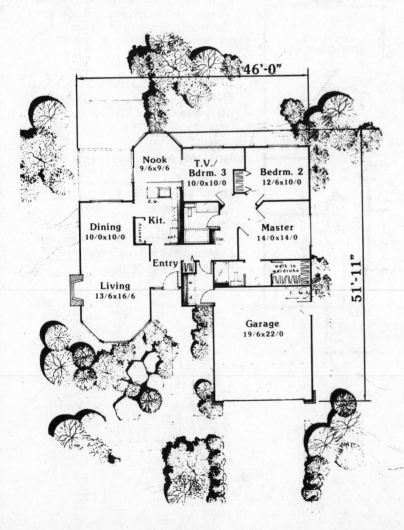

Compact and Luxurious

- The best from the past and the present is bundled up in this compact design, reminiscent of a New England saltbox.
- The cozy kitchen has a center island with a breakfast counter and a built-in range and oven. The corner sink saves on counter space.
- A decorative railing separates the formal dining room from the sunken living room.
- The living room features a vaulted ceiling, built-in shelves, a central fireplace and access to a large rear deck.
- The upper-floor master suite boasts a spa bath, a separate shower and a walk-in closet.

Plan H-1453-1A

Bedrooms: 3		**Baths:** 2
Living Area:		
Upper floor		386 sq. ft.
Main floor		1,385 sq. ft.
Total Living Area:		**1,771 sq. ft.**
Garage		409 sq. ft.
Exterior Wall Framing:		2x6

Foundation Options:
Crawlspace
(Typical foundation & framing conversion diagram available—see order form.)

BLUEPRINT PRICE CODE: **B**

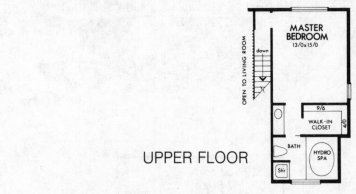

UPPER FLOOR

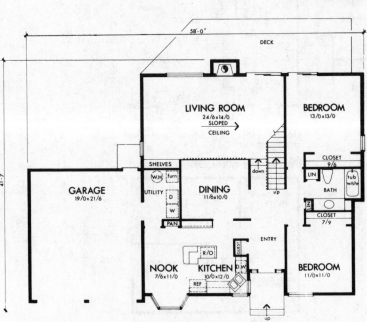

MAIN FLOOR

TO ORDER THIS BLUEPRINT,
CALL TOLL-FREE 1-800-547-5570

Plan H-1453-1A

PRICES AND DETAILS
ON PAGES 12-15

277

P-524-5D Exterior

P-524-2D Exterior

Spacious Great Room

- This same floor plan is available with two different exterior treatments, as illustrated.
- In either case, a spacious Great Room is the highlight, with its vaulted ceiling, wide windows and sliding glass doors which open to a deck, and to the view beyond.
- The dining room and kitchen also feature vaulted ceilings.
- A loft room adds another sleeping area, and the daylight basement offers even more usable space.

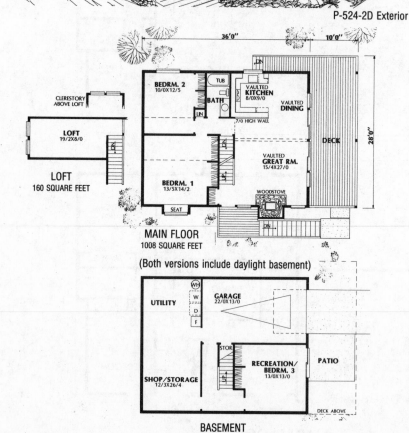

CLERESTORY ABOVE LOFT

LOFT
19/2X8/0

LOFT
160 SQUARE FEET

36'0"   10'0"

BEDRM. 2
10/0X12/5

TUB

BATH

LN

VAULTED KITCHEN
8/0X9/0

VAULTED DINING

7/0 HIGH WALL

DECK

28'0"

VAULTED GREAT RM.
15/4X27/0

BEDRM. 1
13/5X14/2

SEAT

WOODSTOVE

DN

MAIN FLOOR
1008 SQUARE FEET

(Both versions include daylight basement)

WH

UTILITY

W
D
F

GARAGE
22/0X13/0

SHOP/STORAGE
12/3X26/4

STOR

RECREATION/ BEDRM. 3
13/0X13/0

PATIO

DECK ABOVE

BASEMENT
FLOOR AREA 722 SQUARE FEET
(Not counting garage)

Plans P-524-2D & -5D

Bedrooms: 3	Baths: 1
Space:	
Loft:	160 sq. ft.
Main floor:	1,008 sq. ft.
Lower level:	722 sq. ft.
Total living area:	1,890 sq. ft.
Garage:	286 sq. ft.
Exterior Wall Framing:	2x4

Foundation options:
Daylight basement.
(Foundation & framing conversion diagram available — see order form.)

Blueprint Price Code:	B

Master Suite with Fireplace, Deck

- This brick-accented two-story has front stacked bay windows, a three-car garage and staggered rooflines.
- Inside you'll find large, open living areas oriented to the rear and fireplaces in the living room, sunken family room and master bedroom.
- Both the family room and study open out to a rear patio; the island kitchen and bayed nook join the family room, which also offers a wet bar.
- Room for two to three bedrooms plus the master suite with private deck and lavish, skylit spa bath is found on the upper level.

Plan P-7751-3A and P-7751-3D

Bedrooms: 3-4	Baths: 2 ½
Space:	
Upper floor	1,411 sq. ft.
Main floor	1,737 sq. ft.
Total Living Area	**3,148 sq. ft.**
Basement	1,737 sq. ft.
Garage	677 sq. ft.
Exterior Wall Framing	**2x6**
Foundation options:	**Plan #**
Daylight Basement	P-7751-3D
Crawlspace	P-7751-3A
(Foundation & framing conversion diagram available—see order form.)	
Blueprint Price Code	**E**

UPPER FLOOR

BASEMENT STAIR LOCATION-P-7751-3D

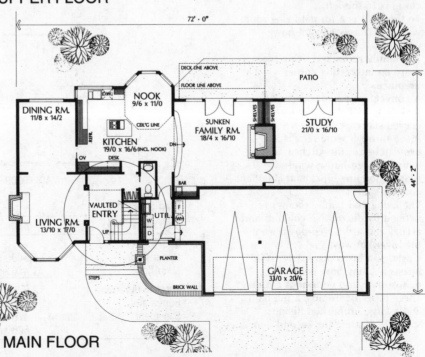

MAIN FLOOR

Oriented for Scenic Rear View

- That elegant look of the past is found in this expansive post-modern design.
- A two-story vaulted entry leads to spacious formal entertaining areas.
- A dining room with built-in China closet is to the left.
- To the right is a formal living room with a strikingly elegant bow window.
- The family room and living room share an interesting corner fireplace.
- A convenient powder room is tucked away behind the sweeping curved staircase.
- A see-through wine rack is an eye-catcher in the kitchen, along with its green-house window, island chopping block and abundant counter space.
- The living and family rooms are defined by decorative columns and arches and are a step-down from the foyer/hallway.
- Upstairs, a luxurious master suite boasts a sunny bow window, deluxe bath and enormous closet.
- Three other bedrooms, a full bath and a large unfinished "bonus space" complete the second floor.

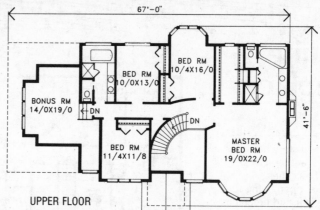

UPPER FLOOR

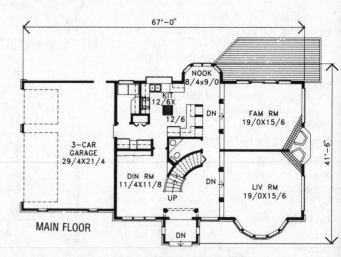

MAIN FLOOR

Plan SD-8819

Bedrooms: 4-5	Baths: 2½

Space:

Upper floor:	1,500 sq. ft.
Main floor:	1,476 sq. ft.

Total living area:	2,976 sq. ft.
Bonus area:	266 sq. ft.
Basement:	approx. 1,476 sq. ft.
Garage:	626 sq. ft.

Exterior Wall Framing: 2x6

Foundation options:
Standard basement.
Crawlspace.
(Foundation & framing conversion diagram available — see order form.)

Blueprint Price Code: D

Deluxe Private Master Bedroom Suite

Living area:	1,380 sq. ft.
Utility & storage:	84 sq. ft.
Garage:	440 sq. ft.
Porch:	80 sq. ft.
	1,984 sq. ft.

PLAN E-1311
WITHOUT BASEMENT
(BOTH CRAWLSPACE AND
SLAB FOUNDATION AVAILABLE)

Exterior walls are 2x6 construction.

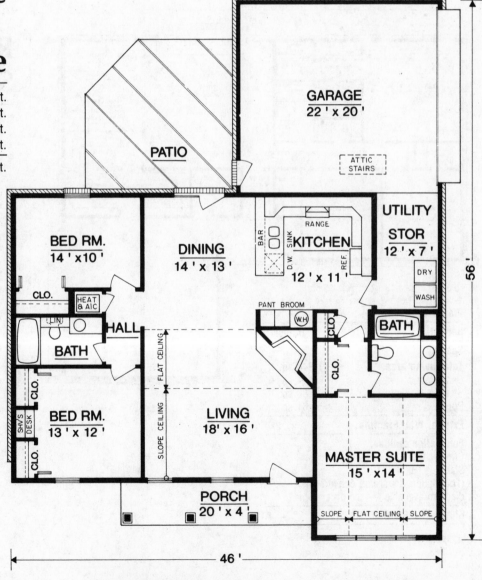

TO ORDER THIS BLUEPRINT,
CALL TOLL-FREE 1-800-547-5570

Blueprint Price Code A
Plan E-1311

PRICES AND DETAILS
ON PAGES 12-15

281

Plan E-1307

Bedrooms: 3	Baths: 2

Space:

Total living area:	1,346 sq. ft.
Garage:	441 sq. ft.
Storage & utility:	88 sq. ft.
Porch:	61 sq. ft.

Exterior Wall Framing: 2x4

Foundation options:
Crawlspace.
Slab.
(Foundation & framing conversion
diagram available — see order form.)

Blueprint Price Code: A

Roomy One-Story Home

- Economical to build and maintain, this home includes many features often found only in larger houses.
- The large living room includes a massive fireplace and beamed, vaulted ceilings, and visually flows into the raised dining room.
- The kitchen is large and offers abundant counter space. A handy utility room adjoins the kitchen.
- The master suite features a large walk-in closet and private bath.
- The two secondary bedrooms also have large closets, and share a second full bath.
- An efficient but still inviting entryway leads off the covered porch.

 Plan E-1307

Elegance at Every Turn

- For a home that is truly outstanding in both beauty and space, this design is hard to beat!
- Elegance is found in every corner, from the spectacular curved stairways in the foyer to the luxurious master suite.
- The huge central living room features a vaulted ceiling, decorative entry columns and a dramatic fireplace.
- The gourmet kitchen and breakfast nook are hidden behind double doors. The kitchen has a cooktop island, a walk-in pantry and a snack counter. The octagon-shaped nook opens to the backyard and adjoins a large sunken family room.
- Up one flight of stairs is the master suite and a quiet den with built-in bookshelves. The master bedroom is entered through elegant double doors and offers a sunny sitting area and a skylighted private bath with an exciting garden tub, a separate shower and a toilet room with a bidet.
- A second stairway accesses two more bedrooms, each with a private bath.

UPPER FLOOR

MAIN FLOOR 92'-2"

Plan R-4029

Plan R-4029	
Bedrooms: 3	**Baths:** 4½
Living Area:	
Upper floor	972 sq. ft.
Main floor	3,346 sq. ft.
Partial basement	233 sq. ft.
Total Living Area:	**4,551 sq. ft.**
Garage	825 sq. ft.
Exterior Wall Framing:	2x6

Foundation Options:
Partial basement
(Typical foundation & framing conversion diagram available—see order form.)

BLUEPRINT PRICE CODE: G

TO ORDER THIS BLUEPRINT,
CALL TOLL-FREE 1-800-547-5570

Plan R-4029

PRICES AND DETAILS
ON PAGES 12-15

283

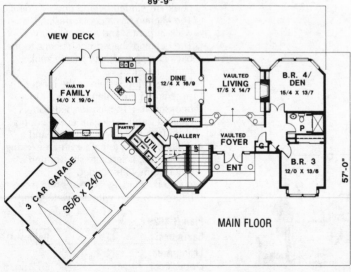

UPPER FLOOR

89'-9"

VIEW DECK

3 CAR GARAGE
35/6 X 24/0

VAULTED FAMILY
14/0 X 19/0+

KIT

DINE
12/4 X 16/9

VAULTED LIVING
17/5 X 14/7

B.R. 4/ DEN
15/4 X 13/7

PANTRY

UTIL

GALLERY

VAULTED FOYER

ENT

B.R. 3
12/0 X 13/6

SUFFET

57'-0"

MAIN FLOOR

Designed with Elegance in Mind

- This expansive home boasts 3,220 sq. ft. of living space designed with elegance in mind.
- The front of the home is finished in stucco, with the rest in lap siding for economy.
- The vaulted foyer leads directly into an impressive sunken and vaulted living room, guarded by columns that echo the exterior treatment.
- The formal dining room is visually joined to the living room to make an impressive space for entertaining.
- An unusually fine kitchen opens to a large family room, which boasts a vaulted ceiling, a corner fireplace and access to a sizable rear deck.
- In the front, the extra-wide staircase is a primary attraction, with its dramatic feature window.
- A terrific master suite includes a splendid master bath with double sinks and a huge walk-through closet.
- A second upstairs bedroom also includes a private bath.

Plan LRD-11388

Bedrooms: 3-4	Baths: 3
Living Area:	
Upper floor:	1,095 sq. ft.
Main floor	2,125 sq. ft.
Total Living Area:	**3,220 sq. ft.**
Standard basement	2,125 sq. ft.
Garage	802 sq. ft.

Exterior Wall Framing:	2x6

Foundation Options:
Standard basement
Crawlspace
Slab
(Typical foundation & framing conversion diagram available—see order form.)

BLUEPRINT PRICE CODE: E

Vaulted Master Suite Upstairs

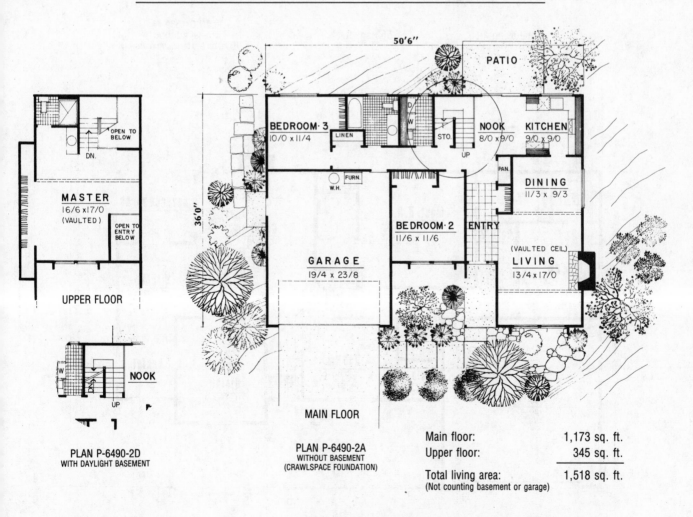

MASTER
16/6 x 17/0
(VAULTED)

OPEN TO BELOW

DN.

OPEN TO ENTRY BELOW

UPPER FLOOR

NOOK

W

UP

PLAN P-6490-2D
WITH DAYLIGHT BASEMENT

50'6"

PATIO

BEDROOM·3
10/0 x 11/4

LINEN

NOOK
8/0 x 9/0

KITCHEN
9/0 x 9/0

STO.

UP

D W

PAN.

FURN.

W.H.

DINING
11/3 x 9/3

36'0"

BEDROOM·2
11/6 x 11/6

ENTRY

GARAGE
19/4 x 23/8

(VAULTED CEIL.)
LIVING
13/4 x 17/0

MAIN FLOOR

PLAN P-6490-2A
WITHOUT BASEMENT
(CRAWLSPACE FOUNDATION)

Main floor:	1,173 sq. ft.
Upper floor:	345 sq. ft.
Total living area:	1,518 sq. ft.

(Not counting basement or garage)

TO ORDER THIS BLUEPRINT,
CALL TOLL-FREE 1-800-547-5570

Blueprint Price Code B
Plans P-6490-2A & -2D

PRICES AND DETAILS
ON PAGES 12-15   285

Great Room Features Cathedral Ceiling

Total living area:
(Not counting garage)

1,559 sq. ft.

PLAN Q-1559-1A
WITHOUT BASEMENT
(SLAB-ON-GRADE FOUNDATION)

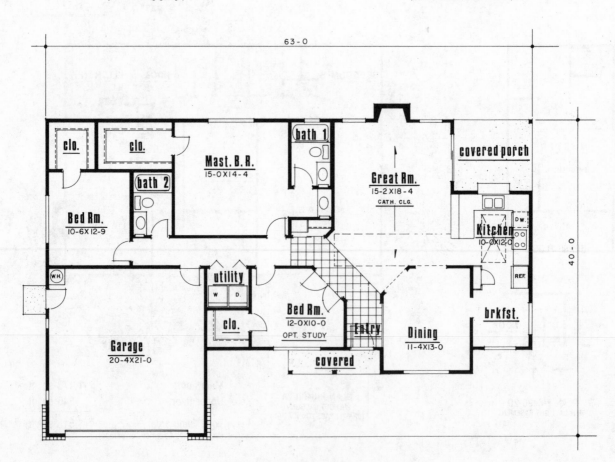

Blueprint Price Code B

Plan Q-1559-1A

Flamboyant Floor Plan

- A host of architectural styles went into the making of this interesting design, from country and Victorian to contemporary. A mixture of gable and hip roofs, a bayed front porch and several differently shaped windows give the exterior plenty of impact.

- A dramatic open floor plan combines to make the home stylishly up to date. High ceilings throughout much of the main level add to the flamboyant floor plan.

- The fantastic family room features a soaring ceiling, a fireplace and an abundance of windows. The adjoining breakfast room has a cathedral ceiling and is open to the kitchen. The attached sun porch is enclosed in glass, with skylights in the sloped ceiling. Formal dining is reserved for the unusual dining room at the front of the home.

- The first-floor master suite boasts a cathedral ceiling, lots of closet space and an irresistible garden tub.

- Three bedrooms and a full bath make up the second level. Each of the bedrooms has a walk-in closet.

Plan AX-1318

Bedrooms: 4	Baths: 2 ½
Space:	
Upper floor	697 sq. ft.
Main floor	1,642 sq. ft.
Total Living Area	**2,339 sq. ft.**
Basement	1,384 sq. ft.
Garage	431 sq. ft.
Exterior Wall Framing	2x4

Foundation options:

Standard Basement

Crawlspace

Slab

(Foundation & framing conversion diagram available—see order form.)

Blueprint Price Code	C

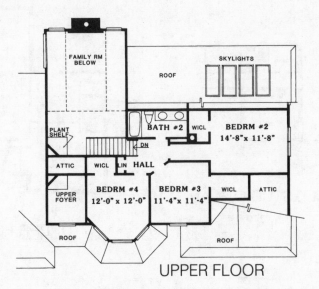

UPPER FLOOR

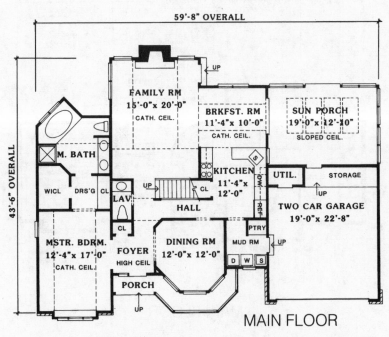

MAIN FLOOR

ALT. STUDIO PLAN

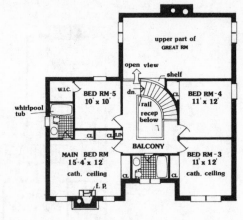

UPPER FLOOR

Floor Plan Offers Options

- This exquisite design offers elegant exterior detailing and a versatile interior floor plan.
- The open, two-story reception area reveals a classic curved staircase.
- A formal living room with a brick fireplace and an open dining room flanks the foyer.
- The roomy gourmet kitchen opens to a dinette/Great Room combination enhanced by a fireplace, a sloped ceiling and wooden French doors that open to the rear terrace.
- The main level may also include the master bedroom with private bath. The alternate floor plan uses this space as a home office or studio.
- The upper level houses three secondary bedrooms and the alternate master bedroom with fireplace and cathedral ceiling.

Plan AHP-9350

Bedrooms: 4-5	Baths: 3½
Space:	
Upper floor	870 sq. ft.
Main floor	1,541 sq. ft.
Total Living Area	**2,411 sq. ft.**
Basement	1,090 sq. ft.
Garage	442 sq. ft.
Exterior Wall Framing	2x4 or 2x6

Foundation options:
Partial Basement
Crawlspace
Slab
(Foundation & framing conversion diagram available—see order form.)

BLUEPRINT PRICE CODE	C

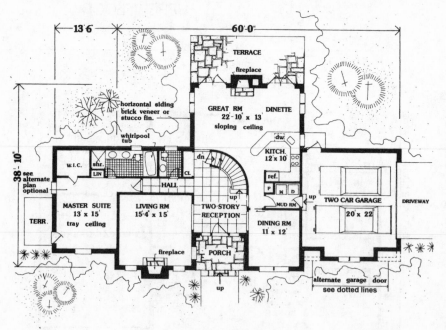

MAIN FLOOR

TO ORDER THIS BLUEPRINT, CALL TOLL-FREE 1-800-547-5570   **Plan AHP-9350**   *PRICES AND DETAILS ON PAGES 12-15*